Rethinking
ASIA

Political and Social Change

Rethinking Asia
Political and Social Change

May 2, 2017
Copyright © 2017 by Center for Asia Leadership Initiatives
Printed in Seoul, Korea

A Publication of the Center for Asia Leadership Initiatives
Acumen Publishing
14 Nancy Lane Waltham MA 02452 USA

Center for Asia Leadership Initiatives
Website: www.asialeadership.org
Facebook: www.facebook.com/asiagroup

Asia Leadership Trek
Website: www.asialeadershiptrek.org
Facebook: www.facebook.com/asialeadershiptrek
Twitter & Weibo: @Asia_Trek

All rights reserved. No part of this book may be reprinted or reproduced or utilized in any form or by any electronic, mechanical, or other means, now known or hereafter invented, including photocopying and recording, or in any information storage or retrieval system, without permission in writing from the publisher.

Library of Congress Control Number 2017938911
KDP ISBN: 979 8-3407940-0-0
US $13.99

For inquiries on partnership or sponsorship, or purchase of the publication, please email us at: cali@asialeadership.org

Political and Social Change

Essays by Harvard, Tufts, and Columbia University students who journeyed through 18 cities in 12 countries in Asia

RETHINKING ASIA

3

Edited by Hungsoo S. Kim

ACUMEN™
PUBLISHING

To all the aspiring leaders of this world

| Table of Contents |

•••

About the Editor   9
About the Contributors   11
Foreword   15

Introduction
| Introduction | Asia Leadership Trek – An Experiential Learning Journey
    _ **Hungsoo S. Kim**   19

Part 1 • Key Leadership Insights from ALT
| Chapter 1 | What Great Leaders I Have Met Do Differently
    _ **Hungsoo S. Kim**   29

Part 2 • Asia Leadership Trek 2016
| Chapter 2 | Malaysia: Resilience amidst Diversity
    _ **Rachel Lipson**   43

| Chapter 3 | Opportunities and Challenges for the Tourism and Garment Industries in Cambodia

_ **Annie Yu Kleiman** 67

| Chapter 4 | Bangladesh's Awakening

_ **Benjamin Goh** 95

Part 3 • Asia Leadership Fellowship 2016

| Chapter 5 | The Purpose of Education

_ **Lisa Lee** 115

| Chapter 6 | Developing a Method for Acquiring 21st Century Skills

_ **Lisa Lee** 145

Part 4 • Asia Leadership Trek VII

| Chapter 7 | Reflections on Kyrgyzstan after Ten Years of Absence

_ **Umar Shavurov** 171

| Chapter 8 | Tajikistan in Transition: Observations at the Crossroads of East and West

_ **Sarah Golkar** 189

| Chapter 9 | Kazakhstan: A Country That Punches Above Its Weight

_ **Katarina Sabova** 209

| Chapter 10 | Uzbekistan's Future at a Crossroads: The Historic Political Leadership Challenges and Opportunities Facing a Proud Nation

_ **Justin Hartley** 227

Part 5 • Afterword

| Chapter 11 | Revisiting the Asia Leadership Trek's Origins and Objectives

_ **Hungsoo S. Kim** 251

| Chapter 12 | The Legacy of the Asia Leadership Trek

_ **Hungsoo S. Kim** 271

Editor's Acknowledgments 293
Appendix I: Trek and Fellowship Itinerary 303
Appendix II: List of Trekkers and Fellows 325
Appendix III: List of Conference Topics 333
Appendix IV: List of Contributors 337

| About the Editor |

•••

Hungsoo S. Kim, a Korean national, is the Co-founder and President of the Center for Asia Leadership Initiatives. Passionate about nurturing and empowering talents in Asia, he has been actively engaging various stakeholders in developing and running over twenty-five programs in more than twenty-two countries in Asia to help emerging leaders explore opportunities to be socially responsible in facing the region's complex challenges. These programs fall under the Center's four main initiatives, namely the Asia Leadership Trek, a public diplomacy arm for scholars at Harvard, Stanford, MIT, and Fletcher; the Asia Leadership Institute, a leadership capacity-building arm; the Acumen Case Center, a research and content development arm; and Acumen Publishing, a publication arm. Hungsoo oversees these initiatives, along with a team of twenty comprising Faculty and Teaching Fellows from Harvard and Stanford University, and administrators at the main office in Boston, U.S., and the Asian regional headquarters in Kuala Lumpur, Malaysia.

As part of his continuous endeavor toward grooming leaders of tomorrow, Hungsoo recently joined the Asia Future Institute, a Seoul-based policy and leadership think tank, as Executive Director to instill in Korean and Northeast Asian talents the drive and passion to create positive social change through effective leadership. He prides himself on accelerating efforts to reach out to all forty-eight countries in Asia by 2022. Hungsoo's areas of research and training, among others, include 'Negotiation and Mediation,' 'Adaptive Leadership,' 'Persuasion and Influence,' and 'Creative Confidence.' To date, some twenty-five thousand burgeoning and established leaders from the government, non-profits, and corporate world in Asia have benefited from these programs.

Prior to establishing the Center, Hungsoo worked for twelve years in varying sectors from strategy consulting and social entrepreneurship to international development, politics, and government. He has also served as a policy aide in the United Nations in New York representing Korea, and as a project analyst at UNESCO in Paris. He currently sits on the board of two non-profit organizations, and has served as a visiting scholar at the Asia Center at Harvard University and at the Kellogg School of Management in Northwestern University. Hungsoo holds a Masters of Public Administration from the Harvard Kennedy School of Government; Masters in International Cooperation from the Graduate School of International Studies, Seoul National University; and completed his undergraduate studies with two majors in U.S. and International Law, and International Politics with a minor in Economics from Handong University.

Previously, Hungsoo was the editor of four books, namely *Rethinking Asia Vol. 1: Education and Innovation*, *Rethinking Asia Vol. 2: Entrepreneurship and Economic Development*, *Finding the Leaders in Us: New Goals for the Future*, and *Redefining Success: Learning to Lead for Change*. He is the editor of three upcoming books scheduled for release in May entitled, *Rethinking Asia Vol. 3: Social and Political Change*, *Next Generation Leadership: Empower Youth to Shape the Future of Asia*, and *Leaders in Development: Enhancing Your Leadership Effectiveness in a Changing World*.

| About the Contributors |

•••

Hungsoo S. Kim is the Co-founder and President of the Center for Asia Leadership Initiatives. Passionate about nurturing and empowering talents in Asia, he has developed and organized over twenty-five programs in more than twenty-two countries in the region to help budding leaders enhance their leadership competencies to navigate challenges in the 21st century. Hungsoo aims to engage with youth in all forty-eight countries in Asia by 2022 and inspire them to enact change in the world.

Rachel Lipson is currently enrolled as a joint degree candidate at Harvard, pursuing an MBA from Harvard Business School and a Master's in Public Policy at the Kennedy School. She was a David M. Rubenstein Fellow at the Center for Public Leadership and currently works as a Research Assistant for Professor Lawrence Summers through the Mossavar-Rahmani Center for Business and Government. Before beginning graduate school, Rachel spent two years at the World Bank, working on governance in the Middle East and North Africa. Prior to that, she worked on research projects at the Council on Foreign Relations, the Earth Institute at Columbia University, and the Tobin Project. Rachel also served as a field organizer and Deputy Training Director in North Carolina on Former President Barack Obama's 2012 re-election campaign. She holds an *A.B. magna cum laude* in Government from Harvard College, with a Citation in Spanish. Her senior thesis research on ethnic diversity and education governance was placed in the University Archives as a winner of the Hoopes Prize for outstanding scholarly work at Harvard.

Annie Yu Kleiman recently earned her Master's degree from The Fletcher School where she focused on international security studies and human security from a gender perspective. She served in the U.S. Air Force for eleven years, and was deployed four times to Southwest Asia, Iraq, and Afghanistan.

Benjamin Goh is a Master in Public Policy candidate at the Harvard Kennedy School. He is interested in issues surrounding governance and development, especially how the Internet shapes public opinion and the implications of "smart city" technologies. Benjamin graduated *summa cum laude* from New York University (NYU) with double honors in Economics and International Relations. Passionate about research, he was named the Ellie and David Werber Research Scholar in Social Sciences at NYU, and received the Fiona McGillivray Prize for his senior thesis on the political economy of Internet surveillance. He is the author of *Succeed at School* (Active Learning, 2011) and regularly contributes articles on current affairs in Singapore and Southeast Asia.

Lisa Lee is the founder and CEO of Case.by.Case (learncasebycase.com), an international educational services company that designs innovative skills based curriculum and programming for 21st century learning. Lisa began her career on Wall Street as an equity trader and investment analyst. During the financial crisis of 2008, she realized that education is the only investment that cannot be taken away, and made the subsequent switch to education, spending over six years teaching students of all ages and backgrounds. She also lived and taught in Kazakhstan for over two years. Lisa received her Masters of International Education Policy from the Harvard Graduate School of Education, focused on innovation and 21st century skills education. She continues to develop innovative content in the Harvard area.

Umar Shavurov recently moved back with his family to his homeland, Kyrgyzstan after a ten-year voyage overseas. He is engaged in a variety of freelance advisory engagement on private sector development regulation, and tax policy and administration with governments around the world, as well as a range of education projects in Kyrgyzstan. Between 2013 and 2016, Umar was based in Bogota, Colombia as part of the World Bank Group (WBG) to assist the Colombian Government on business tax simplification agenda. He brings extensive experience in both private and public sector development in Central Asia, West Africa, and Latin America. A Former Rotary World Peace and Mason Fellow, Umar has played a leading role in reforming over a dozen countries according to the WBG's flagship report, *Doing Business Report.*

Sarah Golkar graduated in 2016 with a Master of Arts in Law and Diplomacy from The Fletcher School at Tufts University with concentrations in international security studies and international political economy. Prior to this, Sarah spent five years working in Washington, D.C. as a foreign affairs specialist focused on the Middle East. She holds a Bachelor of Arts degree in Middle Eastern Studies and Government from the University of Texas, Austin.

Katarina Sabova is a second-year MBA student at Columbia Business School. She has previously worked as a management consultant with McKinsey & Company in Europe and Africa, and as a product manager for Symphony, a communication platform startup in Silicon Valley.

Justin Hartley is an in-house faculty in Leadership and Communications at the Center for Asia Leadership Initiatives, Research Fellow at Harvard University's Center for Public Leadership, as well as a Teaching Assistant at the Harvard Kennedy School for the subject 'Authentic Leadership' and its most popular course, "The Making of a Politician." Prior to that, he was a Visiting Scholar at Harvard University's Shorenstein Center on Media, Politics and Public Policy. As a Fulbright Scholar, John F. Kennedy Fellow, and Executive Vice President of the Kennedy School Student Government, Justin graduated with a Master in Public Administration, achieving straight As.

| Foreword |

•••

Asia is truly becoming ever more important. It is the world's largest and most populous continent, with its economy becoming an increasingly crucial engine of growth even as the world is currently undergoing a heavy recession. I have come to learn about the Asia Leadership Trek (ALT) back in January 2014 when Hungsoo shared with me his vision and plans for the future. I have been very fascinated with this. Ever since then, I have seen it grow and expand into a successful initiative that is fast gaining interest among the Harvard community. In my last encounter with Hungsoo in Singapore, I was thrilled to learn that their eleventh Trek was bound to happen in a few months' time. To date, about three hundred Trekkers or Harvard scholars from around sixty countries have experienced this high value-add program.

The ALT is a significant program in today's globalized world because it aims to explore Asia's crucial role in venturing new frontiers and fostering fresh approaches to promoting growth and creating opportunities for global citizens. In this context, the Trek provides education as a platform to mobilize collaborative actions with different stakeholders—from the grassroots to the decision makers and thought leaders—at various levels to generate effective mutual learning experience for all. The Trek offers Trekkers a chance of a lifetime to gain invaluable insights into the challenges, opportunities, and latest trends affecting Asia through meetings with stakeholders in government, business, and social enterprises. I am certain that many have walked away with great lessons and takeaways from this month-long study tour, and have applied what they have learned to the betterment of the community at large.

As a professor on leadership, I have been engaging with all kinds of leaders for the past three decades. I have been a strong proponent of teaching today's leaders the importance of becoming change agents that involves adopting fresh perspectives, initiating new ways of working together, implementing bold new actions, and continuing to deliver results in the face of new and often

overwhelming demands. In order to initiate change, it is more important than ever to go beyond the classroom and explore unchartered territory. It is crucial for 21st century leaders to have the ability
to put into practice or integrate what they have acquired into their personal and professional lives. In this context, the ALT serves as an amazing platform to bring the Trekkers out of their comfort zone, placing them in various environments and enabling them to explore the dynamic energy of different people and cultures. Through this, they will have the chance to gain greater insights and skills into creating opportunities via extensive learning and networking efforts they encounter. The Trek also gives Trekkers an avenue to share their skills, knowledge, and experiences with communities in the places that they visit through public service engagement. At the same time, they will have the opportunity to mingle with the locals and listen to their stories. It is an incredible platform for mutual learning and empowers the local community to enhance their personal development.

All of these efforts will plant the seeds that bear fruit for a brighter tomorrow. But what guarantees success? It requires a joint effort between all of us to impart the core competencies to be fully motivated and socially aware of the challenges that we face today. It also requires us to identify opportunities that enable us to brainstorm and develop plans that can turn downsides into upsides. I hope all of us will stand united by this common desire to make our world a better place, believing that we have a unique opportunity and responsibility to contribute and make a difference.

I applaud all of those who have taken part in writing and sharing their experiences with the readers. Your stories and lessons learned will truly benefit all of us.

I wish the ALT great success in all its future endeavors.

Professor Dean Williams
Adjunct Lecturer in Public Policy for the Center for Public Leadership
Harvard Kennedy School

Introduction

| Introduction |

Asia Leadership Trek – An Experiential Learning Journey

Hungsoo S. Kim, Editor
MPA, Harvard Kennedy School of Government

● ● ●

It was a brilliant morning shortly before eight, and I was hurrying down to the lobby to greet my Trekkers before we all headed over to our very first meeting, where we would discuss our study and community-service trip, better known as the Asia Leadership Trek. When I met them, I could see from their faces how thrilled they were to be in Dushanbe, Tajikistan, an unfamiliar place that they would probably not otherwise have visited. For all twenty-five of us, it was our first visit to the region, and we were excited to explore seven cities in four countries—Tajikistan, Kyrgyzstan, Kazakhstan, and Uzbekistan.

As I walked across the tree-lined streets of downtown Dushanbe, I recalled the day four years earlier when I had sat down with my classmates at the Harvard Kennedy School to discuss our exciting plans for a study trip to Korea, which eventually became a month-long adventure in seven Asian countries. Upon returning to Cambridge that summer, with much confidence, I worked closely with numerous

Harvard faculty members and colleagues to nurture and expand this vision. Four years later, the Asia Leadership Trek was reaching its ninth edition. As I made my way from the hotel to the secluded, campus-style headquarters of the Ministry of Economy, Investment, and Finance of the Tajik Republic, I reminisced fondly over past Treks. Thanks to God, I had clocked in over five hundred thousand miles of travel to fifty-eight exotic and thriving cities in twenty-two countries across Asia, journeying with over three hundred faculty members and students from Harvard University, the Massachusetts Institute of Technology (MIT), Stanford University, Columbia University, and Tufts University, who collectively represented over sixty countries. We had met with over two thousand policy-makers, businessmen, social activists, and educators, and visited over six hundred institutions, ranging in their aims from international and community development to security, technological innovation, human rights, and strategy and management. Additionally, we had shared our knowledge and expertise with budding young leaders of Asia through our leadership conferences, which we'd held in nearly fifty locations throughout the region. The Treks were a life-changing experience for me, and the three hundred people who accompanied me felt the same. Even now, they still share with me how their experiences on the Treks changed the way they see the world and interact with people.

One of the key takeaways for me was learning what leadership was all about. As a person educated in both the East and the West, I found that the Treks gave me a wonderful opportunity to analyze the traits of successful leaders. I had witnessed the essence of effective and ethical leadership during my young years in the Philippines, and it was rewarding to meet and engage with numerous other leaders in a wide range of fields throughout Asia—including the Trekkers themselves, from whom I learned constantly.

After ten years, I believe this one-of-a-kind Trek experience has taught me invaluable lessons, greatly enriching the reflections on leadership that I will share in the first chapter of this book. Because this volume is an anthology of articles by nine contributors from different backgrounds, their choices of topic vary. However, all the chapters revolve around leadership in the context of national development, civil society, and public policy.

This is the third publication in the Asia Leadership Trek (ALT) series. This time, I have compiled reflections from the three 2016 Treks into one book. The first of these Treks was held in January and included visits to Shanghai, Singapore, Johor Bahru, Kuala Lumpur, Siem Reap, Phnom Penh, and Dhaka. The Asia Entrepreneurship Trek, in March, went to Seoul, Tokyo, and Taipei. Lastly, the Central Asia Leadership Trek, in June, brought Trekkers to Dushanbe, Bishkek, Osh, Almaty, Astana, Tashkent, Samarkand, and Dhaka. Together these three journeys demonstrated that Asia is far from homogenous but is rather a region in which distinct nations, each with its own social, economic, political, and religious norms and challenges, interact in complex ways that are influenced by power and history. In Taipei, we sought to understand the transition of power and initiatives toward a creative economy, embracing startups and information technology. In Tashkent, Bishkek, and Dushanbe, we examined leaders' abilities to envision the future and to discern what elements are most needed for effective public leadership. In Seoul and Tokyo, we delved into how leaders leap forward within mature economies.

In Astana and Kuala Lumpur, we explored how emerging economies can spur growth while preventing a middle-income trap. In Shanghai, Singapore, and Phnom Penh, we witnessed firsthand how public leaders integrate diverse sectors of society for the institutional and economic advancement of their nations. In every country we visited, the leaders faced daunting challenges, including high levels of illiteracy, slowing economic momentum, high unemployment rates, oppressive neighboring powers, high inflation rates, and rising social intolerance. Some spoke about their concerns regarding rapid development, which comes with the dangers of environmental degradation, corruption, materialism, and increased uncertainty about the future. Yet all of the leaders we met shared one thing in common: they saw more opportunities than challenges in front of them—and this optimistic view is central to ensuring progress. On the Treks, we concluded that the most important elements of leadership are talent, transparency, and well-functioning governance mechanisms, all used to bring about meaningful and positive change.

The first ten chapters, including mine, delve into the Trekkers' journeys of exploration and self-discovery. In Chapter 1, I talk about the factors of effective leadership that I have identified in my four years of Trekking. In Chapter 2, Rachel Lipson investigates the challenges and opportunities presented by Malaysia's place in the international system; the latest issues affecting the country, particularly the youth and the education system; and developments in Malaysia's media landscape. Annie Yu Kleiman, in Chapter 3, gives her insights on trends and prospects in the tourism and garment industries in Cambodia. In Chapter 4, Benjamin Goh provides his observations on Bangladeshi people, culture, and society, as well as on the nation's aspirations. Chapters 5 and 6 highlight Lisa Lee's experiences during her stint as a Teaching Fellow during the Trek. In Chapter 7, Umar Shavurov reflects on the dramatic changes in his home nation of Kyrgyzstan after an absence of ten years and on his hopes of contributing to the future of his country. Sarah Golkar, in Chapter 8, explores the collisions of past empires with modern republics in Central Asia and the political cultures theses collisions create, with a focus on Tajikistan. In Chapter 9, Katarina Sabova shares her fascination with Kazakhstan and examines the nation's ambitions to enter the global arena. Chapter 10 offers Justin Hartley's observations on Uzbekistan's political leadership and the opportunities that lie ahead for the country.

In the summer of 2016, the Center for Asia Leadership Initiatives (CALI) focused on public service through its Teaching Fellowship program at the Center's Asia Leadership Institute, which aims to provide students and professionals in Asia with access to cutting-edge leadership training and academic and cultural experiences. Five Teaching Fellows, all Harvard University graduates, gave workshops on leadership, public speaking, and entrepreneurial skills during our week-long leadership programs in Ulaan Baatar, Kuala Lumpur, Incheon, and Pohang. Some of the highlights included our Mongolia Leadership program for Executives, held in the capital for the third time, with a handful of leaders from the Asia Development Bank, World Bank, World Vision, and other organizations, as well as the Third Trilateral Leadership Summit, which gathered promising young individuals from China, Japan, and Korea in Incheon, Korea. We also held our first Leadership School program for young people of Korean descent from the Central Asian region, jointly held with the Korea

Development Bank Foundation. Other programs were held in Kuala Lumpur, Malaysia, bringing together promising leaders, both young and mid-career. All of these programs helped us to achieve our objective of benefiting the Asian community at large and enhancing local Asian communities' ability to overcome challenges through mentorship, inspirational stories on leadership, discussions of best practices, and workshops on leadership, education, and entrepreneurship. Each program was based on the latest research and ideas taught to global leaders at Harvard University.

To highlight this aspect of CALI's mission, Lisa Lee, one of our Teaching Fellows, contributes two chapters in this book, sharing her experiences of teaching workshops on "Authentic Leadership," "Building 21st Century Skills," and "Design Thinking and Innovation" in three countries, to over three hundred participants from fifteen countries. In her chapter entitled "The Purpose of Education," she discusses the importance of equipping students with 21st-century skills—critical thinking, problem solving, creativity, communication, and leadership—to develop agile leaders who can address today's ever-changing challenges. Her following chapter, entitled "Developing a Method for Acquiring 21st Century Skills," describes the program that she piloted with CALI to instill 21st century skills in students and offers her reflections on its impact in Asia.

Here at CALI, we put this book together because we wanted to give those who couldn't take part in the Trek and the Teaching Fellowships an opportunity to experience Asia the way we did: diving deep into learning about Asia's challenges and opportunities through direct engagement with Asian leaders in business, government, and social enterprise, while at the same time inspiring individuals to become capable and ethical leaders of today and tomorrow. I hope you enjoy these essays, which combine moving personal reflections with informed policy analysis, and walk away with some new insights as well as the visceral experience of the two Treks and six Fellowships.

In the book's Afterword, I write about what distinguishes the Asia Leadership Trek from other programs and the ALT's future goals and directions. Entitled "Revisiting the Asia Leadership Trek's Origin and Objectives," the Afterword explains what motivated me to initiate the ALT and why education and leadership are crucial to the success of Asian economies in the 21st century. It also describes in detail how I wish to achieve these goals—the ALT is just a starting point for greater plans and opportunities in the future.

I hope that this book, in addition to giving you insights into Asia's complex societies, will help you meet your personal challenges, whatever they may be. Kudos to the book contributors, and I wish all readers happy reading!

Part 1

•

Key Leadership Insights from ALT

| Chapter 1 |

What Great Leaders I Have Met Do Differently

Hungsoo S. Kim, Editor
MPA, Harvard Kennedy School of Government

• • •

We all know that we would like to be around cool people. I once read an article from *The Huffington Post* introducing a study by Professor Amy Cuddy at Harvard University, which illustrated two factors that instantaneously determine our judgments about other person: "Can I trust this person?" and "Can I respect this person's capabilities?"[1] I viewed these questions as assessing humility and competence respectively, with the former higher in value than the latter.

During the past ten Treks, I have met many leaders who left lasting impressions on me. They come from all over Asia, and they number now in the thousands. (To learn who some of they are, look at the Appendix at the end of this book.) The main objective of this chapter is to share the many factors of effective leadership that I discovered in

---

1 "How to Master the Art of the First Impression." http://www.huffingtonpost.com/dr-travis-bradberry/how-to-master-the-art-of_b_9548610.html.

them.

The first factor is crisis management. During the Asia Leadership Treks, not a single person we met said, "My journey was smooth and sound at all times. There was no crisis in my life." Instead we often heard, "Had there not been a crisis in my life, you wouldn't see me where I am today." Crisis was an everyday companion in their leadership journeys, and dealing with crisis was part and parcel of their everyday lives. For many of them, crisis in whatever form came from nowhere, without any advance notice. But when it came, they didn't shy away from it; rather, they faced it with courage and valor. Clearly, these leaders saw crises as opportunties to become better leaders, exposing their strengths and weaknesses, and molding their characters and capacities. Moreover, they persevered, knowing that crisis is by nature ephemeral. They turned each crisis into an opportunity and managed it with boldness and presence of mind. One well-known entrepreneur in Hong Kong told us, "One should not dodge the problem but rather face it with a 'wise thinking' mindset." When a crisis is over, provided we have responded to it with strength and initiative, we will be left with improved decision making skills, a better knowledge of how to use resources, and the experience needed to avoid perils in the future. A parliamentarian in Japan said, "One day, you will look back at moments like these and feel proud of how far you have come, and realize that a crisis is nothing more than 'a handful of sand in the desert.'" Many of the leaders we met said that crisis or adversity was what made them who they are today. All of them agreed that overcoming adversity unleashed the power of resilience in them.

The second factor is creativity. The Trekkers and I met a policy-maker in education from Singapore, who shared an interesting perspective on fostering creativity. He said that while creativity can forge unique ideas and contribute to solving the world's problems, many people do not live up to their creative and inventive potential. He emphasized the need to start training ourselves to think creatively in order to produce ingenious ideas and apply them in our daily lives. One way of achieving this is to find a balance between reflecting on your personal development and engaging in new ideas and different perspectives. Listening to your inner self and learning from others can help generate groundbreaking ideas and insights that may in turn point to a solution for whatever challenges you face. Many business leaders on the Treks talked about how important it is to possess a problem solving mindset, and how spending time alone enables them to reflect, refresh, and refuel themselves for the challenges ahead. Talking and listening to your allies can also play an important role in finding your next big business idea.

The third factor is emotional control. By emotion, in this context, I mean darker feelings: rapacity, rage, unjustified desires. Managing your emotional health is critical for effective leadership. Many of the leaders we met said that they have witnessed the fall of budding and incumbent leaders whose emotions got in their way, contributing to their downfall. Anger, impulse, vengeance, and hatred act as stumbling blocks in the quest to become a well-respected leader. Fortunately, reflection and self-awareness can help us exercise control and overcome our immediate impulse to lash out. They can be achieved by finding stillness in prayer, which will inevitably lead to mental and physical rejuvenation. Spending time in reflection will also boost your personal growth and help you develop a better understanding of your own strengths and weaknesses.

The fourth factor is mental and physical health. We met a banker in China who shared a famous quote by Deng Xiaoping, one of the founders of modern China: "To seek longevity, humans need to take at least 10,000 steps every day." Another educator from Nepal had an interesting insight about the meaning of each letter in the word "humans." According to him, in order for humans to live a healthy life, they need "happiness" (h); "understanding" of themselves and others (u); "moderation," "meaning," "morality," and good "management of time" (m); a good "attitude" (a); a life well-aligned with "nature" and "nutrition" (n); and a commitment to community "service" (s). This interpretation of the word "humans" affected me deeply. The educator advised us to practice all of the elements to stay healthy, both physically and mentally, because good health is imperative in becoming a great leader for one's family, community, and country.

The fifth factor is competence. Fluency in many languages was widely used as an example by the leaders we spoke with. I am familiar with four languages, including Korean, English, Chinese in writing, and intermediate French. I was surprised to find out that many business and political leaders in Mongolia, Nepal, Malaysia, India, and Kazakhstan conduct their daily activities in four to five languages. To them, language is a key asset in effective leadership, greatly enhancing their ability to connect with others. Cultural literacy and global awareness are also important components of leadership competence. One Korean business executive told us that people love and appreciate it when someone from another community or country shows that they have a genuine interest or even a small wealth of knowledge about their culture, language, or their most talked-about current affairs—which aligns with Robert Cialdini's 'liking' concept which says that people favor those who are like them. Showing that you've taken the time to learn about other people's viewpoints gives you a head start in gaining their confidence and demonstrates your competence by highlighting your initiative and responsibility. Gaining people's trust in turn enables leaders to learn more about their feelings, train of thoughts, values, and even cultural assets. After pondering this factor of leadership—especially the importance of knowing multiple languages—I regret not having learned more languages in my youth, but I hope to pick up another one in the future.

The sixth factor is ethics. Many leaders deplore the prominence of unethical leadership in this day and age. The trust level in public and corporate leaders in most of the places we visited on the Treks was very low. The public believes that most business leaders in their countries—India, Nepal, and the Philippines in particular—have achieved their success solely through bribery and monopolizing access to economic opportunities. One Korean National Assemblyman mentioned that the low level of trust and of ethical standards has caused an increase in social cost. The Samsung Economics Research Institute's recent report entitled 'Social Conflict Index and Economic Growth' reported that Korea was recently ranked fifth among Economic Co-operation and Development (OECD) countries that have had to pay a high price in managing social issues. In other words, about 27 percent of the per capita income was spent in managing various social issues in Korea. Nor is this problem limited to Korea. Through our discussions on the Treks, I learned that maintaining a high level of ethical standards is vital not only to eliminating public distrust but also to creating momentum for a healthy and thriving society. An executive from a Japanese automaker noted that integrity and humility are important in establishing high standards of ethical conduct. Another successful businessman, in Malaysia, emphasized integrity, humility, and excellence as core values of his company. Lastly, a scholar and public official from Singapore introduced to us the idea of "M.P.H.," which stands for meritocracy, pragmatism, and honesty, all crucial elements to sustaining the well-being of Singaporean society. Looking at Singapore's accomplishments, one can easily believe that "M.P.H." has contributed to their past victories, their current success, and their promising future.

The seventh factor in effective leadership is building networks across boundaries. Dean Williams, a professor at the Harvard Kennedy School who conducted leadership seminars at a CALI program in October 2016, explained the importance of networks in this way: "Leadership is about crossing boundaries, breaking fault-lines, building bridges, and leading changes." One Cambodian businessman in the garment industry told us that today's business leaders are caught up in so many things and pulled in so many different directions that they forget about their surroundings and the people they work with, including employees and constituents, neglecting to appreciate and acknowledge their contributions. It is always important to customize our interactions with the people around us. We need to be aware of what makes them tick. So, make yourself available and accessible for one-on-one meetings. Inject life into your line of work and offer advice or lessons to people in need. To me this means not only meeting and engaging with the people around me but also being a resourceful facilitator for connecting other people to each other. Two different leaders on the Trek, a Malaysian senior executive and a business owner from India who runs a successful educational institution, told me that they saw themselves as chief facilitators, connecting the dots between people, information, and resources and thus enabling the people they work with to do their jobs well. By facilitating connections, they bring greater value to their communities, and at the same time they can identify greater opportunities for themselves, their companies, and others.

The eighth factor is the use of multiple perspectives. And this came in two ways. First was seeking out knowledge of both the big picture and more granular, on-the-ground perspectives. This was about thinking long-term, but also living to your fullest each day by adding values to where they fit. Second, good leaders were also stellar with taking perspectives. Most of the leaders we met with agreed that many people, these days, value skills and jobs that allow them to contribute to their societies. They felt that an organization should clearly present its meaning and purpose in order to foster social engagement. The leaders are responsible for promoting this mission and engaging stakeholders continuously, and only leaders who understand and employ multiple perspectives are able to make this happen. Many people we spoke with also argued that today's leaders rely too much on incentives—bonuses and increments for companies, and intermittent public promises for politics—which can spoil people's expectations. They reiterated that leaders must inspire people with a vision, set challenging goals for companies and society as a whole, and boost people's confidence levels so that they believe in themselves. The use of layman's terms is important in articulating a clear purpose that will resonate well, set high expectations, and convey the leaders' competence and commitment.

The ninth factor is performance. Numerous interviews with various leaders in Asia have taught me that an effective leadership was about knowing how to both manage the process, and generate right and meaningful outcomes. We live in an age when people judge each other by how much and how well they perform, using various quantitative standards. And yes it is therefore important for leaders to know how to plan, execute, and attain expected outcomes. However, to perform well as measured by the outcomes we generate, equally or more important was knowing how to manage the processes right to reach there. And this latter included both quantitative and qualitative aspects in which it required novel approaches, non-traditional team efforts, as well as the right standards and code of ethics, given today's tasks and problems characterized by complexity and uncertainty. This latter, especially, were critical in ensuring good and sustainable performances and vital to meeting goals that provides credibility and trust to the stakeholders we served. All effective leaders I had met knew how to build high-impact teams and create an environment conducive to collaboration.

The tenth factor is service for others. I once came across with two articles online, one from *Corporation for National & Community Service,* and another from the *National Philanthropic Trust,* noting of these interesting facts: in 2014, a quarter of Americans gave shares of their time to volunteer for the public, while two-thirds gave their helping hands to their neighbors; the average annual household contribution of American, in 2015, was US$2,974, totaling US$373.25

billion—which is almost the size of the Thailand economy[2]; and 98.4 percent of high income household in the U.S. gave to charity, with nearly two-thirds of them donating to 'give back to the community.' I have no doubt that these were given to strive to alleviate poverty, increase literacy, and build people's capacity both domestic and international. On the Treks, I had the honor of meeting leaders who were very active in the realm of service. I met several entrepreneurs who donated their wealth to establish educational institutions, providing high-quality education through scholarships to promising youth from underprivileged families. Their actions demonstrate their belief that education is crucial in breaking the chains of poverty. Others focused on building hospitals, combining for-profit and not-for-profit models, especially in remote areas, to give the underprivileged access to medical care. Still others spent four hours a week at orphanages, taking care of orphans and disadvantaged youth. All of these service leaders shared one thing in common: they sought and found true happiness through giving their resources, time, and energy to their communities. In fact, giving to others not only led to their own greater happiness and health but also positively impacted their businesses.

A workshop I once attended at the Kellogg School of Management at Northwestern University described three determinants to happiness: set point, life circumstances, and intentional activity. The first is given to us; it refers to what is determined for us before our birth: our parents' jobs, our family's wealth, the education we will receive, etc. Our set point constitutes 50 percent of what determines our happiness. Our life circumstances refer to demographic variables:

---

[2] The World Bank statistics, 2015.

age, marital and employment status, income, possessions, etc. They constitute only 10 percent of what determines our happiness. Our intentional activity, constituting the remaining 40 percent of what determines our happiness, refers to the practices we deliberately engage in. It includes our willingness to adopt a positive attitude, do acts of kindness, engage in physical exercise, and strive toward personal and professional goals. The division of influence among these three factors struck me deeply, for it suggests that at least 40 percent of our happiness is under our control. And I have certainly felt in my own life that doing intentional good leads to genuine and prolonged happiness.

Last but not least among the central factors of effective leadership are vision and people. Many leaders told us that sharing and projecting vision is essential in leaders, since, without vision, we can never navigate the ship to reach our destination. In our meetings, however, many of them also added that while a leader could determine the vision, teamwork, or a good pool of people exercising leadership was what got to realize it than just a vision itself. I asked several of the people we met to name the leaders they found most inspiring. Quite a number replied that the best leaders are those who spend a large portion of their time listening. Such leaders posed problems and challenges, then invited their teammates to help generate visions and solutions. This tactic was also aligned with the idea of leaders as coordinators or facilitators. Nevertheless, though vision should be generated through teamwork, leaders are responsible for making that vision crystal clear. Without a clear goal, your effort may end up going in the wrong direction.

Having completed ten rounds of Treks to fifty-eight cities in twenty-two countries, I can humbly say that I have grown in knowledge and capacity and matured in character. Yet the more I see, hear, and learn, the more I feel that I know nothing. What I cherish most in the Treks is this: genuinely understanding the world I live in, eagerly learning about myself as well as others, humbly discovering new causes to invest my life in, and boldly bolstering the momentum of my endeavor to create a better world for all. I am truly grateful that I can offer the readers of this book some of the important leadership lessons I learned on my journeys with the Asia Leadership Trek.

I would like to end my chapter with a poem called "Success," derived from the writings of the American writer Bessie Anderson Stanley:

> To laugh often and much;
> To win the respect of intelligent people
>   and the affection of children;
> To earn the appreciation of honest critics
>   and endure the betrayal of false friends;
> To appreciate beauty; to find the best in others;
> To leave the world a bit better,
>   whether by a healthy child,
>   a garden patch,
>   or a redeemed social condition;
> To know even one life has breathed easier
>   because you have lived.
> This is to have succeeded.

Part 2

Asia Leadership Trek 2016

| Chapter 2 |

Malaysia:
Resilience amidst Diversity

Rachel Lipson
MBA, Harvard Business School
MPP, Harvard Kennedy School of Government

• • •

This essay consists of six sections. The first will give a brief overview of the Malaysian economy, trends in the country's industries, and its job market—all of which serve as important background for the meetings and discussions that took place during the 2016 Asia Leadership Trek (ALT). The second part will explore Malaysia's relations with some key countries and will discuss the challenges and opportunities presented by Malaysia's place in the international system. The third section will briefly present the current corruption scandal rocking the country. I will explain the intersection of this issue with developments in Malaysia's media landscape and provide information to enhance understanding of the Malaysian press. The next section will review some of the issues affecting the youth in Malaysia, particularly the country's education system. Finally, in the conclusion, I will step back and evaluate some of the takeaways from the Trek in the larger context of Malaysia's opportunities and challenges.

Malaysia's Economy

Malaysia's economic growth rate and strong fiscal performance over the past thirty-five years are significant in both historical and relative terms. The charts below display some of the impressive economic trends that have occurred in the country since 1980:

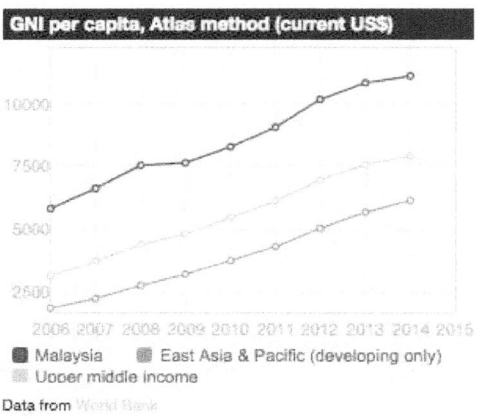

Figure 1 Malaysia's GNI per capita performance relative to other developing countries in the region

From 1980 to 2013, nominal gross domestic product (GDP) in Malaysia grew 17.5 times, from RM53.3bn to RM984.5bn.[1] Dur-

---

1 Khazanah Research Institute.

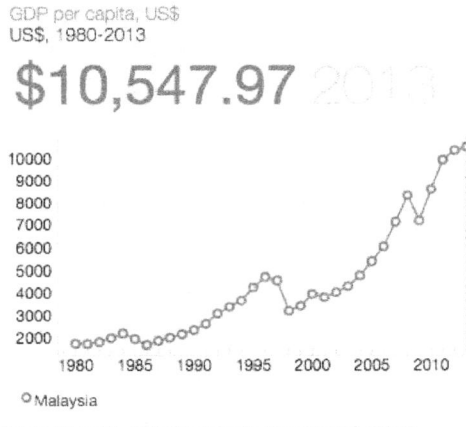

Figure 2 Malaysian GDP per capita growth, 1980-2013. Source: World Economic Forum

ing the same period, nominal GDP per person grew 7.6 times, from RM3,841 per year to RM32,984. Malaysians have been able to translate this growth into measurable improvements in their ability to consume and enjoy higher standards of living. For instance, 98 percent of Malaysian households now own a TV, while 95 percent have a mobile phone. Moreover, 57 percent of Malaysians subscribe to paid television programming.[2] In the Trek's meeting at Sunway Group, we learned that Malaysia has over sixty-five million square feet of shopping malls. From the 1980s onward, one hundred new shopping malls have been built every decade in Malaysia.

During many of the ALT's meetings, our speakers and hosts lauded

---

2   Khazanah Research Institute.

the country's economic accomplishments. In our visit to Bank Negara Malaysia, the Central Bank of Malaysia, Mr. Muhammad bin Ibrahim, the then Deputy Governor of Bank Negara, described how Malaysia had successfully weathered the shocks of the East Asian Financial Crisis in the 1990s, providing a model for reforms and resilience for many other countries in the region. Realizing that Malaysia was overly dependent on its banking sector, the financial services industry diversified in order to encompass much more than just banking. The bond market in Malaysia has tripled over the past fifteen years, and today the banks in Malaysia are regional leaders. The country is also a global leader in Islamic finance, a situation that many stakeholders we met viewed as a major opportunity for the country. Mr. Muhammad additionally cited the impressive achievement that 96 percent of Malaysia's citizens currently have access to financial services.

Soon after its independence, Malaysia became and has remained one of the world's most open economies. In 2015, the country ranked #15 in the world in the World Bank's "Ease of Doing Business" Rankings.[3] Trade has been an integral component of Malaysia's strong development results. According to Khazanah Research Institute, one of the organizations that we visited, Malaysia's trade as a percentage of GDP has consistently been greater than 100 percent dating back to 1988.[4] In 2014, Malaysia's total trade was 131 percent of GDP. Malaysia is one of the signatories to the Trans-Pacific Partnership (TPP) agreement and, as of February 2016, will be one of the thirteen original members of the ambitious pact.

---

3   http://www.state.gov/e/eb/rls/othr/ics/2015/241648.htm.
4   http://www.slideshare.net/KhazanahResearchInstitute/slideshelf.

Malaysia's overarching economic goal, as described by the government, is to transform the country into a high-income nation by 2020. The World Bank defines high-income countries as those with a gross national income (GNI) per head, of at least US$12,736. According to 2014 data, Malaysia's GNI per capita stood at US$10,760. Still, challenges remain as Malaysia's economy moves toward this ambitious objective. The Economist Intelligence Unit forecasts that Malaysia's real GDP growth will decelerate to 4.3 percent on average in 2016, from an estimated 4.8 percent in 2015, which itself was down from 5.9 percent in 2014. In addition, the government faces a number of major economic obstacles, including the decline of its currency, downward trends in the commodity market, and a growing budget deficit.

Challenges also exist in the country's approach to economic inequality and diversity. One of the policy hallmarks of Malaysia's multi-ethnic nation has been a prolonged attempt by the government to create more broadly shared prosperity, and in particular, to promote more inclusive economic opportunities for the country's many ethnicities. Following race riots in the 1960s, Malaysia's 1969 New Economic Policy (NEP) sought to "create a more equitable society by the eradication of poverty and restructuring the society by eliminating the identification of race with economic function."[5] This policy was specifically aimed at supporting the Malays or *bumiputeras,* who were identified as the most economically disadvantaged ethnic group in Malaysian society. Today, Malaysia's population consists of 60 per-

---

5 Hena Mukherjee, "Access to and Equity in Higher Education - Malaysia." Feb 2010. siteresources.worldbank.org/EASTASIAPACIFICEXT/Resources/226300-1279680449418/HigherEd_MalaysiaEquity.pdf.

cent *bumiputeras* (ethnic Malays and indigenous groups), 23 percent ethnic Chinese, and 7 percent ethnic Indian, with the remainder of the population belonging to other races. Though *bumiputeras* have historically lagged behind in education and business, by law, they continue to receive access to cheaper housing, priority in government jobs, preferential access to higher education, and priority for business licenses. Additionally, all companies listed on Malaysia's stock market must have at least 12.5 percent *bumiputera* ownership—a number decreased from 30 percent under the current Prime Minister's tenure—and the National Development Policy requires preferential treatment of the *bumiputeras*, who are entitled to at least 30 percent of any privatized entity's equity.[6] This essay will discuss some of the implications of this policy, especially with respect to education, in later sections.

The Exchange Rate and Commodities Market

One major challenge discussed during many of the Trek's meetings was the effect of currency depreciation. The Malaysian ringgit has decreased in value by some 20 percent against the US dollar since the start of 2015.[7] At the time of writing, one Singapore Dollar was trading for close to three Malaysian Ringgit.[8] During the Trek, we met some Singaporeans who explained that they would cross over the

---

6 http://www.wsj.com/articles/malaysias-leader-at-center-of-a-storm-1444963838; http://www.state.gov/e/eb/rls/othr/ics/2015/241648.htm.
7 Economist Intelligence Unit.
8 http://www.themalaysianinsider.com/business/article/ringgit-rebounds-on-improved-risk-appetite.

border to shop in Malaysia because prices there are so cheap. According to *Reuters*, Malaysia's ringgit was Asia's worst currency performer last year, hurt by the political instability (described in later sections), capital outflows, and the global commodity price slump.[9] While this development has made Malaysian exports more competitive abroad, it hurts Malaysian consumers, who import a large number of products from abroad. Unfortunately, the risk to the ringgit is not finished yet: in our discussions with students and policy makers, many cited the continued risk decreases in demand from China and potential rate increases in the United States may further damage the value of the ringgit.

The decrease in oil and gas prices has also been a major contributor to the ringgit's decline. Malaysia's oil and gas sector is the government's largest and most significant source of revenue. Income from Malaysia's large commodity resources—much of which sit in contested areas of the South China Sea—and from a strong liquefied natural gas industry add up to over 30 percent of the government's revenue.[10] Malaysia is the second-largest source of natural gas exports in the world, although the country is actually a net importer of oil. Many of the stakeholders that we met with expressed concern that the continuing turmoil in energy markets would hurt Malaysia in the coming years.

The Future of Malaysian Jobs

---

9   http://www.reuters.com/article/malaysia-economy-lng-idUSL8N15B0PE.
10 http://www.export.gov/malaysia/doingbusinessinmalaysia/index.asp.

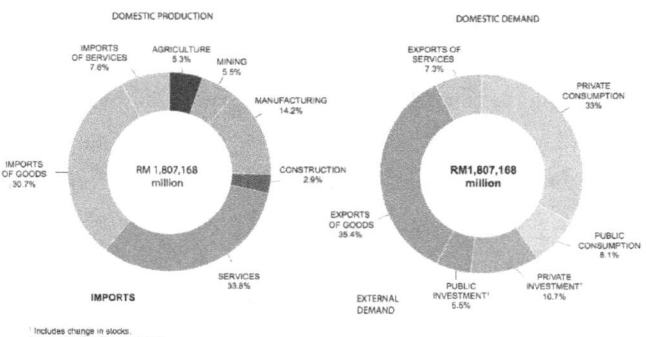

THE ECONOMY 2016
AT CONSTANT 2010 PRICES

Source: Ministry of Finance, Malaysia

One of the most pressing issues discussed at the Trek's meetings with public and private stakeholders was the need to equip and prepare Malaysians for the next generation of job growth. As the country's income level and quality of life increases, there will be a need for Malaysians to enhance their skill sets and move up the value chain accordingly. Relative to its current competitors, however, Malaysia's workforce is not as well-educated as it needs to be. The Khazanah Research Institute has found that jobs with the highest pay in Malaysia (managers and professionals) are currently far less numerous than lower-paying jobs in areas such as services and sales. Malaysia currently has 6.6 million people working as clerical support workers; craft workers; plant and machine operators and assemblers; skilled agricultural, forestry, and fishery workers; and elementary workers. All of these are low-wage professions compared to professionals and technicians, but there are three times as many jobs available in these functions as there are in the higher-paying fields.[11]

The electrical and electronics sector is one of the key industries in the Malaysian economy. Production in this sector makes up one quarter of the country's manufacturing output and is responsible for approximately 33 percent of Malaysia's total exports.[12] However—as we were told by the Advisor to the Chief Minister of Johor, the Minister of Higher Education, and the then Deputy Governor to Malaysia's Central Bank—companies in Malaysia have not been able to rival external competitors in terms of worker productivity and the manufacturing of higher complexity products. The country's industrial sector needs to modernize and move toward higher value production. In addition, Malaysia is trying to develop a more vibrant service sector, one that would offer incomes comparable with those in neighboring Singapore.

To do this, Malaysia will need to increase its capacity building, and technical and vocational training. The need is particularly great in rural and underserved areas. For instance, when we went to Sunway's Southern Regional Office, multiple managers cited the lack of skilled and qualified labor in that part of the country as one of their largest and most difficult challenges. Some had to offer incentives of higher salary to induce current employees to move from Kuala Lumpur to these outer regions, because they could not find local labor with the skills required. Many employers also lamented the decline in English language skills among Malaysia's young workforce. Recently, Sarawak Chief Minister, Mr. Adenan Satem publicly blamed the lack of focus

---

11 http://www.slideshare.net/KhazanahResearchInstitute/slideshelf.
12 Economist Intelligence Unit.

on English in schools as a cause of unemployment: "We are producing thousands of graduates every year who can't find jobs because they are not proficient in English. They can't string 10 words together [in English]."[13] On the Trek, we heard similar sentiments expressed by a number of public and private figures.

Location, Location, Location

This year, for the first time, the Trekkers had the opportunity to visit Johor Bahru, a city of five hundred thousand people that sits on Malaysia's border with Singapore. While many of the people we met with discussed the challenges of Singapore's proximity—for instance, the Special Advisor to the Chief Minister of State described the consistent loss of Malaysian human capital and top talent to Singapore because of wage differences—in general, Malaysia's geographic position next to one of the top performing economies on the planet is an opportunity that needs to be tapped. The government, recognizing this, has made the State of Johor a top priority for economic development and investment.

In Johor, we visited the State Government, where we learned about Johor's potential to become Malaysia's next economic powerhouse; Sunway Iskandar, one of Malaysia's largest and most promising integrated township projects; and Medini Iskandar, the flagship development in Iskandar Malaysia, where we learned about the region's growth plan. One development item that will be key to Johor's

---

[13] http://www.themalaysianinsider.com/malaysia/article/to-ignore-english-is-to-be-impractical-says-adenan.

growth is the proposed high-speed rail link, which would connect Singapore to Kuala Lumpur. The train line is projected to run right through Johor and would make commuting much easier for those wishing to take advantage of Malaysia's cheaper housing and cost of living while working in Singapore and earning higher wages.

ASEAN

Similar to the importance of Malaysia's strong economic ties with Singapore, a common opportunity cited by many of the people we met was the Association of Southeast Asian Nations (ASEAN). In November 2015, Malaysia, along with nine other countries (Brunei, Cambodia, Indonesia, Laos, Myanmar, the Philippines, Singapore, Thailand, and Vietnam) formally established the ASEAN community, which revolves around economic affairs, foreign affairs, and security interests, as well as the socio-cultural aim of building people-to-people connections.[14] As a result of ASEAN, regional integration is now a major priority for Malaysia's government, alongside its private sector and civil society.

While the Trek's meeting with Mr. Le Luong Minh, the 2015 Secretary-General of ASEAN, unfortunately had to be canceled, the importance of Malaysia's membership and role in ASEAN was revealed in many of our meetings. The universities in the countries we visited all highlighted their people-to-people connections with other member states. The Central Bank spokespeople talked about the importance of economic ties with neighboring countries. Lastly,

---

14 Economist Intelligence Unit.

Sunway Group discussed their expansion into other ASEAN markets.

Relations with China

Malaysia's largest trading partner is Singapore, but its largest export market is China. While the United States has been historically a top investor in Malaysia, China's presence in the Malaysian economy has skyrocketed over recent years. The relationship between the two countries is complicated: while their history of interaction is long and deep, Malaysia is viewed by other nations, including the United States, as one of the main counterbalances to China in the region. Malaysia has also participated in the region's disagreements with China over land and borders in the South China Sea. Nevertheless, China has begun to invest heavily in Malaysia as a result of its "One Belt, One Road" initiative, which aims to strengthen infrastructure on China's trade routes. At our meeting at the Chinese-language newspaper *Oriental Daily News*, the editor noted that Chinese officials visit Malaysia approximately once a month to promote trade and investment between the two countries.

Malaysia's relationship with China is further complicated by the many descendants of Chinese migrants residing as citizens in Malaysia, who largely still speak Mandarin and identify as ethnically Chinese. During the unrest of the Summer of 2015 (see later section), relations between the Chinese and Malaysian governments heated up to an unusually controversial level. China's ambassador to Malaysia, Dr. Huang Huikang, visited Kuala Lumpur's Chinatown the day before a large rally and said that if either authorities or demonstrators targeted ethnic Chinese, "We will not sit idly by." He added, "We hope that

Malaysia will maintain its social stability."[15] While his concerns were perhaps warranted given the recent increase in anti-Chinese rhetoric, his statements were not well received by many Malays and nationalist officials in the Malaysian government, who perceived them as a preposterous interference in Malaysia's internal affairs.[16]

During our Trek, we witnessed for ourselves many aspects of China's complex relationship with Malaysia. In Johor Bahru, we saw that many Chinese companies had bought cheap land and were rapidly developing condominium and apartment complexes near the waterfront, posing a direct challenge to Malaysian developers. We also spoke with Chinese Malaysian students about the ambiguity and occasional indifference in their views of China.

It is clear that China's presence in the Malaysian economy will be an influential factor for years to come. Malaysia's management of this relationship and of its cultural and business interactions with China will go a long way toward determining whether China becomes a challenge or an opportunity for Malaysia in the future.

The Recent Corruption Scandal

One of the most interesting and influential developments in Malaysia over the past year has been the high-profile corruption scandal involving the Prime Minister, Najib Razak, and the state-run investment firm, 1Malaysia Development Berhad (1MDB). The scandal

---

15 http://www.themalaymailonline.com/malaysia/article/chinas-envoy-to-malaysia-visits-petaling-street-day-before-rally.
16 http://blogs.cfr.org/asia/2015/10/13/chinas-charm-offensive-continues-to-sputter-in-southeast-asia/.

was present as an implicit or explicit backdrop in a large number of the Trek's meetings. The impact of the scandal has been so far-reaching that it has fostered substantial uncertainty about Malaysia's political and economic future.

In brief, Mr. Najib—who, under Malaysia's unique political system, chairs the Ministry of Finance, which in turn oversees 1MDB—was accused of funneling close to US$700 million from 1MDB to personal accounts. While there had been past rumors about the troubled fund and the massive mismanagement of its finance, the scandal didn't fully break until a *Wall Street Journal* exposé in July 2015 detailed the extent of the accusations against Mr. Najib and implicated his personal involvement.[17] The *Journal* article reported that a paper trail traced the US$700 million to Mr. Najib's personal accounts via agencies, banks, and other companies linked to 1MDB. In response, the Prime Minister said that the money came from a donation, and the country's Anti-Corruption Commission specified that it came from an anonymous donor from the Middle East. These claims have not allayed the concerns of most of the citizens whom we met during the Trek. The scandal has resonated with thousands of Malaysians, many of whom are having trouble keeping up with the rising rents and cost of living in Kuala Lumpur. Some also expressed bitterness at having to pay so much of their income in taxes while their leaders allegedly steal the public's resources.

Shortly after the Trek concluded, on January 26, 2016, the Prime Minister was formally cleared of the corruption allegation by the At-

---

17 http://www.wsj.com/articles/malaysias-leader-at-center-of-a-storm-1444963838.

torney General's Office.[18] Malaysia's Attorney General, Mr. Mohamed Apandi Ali, announced at a press conference that the funds deposited into the Prime Minister's bank account were indeed a donation from Saudi Arabia's royal family and that no criminal offense had been committed.[19] However, while this announcement concluded the domestic investigation into impropriety, it did not mark the end of the scandal. Many Malaysians and members of the international community remain skeptical. 1MDB remains under investigation by Swiss prosecutors, and Malaysia's Anti-Corruption Commission announced the day after the Attorney General's statement that it would appeal the decision and ask an independent government panel to review the case.[20]

Inevitably, the scandal will continue to cast a cloud over Malaysia's politics, as well as Mr. Najib's tenure in power, and it may discourage foreign investors concerned about the country's political stability from investing in Malaysia.[21]

---

18 http://www.theguardian.com/world/2016/jan/26/malaysian-pm-najib-razak-cleared-corruption-gift-saudi-royals.
19 It is relevant to note that the previous Malaysian Attorney General, along with a Deputy Minister who was critical of the Prime Minister, had been removed by Najib, seemingly for investigating the scandal's accusations (http://bigstory.ap.org/article/b451da6f51d5418dbc8c835573f712a5/malaysian-pm-axes-deputy-attorney-general-amid-fund-scandal).
20 http://www.wsj.com/articles/swiss-attorney-general-expresses-concern-over-halt-of-malaysian-1mdb-probe-1454083061; www.nytimes.com/2016/01/28/world/asia/malaysia-agency-to-appeal-decision-to-clear-premier.html.
21 http://www.ndtv.com/world-news/malaysia-pledges-to-help-swiss-probe-as-pressure-on-pm-grows-1271800.

The Role of the Press

During the Trek's visit to the *Oriental Daily News* headquarters, we had a chance to explore the Malaysian media's method of dealing with this scandal, as well as with other political issues, in our roundtable discussion of the role and influence of the media in Malaysia's economic development. Our hosts described the difficulties of covering a scandal as large and sensitive as this one, in a country where press freedom is limited. The Deputy Editor and Executive Editor-in-Chief, explained that they had to be very careful in how they covered the issue. Interestingly, the Deputy Editor stated that only an international outlet like *The Wall Street Journal* could expose the full breadth of the problem. They also talked about their methods of framing the issue to protect themselves from official censure—for instance, covering the statements and reactions of the government in the headline and early part of the article, before giving the rest of the information about the nature of the accusations.

Both men explained that the realm of information and media is changing dramatically in Malaysia because of the rise of the internet and social media. According to many of the people we met on our Trek, the government understands that even if it cracks down on formal press outlets like the newspapers, information will still get out to the public, given the current reach of technology in Malaysia. Out of 30.8 million Malaysians, the country has 20.6 million internet users, eighteen million social media users, 140 percent cellphone penetration (coming to 1.4 phones per person), and ten million smartphone

Mohd Rasfan/Agence France-Presse — Getty Images <http://www.nytimes.com/2015/08/30/world/asia/malaysia-protests-najib-razak-1mdb.html>.

users.[22] Malaysia's average number of hours spent on the internet on mobile devices is the highest in Southeast Asia, with 3.1 hours/day/user.

Malaysian newspapers have been quick to respond to this trend. *Oriental Daily News*, for example, has a very active social media presence, with a Facebook page and a Twitter feed. They also put out separate digital and print editions (both in Chinese) and are usually able to present more controversial coverage in their web version than in their paper edition.

---

22 We Are Social; http://aseanup.com/mobile-internet-social-media-malaysia/.

Youth Are the Future of Malaysia

Perhaps the most rewarding part of our Malaysian journey was the interactions we had with the local youth. Today is an interesting time to be a young person in Malaysia. Last year, youth were at the forefront of the organization of massive protests across Kuala Lumpur, rallying for the resignation of Prime Minister Najib Razak in face of the 1MDB scandal. Openly defying a police ban, tens of thousands of mostly young protestors gathered in the capital in August 2015, making broad demands for change and decrying the failures of corrupt politicians.[23] While the Prime Minister did not resign as a result of these protests, many youth whom we talked with during the Trek cited this incident as an example of the changing nature of Malaysia's next generation, which feels a real sense of agency and wants to have its voice heard.

In 2014, President Barack Obama became the first U.S. president in nearly fifty years to visit Malaysia, where he was welcomed with a six hundred-guest state dinner. Signs of this visit, as well as of his follow-up trip in November 2015 for the Summit of ASEAN leaders, were still visible in Kuala Lumpur when we visited. Obama paid much attention to young people during his time in Malaysia. He gave an impassioned keynote address, as well as conducting a lengthy question-and-answer session, at the Young Southeast Asian Leaders Initiative Town Hall, hosted by the University of Malaya in Kuala Lumpur on April 27, 2014.[24] Many of the youth we met on our Trek

---

23 http://www.bbc.com/news/world-asia-34101245.
24 https://www.whitehouse.gov/the-press-office/2014/04/27/remarks-president-obama-young-southeast-asian-leaders-initiative-town-ha.

described this visit enthusiastically. During his remarks, Mr. Obama called multiple times for the young people of Malaysia and in the region to be leaders in bringing about change:

> The great thing about young people is they're impatient. The biggest problem with young people is they're impatient. It's a strength, because it's what makes you want to change things. But sometimes you can be disappointed if change doesn't happen right away, and then you just give up. And you just have to stay with it and learn from your failures, as well as your successes. [...] It's now up to you, the next generation, to make sure that twenty years from now, or thirty years from now, people look back and say, wow, things are a lot better now than they were back then.[25]

While Malaysian youth are certainly promising heralds of change, there will also be major challenges in meeting their growing demands and needs. With quality of life and GDP per capita on the rise, many Malaysians expect more than ever before from their government and society. One topic stood out when we spoke with young people in Johor Bahru, Malacca, and Kuala Lumpur: the division, problems, resentments, and inequities in Malaysia's education system, particularly higher education. Malaysia has a unique educational system in that students tend to attend primary and secondary schools that correspond to their ethnic identities. Dating back to the country's time under British colonial rule, the system offers multi-stream and multilingual schools as well as a range of vernacular schools with their own

---

25 Ibid.

languages of instruction.[26] Thus, national schools use Bahasa Malaysia, Chinese independent schools use Chinese, private and international schools use English, and state religious schools use Arabic and Bahasa Malaysia.[27] Such a system is advantageous in that each ethnic group in Malaysia can maintain a distinct cultural and linguistic identity, and parents can pass on their ethnic traditions to their children via the schools they attend. The downside—which is currently a hot topic in Malaysian society, as we heard from the students we met—is that the system makes it much more difficult for the country's diverse citizens to develop a cohesive and inclusive sense of national identity. Some of the people we talked with felt that the system encouraged continued stereotyping and social division, rather than promoting integration among all Malaysians regardless of ethnicity. Others, however, maintained that the system is an important part of the Malaysian social contract and said that their parents felt it was important to protect their ability to choose what kind of school they wanted their children to attend.

Malaysia's ethnic tensions also play into the country's university system. While in the past, Malaysia used an ethnic quota to designate spots in government-funded universities—primarily to increase opportunities for *bumiputeras*—this system was abolished in 2002. Currently, Malaysia's Education Ministry says that the university admission system is based on merit. However, many students that we met described the university entrance process as "unfair" and "biased."

---

26 Selvadurai et al., 2015. www.ukm.my/geografia/images/upload/2x.geografia-dec15-siva-bi-edam1.pdf.
27 Routledge Handbook of Contemporary Malaysia 2014. https://www.routledge.com/products/9780415816731.

The system is especially complex because there are two different paths to enrollment, "matriculation" and the Malaysian Higher School Certificate (STPM). The "matriculation" path, which is reserved for *bumiputeras*, can be completed in just one year, while STPM, which Indian and Chinese students must follow, takes two years and is considered more difficult because it is equivalent to British A-Levels and linked to the University of Cambridge's local examination syndicate.[28] As a consequence, the number of Indian and Chinese students in public universities has been falling over time, and admission rates overall are declining. In 2013, according to the *BBC* and Senator Jaspal Singh of the Malaysian Indian Congress (which is part of the governing Barisan Nasional coalition), the number of Indians offered a place in government-funded universities had dropped by more than half from a decade earlier, when at least 8 percent of the public university intake were Indians, even though records showed that the number of Indians applying to public universities had not changed.[29]

In response to the controversy surrounding this issue, the government opened up the higher education system to private participation in 1996, through education reform legislation. According to the World Bank, from 1985 to 2008, while primary school enrollment in Malaysia increased by 43.9 percent and secondary school enrollment rose by 84.6 percent, higher education enrollment improved by a whopping 1,339.4 percent.[30] This enormous increase shows the benefits of private participation, which also enabled Sunway, one of our hosts and the home of the Center for Asia Leadership Initiatives

---

28 http://www.bbc.com/news/world-asia-23841888.
29 Ibid.
30 Mukherjee.

(CALI), to grow exponentially. Sunway Education Group, founded in 1987, is owned and governed by the Jeffrey Cheah Foundation, a first-of-its-kind institution within the field of private higher education in Malaysia. Along with its two flagship universities, Sunway also operates a research-intensive medical school, an accountancy center, a hospitality and management school, and an international school. The Trek had the opportunity to visit many of these institutions during our stay. Sunway's educational institutions have been hailed as a model in the country, and two of the schools—Sunway University and Monash University Malaysia—hold the 2013 Rating for Higher Education Institutions in Malaysia (SETARA '13) Tier 5 Excellent ratings. Nevertheless, while the rapid expansion of private universities over the past twenty years has been "widely credited with increasing access to higher education in Malaysia,"[31] experts have expressed concerns about the varying levels of quality provided by such institutions.

In Kuala Lumpur, we met with Mr. Idris Jusoh, the Malaysian Minister of Higher Education, to discuss the government's vision for the future of higher education in Malaysia. The Minister presented the government's priorities for the reform of higher education in the country, including an increased emphasis on preparing tertiary students. He was also enthusiastic about the growing number of international students studying in Malaysia, many of whom come from the Arab world. This year, he said, Malaysia is expected to be ranked twelfth in the world for the highest number of international students.

---

31 http://www.nytimes.com/2011/10/03/world/asia/malaysia-tries-to-rein-in-private-education-institutions.html.

Concluding Thoughts

I departed Malaysia after the Trek with an array of vivid impressions of the country. First, I was touched by its warmth and generosity. Even when meeting with prominent figures with extremely busy schedules, we were always welcomed with a smile and shown the utmost hospitality. The food was delicious, the meeting rooms were always impeccably prepared, and our student guides at Sunway University were polished and polite. More importantly, our questions in meetings were taken very seriously, and we almost always received thoughtful, authentic responses. This left me with a very favorable impression of the Malaysian people and their spirit.

Second, I left both impressed and slightly concerned by the way in which Malaysia handles its diversity. Like the U.S., Malaysia is a multiethnic, multilingual, and diverse country. During the Trek, I realized that grappling with that diversity and turning it into an advantage rather than an obstacle will be one of the country's biggest challenges in the future. On the one hand, after my recent work and travels in the Middle East, I found it extremely laudable that different ethnic groups in Malaysia have been able to live side by side in peace for so many decades, despite clearly existing tensions. In just a few hours in Kuala Lumpur, I could eat exquisite Indian food, visit a world-renowned Islamic Arts museum, and thread my way through market stalls in Chinatown.

Yet, there is still much room for improvement, as demonstrated in our conversations with the various students we met. We spoke with many high achieving young people who had been hurt directly by the affirmative action system in education and who told us that this was causing them to question their prospects for success in the country. Some of the young Chinese students even noted that the current system of favoritism for the majority means that, if given the chance to study and work abroad, they would not feel inclined to come back to Malaysia. The situation poses a profound problem, given the already existing brain drain referred to by the country's leaders. If Malaysia wants to achieve the ambitious goals it has set for itself, it must do a better job of establishing a fair system in which all citizens feel they have access to opportunities and can climb the ladder of success. Nevertheless, today's young generation in Malaysia benefits from decades of gains in income and living standards, and I feel confident that they will successfully take up the mantle of change.

Finally, I realized that, like the U.S., Malaysia is struggling with profound challenges within its political system and institutions. Unlike America, however, the leader at the top of the political system has been personally implicated, which has sparked a rethinking of even the most basic political assumptions throughout the country. In Kuala Lumpur, I led workshops in which I talked about my experiences in community organizing and political campaigns. It was fascinating to witness the rapt attention of the Malaysian students during my sessions, many of whom are questioning, for the first time, the system in which they live and its previously infallible leaders. The present is thus a delicate moment for Malaysia. Both the world and its own citizens are watching. The way in which Malaysia's political parties confront this challenge will tell onlookers a great deal about the country's resilience and its future political possibilities.

| Chapter 3 |

Opportunities and Challenges for the Tourism and Garment Industries in Cambodia

Annie Yu Kleiman
MALD, Tufts Fletcher School of Law and Diplomacy

By any measure, Cambodia has made impressive gains in the last two decades. Rising from the ashes of a brutal genocide and a decades-long civil war, the country has managed to restore and maintain peace and stability, develop an open market economy, and encourage foreign direct investment. The results have been impressive: hovering at around 7 percent, Cambodia's Gross Domestic Product (GDP) is growing at one of the fastest rates in the world and the highest of any post-conflict nation. In line with the United Nations Millennium Development Goals, the poverty rate has been reduced sharply, from 47.8 percent in 2007 to 18.9 percent in 2012.[1] Life expectancy jumped from fifty-four years in 1990 to seventy-two years in 2012, and the maternal mortality rate plummeted from one thousand two hundred deaths per one hundred thousand births in 1990

---

1 "Poverty in Cambodia," *Asian Development Bank*, Sept 8, 2015, http://www.adb.org/countries/cambodia/poverty.

to one hundred seventy deaths per one hundred thousand births in 2014.[2] Furthermore, registration of children in primary schools now stands at 98 percent for girls as well as boys. According to the World Bank, Cambodia is on the threshold of transitioning from a low-income country to a lower-middle-income country, which is defined as US$1,045 Gross National Income (GNI) per capita, using the World Bank Atlas method. The government hopes to turn Cambodia into an upper-middle-income country by 2030 and an upper-income country by 2050—a ten-fold increase in GNI per capita over the next three and a half decades.

To accomplish this, Cambodia will need to continue its strong economic growth and tap into sources of future potential expansion. But is Cambodia's impressive increase in GDP sustainable? Could the country's current economic growth actually be a hindrance in its future progress? In many ways, Cambodia's relatively low Gross National Product (GNP) per capita is a huge economic asset, but this comparative advantage will decrease as the country's GNP per capita—and therefore its price levels—increase. With most of its economy tied to the dollar, Cambodia cannot utilize exchange-rate fluctuations as a buffer to shore up exports when its currency weakens. Instead, it must rely on its relatively low price levels to remain competitive in the global economy. Two commercial sectors, tourism and the garment industry, make up a significant portion of Cambodia's economy, and both depend on the country's low price levels in comparison to developed countries.

---

2 Crothers, Lauren, "Life Expectancy Leaps 18 Years, WHO Says," *The Cambodia Daily* (Phnom Penh, Cambodia), May 16, 2014, https://www.cambodiadaily.com/archives/life-expectancy-leaps-18-years-who-says-58878/.

The Tourism Industry

In the tourism sector, Cambodia regularly appears on lists for "Best Budget Destinations." Its main draws are affordable food, transportation, and accommodations; friendly locals; and the ancient Angkor Wat complex.[3] From my perspective as a short-term visitor on the Asia Leadership Trek, much of Cambodia's economy seemed to rely on foreign visitors spending money on goods or services that cost a fraction in Cambodia of what they do in the visitors' home countries. Less than two minutes from our hotel, there were four massage parlors and spas, charging about one-tenth the price that similar services would command in Boston, Massachusetts. Transportation via tuk-tuk ranged between US$1 and US$4 and was always obtainable, with at least half a dozen tuk-tuk drivers always parked outside our hotel, looking for potential customers. While a few dollars for a ride was a significant cost for many locals, it was cheap by Western standards. That said, prices do seem to be on the increase, as I observed on several occasions, when tuk-tuk drivers sought US$4 for a route I had taken just a few hours earlier for only US$2. Most often, trips from our hotels to the local markets were US$1-US$2 cheaper than the same trip returning to the hotel. It was not clear if the hotels supplemented the tuk-tuks sitting out front or if there was simply a difference in bargaining perception at the local markets.

I visited night markets in both Phnom Penh and Siem Reap.

---

3 "Where to Go in 2015!" *Budget Travel*. Accessed February 20, 2016. http://www.budgettravel.com/feature/10-best-budget-destinations-for-2015,51558/.

While the food stalls catered to the local palate, much of the merchandise seemed geared toward foreign visitors: mass-produced shoes, clothing, jewelry, and knick knacks were offered at a fraction of typical prices in more developed countries. Vendors expertly switched between English, Chinese, and other languages depending on the appearance of the groups of tourists walking by, and at every stand where I paused (and even some where I didn't), I was inundated with suggestions for potential purchases and offers of discounts. A key selling point tapped into the same impulse that "dollar stores" in the U.S. take advantage of: prices are so low that buyers make purchases without seriously considering whether they need, or even truly want, the item in question. Not planning on buying half a dozen scarves with Angkor Wat embroidered on them? Buy them anyway—they're only three dollars each. A pair of sandals for five dollars? A bargain; never mind that they don't fit perfectly.

This economy of impulse buying and cheap, plentiful services has negative effects on both foreign visitors and Cambodians. It makes the locals regard all foreign visitors as walking dollar signs, potential sources of income. Virtually every interaction between locals and tourists has a monetary transaction as the end goal, and nothing more. There is no curiosity about the other person's story, home country, or culture—simply a desire to exchange a product or service for hard cash. For the visitors, the system risks reducing Cambodians to faceless commodities and service providers. Instead of encountering individual human beings worthy of dignity and respect, we are confronted with tuk-tuk drivers, street vendors, and food servers, one much like the others and all trying to offer something in exchange for money. As a result of this effect, the system also tends to turn foreign visitors into jerks—arrogant, dismissive, and secure in our higher spending power. It is easy to feel superior when haggling over a dollar for a magnet or dismissing a tuk-tuk driver because there are three others clamoring for your business. Though most visitors probably don't intend to act offensively, there is a temptation to slip into this entitled behavioral pattern—part defensive, part exasperated—when confronted with constant questions: "You buy something?" "You need a tuk-tuk?" After a while, the vendors' aggressive approach forces one into an irritated refrain of "No, no, we're fine."

In Siem Reap, the negative effects of Cambodia's over-reliance on tourism are on full display. The vendors at the night market were so keen to make a sale that one of them literally pulled me by the hand, refusing to let go while she tried to convince me to buy a dress. At Angkor Wat, we were approached and followed by countless individuals selling coffee, books, magnets, and other trinkets. In one case, I was thinking about buying a piece of artwork, but the seller was so pushy that I decided not to; ironically, he had talked himself out of a deal. Perhaps most disturbing was the sight of the children at Angkor Wat, selling trinkets or begging. Despite official signs advising visitors not to give money or candy to the children, since that encourages them to continue begging instead of going to school, it was hard to walk away from these children. The plaintive sound of a young child calling, "Buy a magnet, one dollllarrrr," in a voice that should have been asking for ice cream or five more minutes with a favorite toy, is heartbreaking. I spent much of my visit to Angkor Wat torn between wanting to give the children money and knowing that doing so would only exacerbate the problem. It was agonizing that, as an individual, I could do nothing to remedy the systemic issues causing those conditions. Somehow the relative gains and costs for a family to send their children to school versus selling trinkets to tourists must be shifted so that school becomes a more viable, more economically appealing option.

The constant barrage of transactional offers was exhausting, one of the few negatives in an otherwise great trip. Yet, while I simply wanted to be left alone to browse in peace, my arbitrary decisions of what and where to buy it might well have dramatically impacted the livelihoods of the stall vendors. It was impossible to know if the eight dollars one vendor wanted for a dress would bridge the gap between his family going hungry or eating well that night, or if a tuk-tuk driver trying to catch my attention desperately needed the income. Unfortunately, any attempt to ascertain such information could be twisted into another sales pitch. The phenomenon led one of my friends to remark, "Go visit Myanmar soon, in the next few years, before it becomes like Cambodia." I noticed this trend while speaking with other friends who had also visited Cambodia—it's a country always spoken of with a caveat: "Cambodia was beautiful, but it was so sad seeing the children beg." "Angkor Wat was stunning, but it seemed like all my interactions with the locals were transactional."

Tourism in Cambodia doesn't have to be like this. With the country's rich history, beautiful scenery, and delicious food, foreign tourists shouldn't need to include caveats when talking about their visit. There are several concrete steps the government can take to improve and expand the tourism industry. In its report entitled "Economic Outlook for Southeast Asia, China, and India 2014: Beyond the Middle-Income Trap," the Organization for Economic Cooperation and Development (OECD) makes three main recommendations for

Cambodia: develop a tourism-specific infrastructure, improve the existing transport infrastructure, and diversify tourist destinations beyond Angkor Wat.

Developing a Tourism-Specific Infrastructure

The OECD report gives kudos to the Cambodian government for developing an online visa application system that's available in twenty-five languages. I can personally attest that the system was convenient and easy to use. I applied for and submitted my payment for the visa online, and I received it via e-mail a few days later. Some members of our group didn't even apply for visas ahead of time, choosing instead to get them upon arrival at the Phnom Penh international airport. That process took only a few minutes and didn't delay our group's departure from the airport. Overall, the process made traveling to Cambodia easy and was much simpler than, for example, China's arcane visa system, which requires one's passport to be presented in person at the Chinese consulate geographically responsible for one's permanent residence.

Nevertheless, some travelers have complained online that the employees at both Cambodian airports overtly ask for tips when processing their visa paperwork or examining their passports. While we did not experience this phenomenon ourselves, I have found anecdotal evidence that requests for tips are more commonly made to Asian, specifically Chinese passengers. Given that tourists from Asia and the Pacific make up the vast majority—approximately 78 percent—of Cambodia's foreign visitors every year, asking for tips does not seem conducive to encouraging growth in the tourism sector. The e-visa program is a good start in minimizing this trend, as it allows travelers to bypass the visa application process at the port of entry, but attempts should still be made to reduce the incidence of airport employees asking for tips. A sign at each immigration desk with the message "Tips not allowed," along with the employee's name and an identification number, would do much to discourage blatant requests. A more technologically advanced system, allowing travelers to report demands for tips online, could hold employees accountable and make enforcement easier.

Of course, regardless of how well designed the tipping prevention system becomes, at the airports or anywhere else in Cambodia, for the system to work the leaders must buy into it. Thus, a large part of the solution rests on government and business leaders convincing their followers that eliminating, or at least minimizing, requests for tips is in the best interest of everyone in the long run. At the same time, attention should be paid to why these requests are being made in the first place. Are employees supplementing their income with tips because they feel their wages are too low? If so, can their employers afford to raise those wages? Where would the additional funds come from? What would be a fair wage? Solving these problems requires a holistic approach, with consideration given to the elements of technology, economics, and human psychology. The long-term payoff, however, would be a better traveling experience for visitors to Cambodia, with a better reputation on the world stage.

Another area ripe for improvement is the regulation of informal vendors. According to a recent *Voice of America – Cambodia* article, the number of vendors in Siem Reap has increased in the past few years. This means that each individual vendor is making less than before, despite the increase in tourists (2.35 million in 2014, compared to 2.23 million in 2013).[4] To my unpracticed eye, it appeared that many of the vendors we encountered were not part of the formal economy and thus not subject to control or regulation. A system regulating their number as well as the quality of products sold would increase profits for the vendors as well as greatly enhance the shopping experiences for foreign visitors.

At the same time, the Cambodian government should encourage the production and sale of unique, locally made, high quality Cambodian products. During the Trek, as we walked around the stalls at the Siem Reap night market, it became apparent that many of the stalls sell the same products. When we travel overseas, my husband and I always purchase a stuffed animal for our daughter in every country we visit. While searching for such a toy at the night market, I found at least half a dozen stalls selling the same toy elephant but none selling a toy that was quintessentially Cambodian. At least four stalls sold paintings—supposedly hand-painted—that looked remarkably similar. After much haggling over what we thought was a unique gift—a bottle of alcohol containing a snake and scorpion—my husband and I turned the corner to find two more stalls selling the same thing. And while I'm happy buying mass-produced products in my daily life, that's not what I'm looking for when I shop for souvenirs in a foreign country. I can't help but feel that I've been taken for a sucker when I purchase what I thought was a unique local item, only

---

4 Bopha, Phorn, "In Siem Reap, a Hustle and Grind for Tourism Dollars," *Voice of America Khmer,* (Phnom Penh, Cambodia), April 30, 2015. http://www.voacambodia.com/content/in-cambodia-siem-reap-a-hustle-and-grind-for-tourism-dollar/2741805.html.

to find it sold throughout the country or—worse—sold in different countries altogether. While it is of course cheaper for the vendors to sell these mass-produced items, the Cambodian government should encourage the production and sale of souvenirs that are representative of the country's unique heritage.

One effective example of such governmental encouragement can be found in Singapore, where many vendors offer figurines of Singapore's national symbol, the merlion—a half-lion, half-fish creature said to represent Singapore's beginning as a fishing village. I assumed initially that the merlion was well-established in ancient Singaporean folklore but then found out that it was created by Singapore's tourism board in the 1960s. Despite this bit of PR contrivance, however, my daughter is now the proud owner of a stuffed merlion, which is unmistakably Singaporean. My husband and I couldn't find an equivalent for Cambodia during the Trek, no matter how many markets we went to. Yet, given Cambodia's rich history and iconography, it should be possible to establish and market certain symbols as quintessentially Cambodian. Such a program could provide funding for local artists to set up stalls at various markets while simultaneously controlling the quality and quantity of the vendors' products.

One other issue greatly affects the Cambodian tourism industry and Cambodia's reputation in the outside world. As soon as our bus left the airport, I was struck not only by the beautiful architecture in Phnom Penh but also by the prevalence of trash on the streets. Plastic bags, bottles, and other bits of garbage were strewn everywhere. During our time there I never observed a trash collection service at work (though I'm sure some system exists), and public garbage cans were few and far between. The amount of garbage detracts from Phnom

Penh's vibrant beauty and could pose a health threat as well. In Siem Reap, I experienced the same thing: I was distracted by the trash on the streets instead of giving my full attention to the interesting sights and sounds around me.

The Cambodian government would need to leverage a clever mix of policies to reduce trash on the streets, pursuing two separate but mutually enforcing goals: first, to change the average citizen's behavior from being willing to litter to refraining from littering, and indeed going out of their way to pick up litter in public spaces; second, to improve public services for trash pick-up, including increasing the availability of public trash receptacles. Reaching both of these goals would require a mix of policies and public education campaigns. The government could pass statutes imposing high penalties for littering, while also increasing funding for new trash cans and pick-up services. Simultaneously, local law enforcement agencies could be instructed to be vigilant about enforcing the statutes. Lastly, a public awareness campaign could be initiated to educate the public about the new statutes and to change their attitude about littering. Civic organizations, such as the Union of Youth Federations of Cambodia, could be enlisted to help, mobilizing their members to engage in volunteer clean-up efforts as well as spreading the message about not littering. The ultimate aim would be to achieve a system of reducing trash on the streets that was sustainable in the long-term and required minimal government expenditure.

While it is ambitious, I know that such a system is possible: Phnom Penh itself offers the proof. While driving through the city on our first day, we suddenly entered a section of the city that was immaculate. The grass was beautifully manicured, and there was not a single piece of garbage in sight. I don't know why this section of the city was so clean, but its existence means that the trash on the streets isn't simply "the way Cambodia is." The neighborhood serves as evidence that the right mix of policies, services, and incentives can make a difference.

Improving Transport Infrastructure

In 2015, Cambodia ranked 105th out of 141 countries in the World Economic Forum's Travel and Tourism Competitiveness Index, behind countries like Rwanda, Honduras, and Iran.[5] While it received high marks for the prioritization of travel and tourism, and for price competitiveness, it fared poorly in air transport infrastructure, ground and port infrastructure, and tourist service infrastructure. Surprisingly, it also scored poorly in cultural resources and business travel, though perhaps the calculations in this category were misleading, as the entire Angkor Wat complex counts as a single World Heritage site. That point aside, the Travel and Tourism Competitiveness Index, much like the OECD report, makes it clear that the travel infrastructure in Cambodia needs to be improved.

Of the approximately 4.5 million tourists who visit Cambodia each year, almost half arrive by air. In 2012, 1.7 million tourists entered Cambodia via the only two airports in the country that can accommodate regular international flights: Phnom Penh and Siem Reap. Both airports need to be expanded to accommodate growing

---
5   World Economic Forum. 2015. *The Travel & Tourism Competitiveness Report.* Geneva: World Economic Forum. www3.weforum.org/docs/TT15/WEF_Global_Travel&Tourism_Report_2015.pdf.

needs. By contrast, Cambodia has some of the lowest road density scores in Southeast Asia: 0.26 in 2012, compared to 0.35 for Thailand and 0.78 for Vietnam in 2009. Natural disasters such as floods are a major challenge for Cambodia's road development efforts, although the government has drastically increased its flood related maintenance and road infrastructure budgets since 2007. While the government is currently working on rehabilitating Cambodia's railways, which fell into disrepair during the civil war, the railway system is several years away from being a viable transportation option for tourists. One line opened to freight traffic in 2010,[6] while another, which will connect to the Thai railway system, is being reconstructed. A third line, connecting Phnom Penh with Ho Chi Minh City, is in the planning stages.

On a more granular level, based on my time in Cambodia with the Trek, I believe that expanding and improving local transportation within Cambodian cities would greatly improve the average tourist's experience. Every time we stepped outside our hotel in Phnom Penh, there were at least four tuk-tuk drivers waiting in front of the building, aggressively offering their services. We would then engage in elaborate negotiations over the price, taking into account where we wanted to go, how many people were in our group, what we had paid for previous trips, and how many other tuk-tuk drivers were nearby, waiting to undercut the price and snap up our business. The process usually left me feeling uncomfortable, with no single party complete-

---

[6] Carmichael, Robert, "Cambodia Takes First Step in Connecting Regional Railways," *Voice of America,* October 24, 2010. http://www.voanews.com/content/cambodia-takes-first-step-in-connecting-regional-railways-105662543/166537.html.

ly satisfied with the transaction. As visitors, we were never sure if we were getting ripped off despite our bargaining, and the tuk-tuk driver was probably disappointed that a group of foreign tourists would haggle over a dollar or two. The other tuk-tuk drivers, who were too slow, too passive, or too far away, were undoubtedly annoyed not to get our business. Overall, it's a system that can be intimidating and frustrating for tourists and is inefficient for tuk-tuk drivers. As far as I could see, most of the drivers spent the majority of their day sitting in their tuk-tuks, waiting for potential customers to show up.

An Uber-like system, allowing customers to call a tuk-tuk using their phone and to see a fare estimate for the trip ahead of time, would solve most of these issues. It would eliminate the need to negotiate a price for every trip, thus cutting out a common source of friction for tourists. Moreover, drivers would not have to be physically present to gain customers, freeing them up for more productive activities elsewhere. By making the monetary transactions electronic, such a system would also help to bring more of Cambodia's population into the formal banking system: currently only about 22 percent of Cambodians over the age of fifteen have an account at a financial institution, one of the lowest rates in the Asia-Pacific region.[7] Last but not least, by eliminating the need for money to change hands between tourists and tuk-tuk drivers, the system would create opportunities for interactions beyond the purely transactional. Instead of haggling over a few dollars, tourists and drivers might engage in more substantive conversations about their respective backgrounds, inter-

---

7   World Bank, "Financial Inclusion Index." http://datatopics.worldbank.org/financialinclusion/country/cambodia.

ests, and cultures.

Diversifying Tourist Destinations

Over half of the visitors to Cambodia each year go to Siem Reap in order to see Angkor Wat, which is by far the country's most popular tourist destination. But Cambodia holds numerous other destinations that tourists would enjoy if they were effectively publicized and marketed. For example, the OECD report recommends the "tropical beaches on the south-west coast and the colonial and historical buildings in Phnom Penh." Steps could also be taken to promote Cambodia as a scuba diving destination. While the Professional Association of Diving Instructors' website lists several excellent dive sites off the coast of Cambodia, the country does not have the strong reputation for scuba diving of other tropical countries, such as Australia or the Bahamas.

One reason for this lack of diverse destinations might be the difficulty of traveling within Cambodia. Some members of the Trek, for example, wanted to stay a few extra days after our visit ended, but they had a hard time traveling from Siem Reap to other destinations. Given that the majority of Cambodia's visitors go to Siem Reap, it makes sense to encourage them to visit other parts of Cambodia in conjunction with their visit to Angkor Wat, and thus improving the transportation infrastructure, especially into and out of Siem Reap, would also help to expand tourism beyond Angkor Wat.

The Garment Industry

It is difficult to over exaggerate the importance of the garment industry to Cambodia's economy. As of mid-2015, the sector employed roughly six hundred thousand workers, approximately 86 percent of whom are female.[8] These workers collectively earn around US$130 million each month, money that is injected into the Cambodian economy from overseas by international clothing companies.[9] Since the majority of the financial transactions in Cambodia take place in US dollars, this influx of funds is an important source of liquidity that helps mitigate the government's lack of monetary policy.

Accounting for approximately 80 percent of the country's exports, the garment industry "remains the backbone of the Cambodian economy" and is the country's largest manufacturing industry as well as the largest foreign exchange earner.[10] Cambodia's market share of garment and footwear exports has grown steadily, from 1.1 percent in 2005 to 1.8 percent in 2014, ranking eighth among the world's top footwear exporters, although it significantly trails two of its regional competitors, Vietnam (ranked second in the world, with 6.9 percent market share) and Bangladesh (ranked fourth, with 5.5 percent market share).[11] The garment industry is also, however, one that "follows poverty" as if on "roller skates…rolling from Latin America to China

---

8   International Labour Organization, "Cambodian Garment and Footwear Sector Bulletin," October 2015.
9   Meeting with GMAC officials, January 15, 2016.
10 International Labour Organization, "Cambodian Garment and Footwear Sector Bulletin," October 2015.
11 Ibid.

to Bangladesh—wherever costs are lowest."[12] Given the increases to the minimum wage in recent years—from US$100 to US$128 per month in November 2014[13] and from US$128 to US$140 per month in October 2015[14]—Cambodia will need to find a careful balance between increasing wage and living standards and suffering possible job losses as a result.

While in Cambodia, my fellow Trekkers and I had the opportunity to meet with

Secretary General Dr. Ken Loo and Mr. Van, Chairman of the Garment Manufacturers Association in Cambodia (GMAC). We discussed several aspects of Cambodia's garment industry, focusing especially on key areas in which Cambodia is competitive and on areas in which it can continue to improve.

Dollarization

All transactions for the Cambodian garment industry are conducted in US dollars, making it easy for international clothing companies, especially those in the US, to do business in Cambodia. In fact, Cam-

---

12 Planet Money. "'Our Industry Follows Poverty': Success Threatens A T-Shirt Business," *National Public Radio*, December 2, 2013. http://www.npr.org/sections/money/2013/12/04/247360787/our-industry-follows-poverty-success-threatens-a-t-shirt-business.
13 Hookway, James and Sun Narin. "Cambodia Sets Minimum Wage Below Union Demands," *The Wall Street Journal*, November 12, 2014. http://www.wsj.com/articles/cambodia-sets-minimum-wage-below-union-demands-1415789944.
14 "Cambodia raises minimum wage for garment workers," *British Broadcasting Company*. October 8, 2015. http://www.bbc.com/news/world-asia-34474397.

bodia possesses Asia's "most dollarized" economy,[15] and US dollars are more widely accepted there than the Cambodian riel, which, at an exchange rate of approximately four thousand riel to one dollar, is commonly used as pocket change for transactions less than a dollar. In many ways, Cambodia's prevalent use of the US dollar makes the garment industry possible: international companies can build factories, hire workers, and pay for exports without having to rely on the Cambodian government to maintain a robust currency exchange system. According to Dr. Loo, it "wouldn't be possible" for the garment industry to function if the transactions weren't in dollars.

Yet, while operating in dollars decreases transaction costs and complexities, Cambodia's reliance on the dollar is a mixed blessing. A strong US dollar makes exports from Cambodia more expensive to the rest of the world, which is increasingly problematic as the US is no longer Cambodia's biggest customer for clothing exports. While the government has taken small steps to encourage the use of the riel—it is used for government salaries, taxes, utility bills, and the Cambodia Securities Exchange—policy makers are hesitant to require its use in all transactions for fear of destabilizing the economy. Other countries provide cautionary examples of such destabilization. In 1982, for instance, when Mexico converted deposits held in dollars into pesos, a large amount of capital flight occurred, slowing growth and increasing inflation significantly. With foreign currency accounting for 83 percent of deposits in Cambodia, a similar effect could be catastrophic for Cambodia's economy.

---

15 Duma, Nombulelo. "Dollarization in Cambodia: Causes and Policy Implications," International Monetary Fund Working Paper, March 2011.

The National Bank of Cambodia will thus move slowly and cautiously in encouraging wider acceptance of the riel, but, according to the Director General of Central Banking at the Cambodian National Bank, the process will continue in the next decade.[16] Despite the lack of a definitive date to implement these plans, if Cambodia's economy continues to grow at a rapid rate and Cambodia reaches its goal of becoming an upper-middle-income country, at some point it will undoubtedly wish to re-establish the use of the riel and reclaim its autonomy in monetary policy, in order to protect itself from shocks to its economy. And as the economy shifts from dollars to riel, the garment industry will need to adjust accordingly, weighing the costs and benefits of the ease of transactions versus export price competitiveness.

ILO Monitoring

The Cambodian government mandates that all factories must submit to monitoring by the International Labor Organization (ILO) in order to receive an export license. This requirement came about in 2001 as a result of a bilateral trade agreement with the United States, which provided an incentive for Cambodia to improve factory working conditions by linking improvements to expanded quotas for Cambodian exports. Though the quotas expired in 2004, the Cambodian government has maintained the monitoring requirement and

---

16 Ismail, Netty Idayu. "Pol Pot Legacy Leaves Cambodian Riel Battling Dollar's Supremacy," *Bloomberg*, March 10, 2016. http://www.bloomberg.com/news/articles/2016-03-11/pol-pot-legacy-leaves-cambodian-riel-battling-dollar-s-supremacy.

today is working with trade unions, the GMAC, and Better Factories Cambodia, the independent monitoring organization developed by the ILO, to improve factory labor conditions. This collaboration has led to improved working conditions in factories across Cambodia and is a key competitive advantage that Cambodian factories can use to attract international buyers.

During the Trek's meeting with GMAC officials, they stressed Cambodia's excellent safety record and the difference between factories in Cambodia and those in Bangladesh, where garment workers earn some of the lowest wages in the world, at approximately $68 per month.[17] In particular, they mentioned the 2013 Rana Plaza collapse in Bangladesh, which killed over a thousand people, the worst disaster in the garment industry's history.[18] Secretary General Loo pointed to Cambodia's much better safety record, emphasizing the requirement that all factories in Cambodia must be single-story buildings, in contrast to Rana Plaza, which was eight stories high.

Nevertheless, there are still some problematic aspects within Cambodia's garment factories. For example, the ILO monitoring requirement exists only for factories seeking to export their products. Better Factories Cambodia therefore exerts very little influence on smaller factories, but these smaller factories frequently act as sub-contractors for larger factories, and it is often in them that the worst working

---

17 Wright, Tom, "Garment Brands Support Workers' Push for Higher Wages," *The Wall Street Journal,* October 14, 2014. http://www.wsj.com/articles/garment-workers-push-for-higher-wages-1413321601.

18 Manik, Julfikar Ali and Nida Najar, "Bangladesh Police Charge 41 With Murder Over Rana Plaza Collapse," June 01, 2015. http://www.nytimes.com/2015/06/02/world/asia/bangladesh-rana-plaza-murder-charges.html?_r=0.

conditions exist.[19] Many Cambodian factories continue to engage in forced overtime: in a study conducted by Human Rights Watch, the majority of interviewed workers reported that they were forced to perform overtime work exceeding the two-hour per day limit imposed by Cambodia's Labor Law, sometimes working until as late as 9 p.m. Workers also reported being subjected to retaliatory actions if they did not perform overtime work, such as being fired, having their wages reduced, or being transferred from receiving a monthly wage to earning wages based on the number of garments they produced.[20]

A number of factories have taken steps to discourage the formation of unions, going so far as to fire union leaders or pressure them with bribes, keep workers on short-term contracts to discourage their participation in unions, and encourage pro-management unions. The Cambodian Ministry of Labor and Vocational Training has also introduced additional bureaucratic requirements to register newly formed unions, which will lengthen the registration timeline and thus present an additional obstacle for workers seeking to unionize. This issue was brought up by the GMAC officials during our meeting with them, but, revealingly, they framed it as an indication of there being too many unions in the garment industry. "Cambodian workers love unions," they told us. "We meet with the leader of a union one day, and six months later the union has split into two and he's the leader of a different union!"

Discrimination against women, who make up the vast majority

---

19   Human Rights Watch, "Work Faster or Get Out," March 11, 2015. https://www.hrw.org/report/2015/03/11/work-faster-or-get-out/labor-rights-abuses-cambodias-garment-industry.
20   Ibid.

of the garment industry workforce, is another acute problem within the industry. Pregnant women face especially heavy obstacles: the difficulty of getting hired if they are visibly pregnant, the lack of accommodations for restroom breaks, harassment for being "slow" and "unproductive," and, perhaps most troubling, the discovery that their short-term contracts will not be renewed so that their employers won't have to pay maternity benefits.[21] Women workers in Cambodia's garment factories also report frequent instances of sexual harassment from male managers and workers, with approximately one in five women reporting that harassment has created a threatening work environment.[22]

The problematic gender dynamic within the industry was visible even during our meeting with the GMAC officials, who were all men. When the issue of harassment was raised, they trivialized the recent mass fainting incidents at factories, stating that probably only one person had actually fainted and that her neighbors had taken advantage of the opportunity to get a break from working. Their statements implied that the workers involved were all female and that the fainting, whether real or feigned, was an indication of feminine weakness. Worse still, when one Trekker asked about the gender balance in union leadership positions, one of the GMAC officials stated that the majority of union leaders were men, even though almost 90 percent of the workers are women, and he seemed unconcerned by this imbalance. "I don't think the women want those leadership positions," he said, adding, "Life is hard."

---

21 Ibid.
22 Ibid

Trade Preferences

The GMAC has stated on record that Cambodia's garment exports are completely reliant on trade preferences.[23] The good news is that Cambodia currently has trading preferences with the European Union (EU), Canada, and Japan. Under the EU's "Everything But Arms" scheme, Cambodia can export all products except for ammunition and arms to the EU, duty free.[24] Despite this advantage, however, during our meeting with the GMAC officials, they candidly stated that in countries where Cambodia does not have trade preferences, such as the U.S., Cambodia is losing market share. The EU recently replaced the U.S. as the biggest importer of Cambodia's garment exports, an indication of how powerful trade preferences can be.

One key difficulty is that Cambodia's garment industry is competing with Vietnam. During our meeting we learned that Vietnamese workers are paid approximately the same wages as Cambodian workers but are roughly 25 percent more productive. While the leaders of GMAC admitted this freely, they did not address why Vietnamese workers were more productive or how lessons from Vietnam's garment industry could be applied to Cambodia's industry. Two major trade agreements—the Trans-Pacific Partnership and the EU-Vietnam free trade agreement—could allow Vietnam to export garments, duty

---

23 Baliga, Ananth, "TPP puts Cambodia's trade, investment in the spotlight," *Phnom Penh Post*, October 7, 2015. http://www.phnompenhpost.com/business/tpp-puts-cambodias-trade-investment-spotlight.
24 Delegation of the European Union to Cambodia, "Cambodia and the EU," http://eeas.europa.eu/delegations/cambodia/eu_cambodia/index_en.htm.

free to the U.S., Japan, Canada, and the EU in the next few years, a change that would greatly enhance Vietnam's competitiveness at Cambodia's cost and clearly shows that Cambodia's reliance on trade preferences is not sustainable in the long run.

The Cambodian garment industry is taking steps to address these concerns, including building an institute to provide leadership training to selected workers and allowing certain management positions currently held by expats to shift to local hires, thereby saving on salary. But there has been little discussion of how to improve the workers' efficiency or how to create new opportunities for the garment industry as a whole. For example, while garments make up the largest share of Cambodia's exports, the sector relies on importing textiles for its raw materials. Of the top ten products imported to Cambodia in 2012, three were textiles—cotton, synthetic fibers, and knitwear—and accounted for 32 percent of the total imports.[25] If the garment industry could expand to include the manufacturing of textiles, the result would be a significant increase in revenue—or at least a decrease in the use of export revenue to pay for imported textiles.

This situation is not new in the garment-making world: Colombia's garment industry recently experienced a similar threat and has taken steps to ensure its own survival. As of December 2013, workers making T-shirts in Colombia were paid about US$13 a day without overtime, compared to workers in Bangladesh who made about US$3 a day, including overtime. While the wage gap is large, Colombia's factories compensate with better technology and greater

---

25 EuroCham Cambodia, "Market Study: The Textile Industry in Cambodia," *Italian Trade Commission*, September 2014.

efficiency: eight people making one hundred forty T-shirts per hour compared to Bangladesh's thirty-two people making eighty T-shirts per hour. Additionally, some of Colombia's factories do everything in-house, including spinning the cotton into yarn, knitting the yarn into cloth, and sewing the T-shirts, making the process faster and easier and reducing the outflow of revenue for raw materials. Lastly, Colombian clothing manufacturing companies have started to move from making low-end clothing for Western brands to making and selling high-end clothing under their own brands, in an attempt, they say, to "control our own destiny."[26] With Cambodia poised to hit a demographic sweet spot, there is every reason for the leaders of the country's garment industry to aim for a similar transformation.

Conclusion

To capitalize on the gains of recent decades, Cambodia cannot simply scale up or do more of the same. It needs to explore fundamentally different ways of doing business, shifting its economy from one that relies on relative poverty to one that can overcome these limitations and move toward a holistic approach to growth. However, in order to do that, Cambodia should first start by maximizing the resources it already has. The country's many interesting and beautiful regions have the potential to serve as effective draws for tourist dollars. Working on developing easier access to these areas and ensuring

---

26 Planet Money. "'Our Industry Follows Poverty': Success Threatens A T-Shirt Business," *National Public Radio*, December 2, 2013. http://www.npr.org/sections/money/2013/12/04/247360787/our-industry-follows-poverty-success-threatens-a-t-shirt-business.

that they remain unpolluted—as well as reducing the pollution levels in already established tourism sites—will help to enhance Cambodia's global reputation and appeal. I look forward to coming back to Cambodia soon, to enjoy not only the history of Phnom Penh and the majesty of Angkor Wat but also the many other tourist sites that they will undoubtedly develop.

The country also needs to diversify its industries, while modernizing and improving its already thriving garment industry. This will require increased cooperation and political participation at all levels: internationally, among agencies, and between the public and private sectors. Internationally, major clothing brands must expand their commitment to ensuring fair wages and adequate working conditions for all workers in their supply chain. At the inter-agency level, the ministries within the Cambodian government must work together not only to develop laws that protect workers and enhance the garment industry's productivity but also to provide adequate monitoring and enforcement. Lastly, the public and private sectors should explore possible areas of cooperation in order to make full use of Cambodia's human resources.

In the past twenty years, Cambodia has overcome nearly insurmountable obstacles to transform itself into a peaceful and secure nation with an open market economy. I have no doubt that it will tackle future challenges with enthusiasm and wisdom.

Bibliography

Baliga, Ananth. "TPP puts Cambodia's trade, investment in the spotlight." *Phnom Penh Post*, October 7, 2015. http://www.phnompenhpost.com/business/tpp-puts-cambodias-trade-investment-spotlight.

Bopha, Phorn. "In Siem Reap, a Hustle and Grind for Tourism Dollars." *Voice of America Khmer* (Phnom Penh, Cambodia), April 30, 2015. http://www.voacambodia.com/content/in-cambodia-siem-reap-a-hustle-and-grind-for-tourism-dollar/2741805.html.

"Cambodia raises minimum wage for garment workers." *British Broadcasting Company*, October 8, 2015. http://www.bbc.com/news/world-asia-34474397.

Carmichael, Robert. "Cambodia Takes First Step in Connecting Regional Railways," *Voice of America,* October 24, 2010. http://www.voanews.com/content/cambodia-takes-first-step-in-connecting-regional-railways-105662543/166537.html.

Crothers, Lauren. "Life Expectancy Leaps 18 Years, WHO Says," *The Cambodia Daily*. May 16, 2014. https://www.cambodiadaily.com/archives/life-expectancy-leaps-18-years-who-says-58878/.

Delegation of the European Union to Cambodia, "Cambodia and the EU," http://eeas.europa.eu/delegations/cambodia/eu_cambodia/index_en.htm.

Duma, Nombulelo. "Dollarization in Cambodia: Causes and Policy Implications," International Monetary Fund Working Paper, March 2011.

EuroCham Cambodia. "Market Study: The Textile Industry in Cambodia," *Italian Trade Commission*, September 2014.

Hookway, James and Sun Narin. "Cambodia Sets Minimum Wage Below Union Demands," *The Wall Street Journal*, November 12, 2014. http://www.wsj.com/articles/cambodia-sets-minimum-wage-below-union-demands-1415789944.

Human Rights Watch, "Work Faster or Get Out," March 11, 2015. https://www.hrw.org/report/2015/03/11/work-faster-or-get-out/labor-rights-abuses-cambodias-garment-industry.

International Labour Organization. "Cambodian Garment and Footwear Sector Bulletin," October 2015.

Ismail, Netty Idayu. "Pol Pot Legacy Leaves Cambodian Riel Battling Dollar's Supremacy," *Bloomberg*, March 10, 2016. http://www.bloomberg.com/news/articles/2016-03-11/pol-pot-legacy-leaves-cambodian-riel-battling-dollar-s-supremacy.

Manik, Julfikar Ali and Nida Najar. "Bangladesh Police Charge 41 With Murder Over Rana Plaza Collapse," June 01, 2015. http://www.nytimes.com/2015/06/02/world/asia/bangladesh-rana-plaza-murder-charges.html?_r=0.

Meeting with GMAC officials, 15 January 2016.

Planet Money. "'Our Industry Follows Poverty': Success Threatens A T-Shirt Business," *National Public Radio*, December 2, 2013. http://www.npr.org/sections/money/2013/12/04/247360787/our-industry-follows-poverty-success-threatens-a-t-shirt-business.

"Poverty in Cambodia," *Asian Development Bank*, Sept 8, 2015. http://www.adb.org/countries/cambodia/poverty.

"Where to Go in 2015!" *Budget Travel*. http://www.budgettravel.com/feature/10-best-budget-destinations-for-2015,51558/.

World Bank, "Financial Inclusion Index." http://datatopics.worldbank.org/financialinclusion/country/cambodia.

World Economic Forum. *The Travel & Tourism Competitiveness Report*. Geneva: World Economic Forum. 2015. www3.weforum.org/docs/TT15/WEF_Global_Travel &Tourism_Report_2015.pdf.

Wright, Tom, "Garment Brands Support Workers' Push for Higher Wages," *The Wall Street Journal*, October 14, 2014. http://www.wsj.com/articles/garment-workers-push-for-higher-wages-1413321601.

| Chapter 4 |
Bangladesh's Awakening

Benjamin Goh
MPP, Harvard Kennedy School of Government

• • •

"So what have you read about Bangladesh?" asked Steven, a fellow Trekker, during our flight from Kuala Lumpur.

I had spent the last three hours of our flight reading about Bangladeshi culture and history in order to prepare for our adventure in the South Asian country. "It used to be called East Pakistan when the British—" I began, but before I could finish my sentence, at least three pairs of eyes peered at us over Steven's shoulders, expressing anticipation and contempt as I tried to give an account of their history. "The British partitioned it away from India," I went on, "with India sitting in the middle between East and West Pakistan—."

"This is a country of culture, unlike the uncivilized people of Pakistan," interrupted one of the men listening to us. The comment wasn't unexpected. In my reading about Bangladesh, its contempt for its supposed arch-rival was frequent: fervent nationalistic tendencies, it seemed, often overrode Bangladeshi civility. I smiled at the man, tacitly agreeing with him lest we get into an unnecessary debate, then turned back to continue the conversation. Steven and I talked about what we understood of Bangladeshi history, while the man next to us held forth to his compatriots: "War... terrorists... killing each other... no sense of identity." The words I picked up from his remarks gave an impression of the great Bangladesh discussing the "backwater" of Pakistan.

National quarrels were not new to me, and I was confident that these conflicts formed only one aspect of Bangladeshi society. While on our flight, on Biman Bangladesh, we experienced a taste of Bangladeshi customs.[1] The flight was the most vibrant I've ever seen: as long as the seatbelt signs were off, everyone walked around talking to one another. The aisles of the aircraft were never clear; once three or four people blocked my way to the bathroom because they were chatting with family members, friends, or other locals they had barely met. The Bangladeshis are a people who favor conversations and emotional connections. I was the only person on the plane sitting alone, getting work done; almost everyone else who wasn't sleeping had stood up to mingle with the other passengers. It made for a noisy airplane ride, but a cheerful one as well.

Their volubility also told me a lot about my fellow passengers' experience of air travel. I could tell from the expressions of some of the people on board that the flight was their first. The man sitting beside me observed my every action because he didn't know how to connect earphones to the flight entertainment system. He was too shy to ask

---

1 Since Biman is Bangladesh's national carrier, I am assuming that the majority of passengers were Bangladeshi.

me for help, but I saw the smile on his face when I showed him how. And while the flight was boisterous and fun for some, for others it was an anxious and unsettling experience.

All in all, within only a few hours, I had not only gained a sense of Bangladeshi patriotism but also discovered an unusually warm and talkative people, many of whom were seeing the world for the first time.

A Middle Power Taking the Middle Road

Bangladesh gained independence in 1971, after a revolution ousted the Pakistani leaders of the territory. The artificial arrangement drawn up by the British that united Bangladesh with Pakistan was unsustainable, since Bangladesh isn't contiguous with Pakistan: India's massive bulk divides them. The British had initially divided up the region according to religious lines, but the Bangladeshis, who are mostly affiliated with the Bengali culture and civilization, never accepted losing their language and culture, and they finally fought for independence under the leadership of Sheikh Mujibur Rahman.

Bangladesh is located east of India and west of Myanmar, through which it gains access to China. In this position, sandwiched between the growing Asian giants of India and China, Bangladesh is greatly influenced by the economic and political situations in these neighboring countries. Added to the fragility and complexity of its development are the one hundred fifty million people who live there: Bangladesh is one of the world's most densely populated countries, making its economic growth difficult to coordinate and its governance tremendously challenging.

Perhaps surprisingly, Bangladesh has no interest in rivaling the great superpowers in Asia. Rather, in our meeting with a representative from the Ministry of Foreign Affairs (MOFA), it became clear that Bangladesh's strategic priority is to ride the wave of their growth to strengthen their own position as a middleman. "Connectivity is key," said one of MOFA's Directors, and Bangladesh certainly plays an active role in connecting the neighboring economic powers to each other. According to Bangladeshi officials, doing so creates immense leverage and bargaining power for this middle power nation because it creates a vested interest in peace, for shared prosperity. Not only does Bangladesh facilitate trade routes between its neighboring countries, it connects its neighbors' infrastructure as well: the power grid in China runs on electricity generated in India that then travels through Bangladesh, making Bangladesh a critical partner for both countries.

Thus, while Bangladesh acts as a cooperative nation, its stance promotes its own domestic interests as well. As a lower-middle-income country, the nation's internal priority is to create jobs. Maintaining economic corridors between its neighbors produces jobs that lure the country's skilled labor, guarding against the brain drain that has plagued many South Asian nations. Currently, Bangladesh is expanding its Chittagong port, supported by China, in order to provide an alternative to the Straits of Malacca as a prominent trade route, a strategy that shows not only Bangladesh's economic potential but also its reliability as a geopolitical stronghold and partner for prosperity in the region.[2]

---

2   Yong, Tan Tai, ed. *Socio-political and economic challenges in South Asia*. SAGE

Despite the country's successful economic policies, however, Bangladesh's national interests have inevitably played into some regional tensions. My American education has ingrained in me the idea that a nation's distress calls for international intervention, but Bangladesh has enshrined in its constitution a policy of non-intervention in any other country's domestic affairs. Indeed, it goes a step further: officials of the foreign service made it clear to me that Bangladesh recognizes the United Nations (UN) as the only legitimate institution to decide on intervention. This is democracy at an international scale: by embracing such a policy, Bangladesh is arguing for the need for accountability in trans-national affairs and displaying faith in the international community to decide collectively what is best for the world.

Similarly, as the country providing the highest number of UN peacekeepers, Bangladesh pays off its social responsibility through the UN. Respecting the international processes in this way lets Bangladesh take the high road and maintain its reputation as a fair, responsible, and reliable player in the region.

A Functioning Democracy: Gender Empowerment

As I roamed the streets of Dhaka, I was attracted by screams and shouts at the end of a block. When I got nearer to the commotion, I saw about eighty ladies sitting by the front porch of the Ministry of Labor, shouting and singing slogans under the guidance of a charismatic leader. My local translator told me that the nurses' union was protesting for a higher wage because their meager wage was insult-

---

Publications India, 2009.

ing to their noble work. Amid the shouting, half a dozen policemen maintained order, but for the most part they left the women free to protest and, in effect, to improve their own lives. As we left the scene to continue to our meeting venue, we heard the voices behind us take on a more masculine tone; a local informed me that men were now joining the protest on behalf of the ladies. The brief interlude offered an eye-opening window into Bangladesh's social and governmental values.

The Bangladeshi government's strong stance on gender inequality is partially due to Prime Minister Sheikh Hasina's personal vision of gender equality, but credit should also be given to the system that enabled the country's first female Prime Minister to be elected after only thirty-eight years of independence. Through a series of programs such as the Vulnerable Group Feeding (VGF) project, which provides allowances and food security to extremely poor women, Bangladesh's gender-empowerment policies, according to many officials, have changed the country's social equilibrium for good.[3] According to State Minister Shahriar Alam, the social changes are particularly visible in the countryside, where women have come out of traditional roles and asserted themselves in society. Women with financial ability are put in a better position to negotiate their future livelihood, including wages, work arrangements, and terms of loans for marriage.

A democratic society must strive actively to protect the vulnerable. Although Bangladeshis have a *per capita* income of only about $1,200, the government has invested so extensively in healthcare

---

[3] http://cri.org.bd/2014/09/01/development-of-women-empowerment-in-bangladesh/.

and education that—as far as these social indicators of well-being are concerned—Bangladesh is equivalent to countries with five to six times its *per capita* income. The government has also given about three hundred million books to the public schools in order to lower the cost of studying and attract more students. Through extensive economic studies, the Bangladeshi government has instituted a policy that grants free food for the poor, while putting in place systems that encourage upward mobility. An infant inoculation rate of 100 percent has dramatically reduced infant mortality rates, and trained birth attendants are guaranteed in every village to prevent the maternal deaths that plague so many poor areas in the world.

The One Family One Farm project, which guarantees minimum subsistence for every family in Bangladesh, ensures a safety net for all Bangladeshi citizens. Such major infrastructure investments, far from creating dependency, instead build a society in which even the poorest citizens can realize at least some of their aspirations. Of course, the government must tread carefully in making such investments, taking into account the desire of many citizens for instant gratification. "It is a gamble," says Minister Alam. "If you decide that you want to do something for the people, make sure you deliver it. If you don't, be prepared to accept the consequences." In sharp contrast with the oft-cited East Asian model of "authoritarian developmentalism" which requires a "strong leader" who can ignore the wishes of the masses, Minister Alam's comments demonstrated that strong leadership and service to the people are not mutually exclusive.[4] Leadership, from this Bangladeshi standpoint, means bringing the nation's people to a

---

4   http://www.grips.ac.jp/forum/DCDA/Chapter02.pdf.

better place, while granting those same citizens the power to evaluate the performance of their leader.

Digital Bangladesh

One of the greatest takeaways from our visit to Bangladesh was that the country seems confident and prepared for the future. In international development literature, much has been written about the perils of the "middle-income trap," a problem besetting many countries that manage to kick-start the industrial process but fail to increase productivity for prolonged periods of time.

Bangladesh's strong foundations in literacy and healthcare facilities encourage the best and brightest members of its society to contribute to its economy, which serves as a strong guard against the middle-income trap. Moreover, during our visit we saw that the government had formed detailed and thoughtful plans for sustained inclusive economic growth.

Dubbed "Digital Bangladesh," the Government Innovation Unit (under the Prime Minister's Office) shared with us their plans for Bangladesh's next stage of development. Firstly, the government will continue investing in basic literacy for its people. Providing three hundred million books to students, as mentioned before, was the first step; the next will be to increase the quality of schools, teachers, and teaching standards, in order to generate more productivity. Secondly, Bangladesh will ride on the current wave of technological advances to maximize its potential. This "digital" trend in Bangladesh is fascinating because the country must develop during an era of global market disruption. Software, data analytics, and algorithms are taking over jobs everywhere in the world, even in developed countries, and middle-income countries like Bangladesh must therefore leapfrog over the development lag in order not to fall by the wayside.

One of the first initiatives we learned about was the use of technological capabilities to deliver better service to villages in Bangladesh. The government is making massive infrastructure investments to provide connectivity throughout Bangladesh. Thereafter, they will use technologies such as geo-imaging and drones to identify the rural population more accurately and to get services to them quickly and efficiently.

In addition to service delivery, the Bangladeshi government is digitizing the country by learning from data. To show that they are ahead of the curve in analytics, the government officials we spoke to cited precise statistics in their answers to our questions. I vividly remember the remarks of Dr. Gowher Rizvi, International Affairs advisor to the Prime Minister and former Director of the Ash Center at the Harvard Kennedy School, on the demographic dividend in Bangladesh. To him, youth will always be engaged as long as they see that government policies affect them positively. Provided that the country's economic growth does not come with rising inequality, he said, social mobility can be preserved and youth will continue to contribute their skills and passion to the building of Bangladesh. And the latest data, according to Dr. Rizvi, shows that this trend is likely to continue.

What struck me most was that the Bangladeshi government is actively taking stock of technological improvements and determining how technology will affect the country. In a liberal, free-market paradigm, such extensive government actions might be seen as too interventionist, but in Bangladesh one soon realizes that targeted government investments are in fact a desirable system. As Dr. Rizvi mentioned to us, capital moves *freely* but not *fairly*, and the government needs to calibrate its movements for maximum social benefit. In particular, the Bangladeshi government keeps tabs on the inflow of funds towards industry in Bangladesh, actively seeking such data out before making investment decisions so as not to crowd out mature industries while kick-starting emerging crucial ones.

The Bangladeshi government is doing a great deal to coordinate resources and plan out the country's development for the next decade. Is it doing too much? Are citizens afraid of government abuse in favor of cronyism? I had genuine worries about the centralized approach to planning, which often comes with potentially massive stakes on the part of the citizens, so I decided to ask a question about excessive government planning. The answer, to my surprise, exhibited absolute confidence that the government has done well and will continue to do well for its people. "The government is the last guarantor of social justice," one official said.

While cynics may deride this as delusion, it soon became clear to me that the relationship between government and citizens in Bangladesh is fundamentally different from the model in the U.S. The Bangladeshi model showed me that a vibrant democracy need not be accompanied by a skepticism for government. Checks and balances can occur within a system government officials fighting for the common good. Fundamentally, what a working democracy needs is a commitment to put aside partisan differences and to fight for the most underprivileged in society—and as was clear from our meetings with people at every level (be they political appointees, bureaucrats, or business owners), differences are secondary to what each Bangladeshi citizen perceives to be the common interest of Bangladesh.

Our Common Society

Where does this strong sense of democratic responsibility come from? During our time in Bangladesh I witnessed a widespread commitment to improving the lives of others. When asked about Bangladesh's relationship with its diaspora, the State Minister dispensed with diplomatic evasion and frankly talked about the difficulty of balancing international relations with national solidarity. What moved me most was the love and care that shone through his polished oratory and his determination to improve the living conditions of his citizens. "We can do better," he said.

We also visited a milk factory owned by a local non-governmental organization (NGO), the Bangladesh Rehabilitation Assistance Committee (BRAC), which works to empower local farmers and women. The milk factory gives local farmers access to urban markets, a business model that proved profitable as well as socially conscious. Expanding internationally seemed like the natural next step for the organization, especially since the cost of goods is much higher in the neighboring countries of Bhutan and China. When we asked about expansion, however, the spokesperson of BRAC did not cite profit or feasibility; instead he simply said. "Bangladesh is a net importer of milk…and we will not expand internationally until that changes."

This solidarity runs beyond government and state relations to form a real and wide-ranging network of support and assistance. At BRAC, we saw a clear effort to empower women by providing them with jobs: almost all of the workers we met at the production plant were women. BRAC, moreover, goes even further, escorting its employees home after night shifts. When I asked the manager why the company decided to do that, he candidly mentioned that since safety for women is a concern in Bangladesh, it is only right for BRAC to protect its female employees and thus stay true to its intentions of empowerment. To some extent this is common sense, but it still came across as refreshing and surprising; in an era when the numbing rhetoric of inclusion seems ubiquitous, it is inspiring to see a company address the substantive, not just the symbolic, issues for empowerment.

Nor was BRAC the only company we encountered that cared about working conditions. The same commitment to a livable working environment was also evident when we visited Generation Next, one of the major garment factories in Bangladesh. Garment factories all over the world are notorious for their poor working conditions, especially since they are usually associated with low-skilled and exploited labor. However, at Generation Next, the ventilation was good and every worker had a clearly defined workspace. Lunchtime began promptly at 1 p.m., and workers did not return before the hour ended, which gave them ample time not only to eat but also to run quick errands—whether it was calling to make sure their kids were home from school or going to the grocery store to get *dosa* for breakfast the next day. This system of trust requires discipline from the workers, but it also inspires mutual respect, something we saw clearly during the afternoon we spent at Generation Next.

My observations of the tightly knit social fabric in Bangladesh can be summed up by this maxim, shared with me by a local student: "Dhormo jar jar, utshob shobar," which translates roughly as "The religion is yours, but the celebration is for everyone." Be it Buddha

Purnima (commemorating Gautama Buddha's birth, enlightenment, and death), Eid-ul-Fitr (the Muslim breaking of the fast), or Durga Puja (worship of the Hindu Goddess Durga), every religious festival in Bangladesh is celebrated by everyone—nor is it considered blasphemous or sacrilegious to prepare food for citizens who follow a different religion. Such a commitment to inclusion cuts across religious differences and also embraces the poor and disenfranchised.

A tightly knit social fabric and strong civil society do not come purely from nationalistic fervor or passed-on wisdom; they are created through daily practice, from the individual all the way to the highest levels of government. The citizens' commitment to each other, beyond immediate self-interest, is what makes Bangladeshi democracy work. At the time of independence, the founding government created self-sufficiency in food and then found good jobs for its people in the garment industry, which still produces 80 percent of Bangladesh's export. While some may scoff at Bangladesh's prolonged engagement in the garment industry, on the assumption that it has created a middle-income trap, in fact the stability created by these good jobs has in turn yielded a demographic dividend for Bangladesh. Along with better healthcare, Bangladesh experienced a baby boom in the 1970s and 1980s, and that boom created a thriving middle class that can and will transform the economy. With fifty to sixty million more people expected in the medium term, Bangladesh's stability will create a significant demand for services and products, which will in turn lead to an economy more focused on domestic consumption, thus creating a dynamic market of one hundred fifty million people.

Stories like that of BRAC show the country's bottom-up commitment to improving the quality of life in Bangladesh, but the main driver of good policy-making is still the government. In order to meet the changing needs of its country, the Bangladeshi government has actively transformed itself. The Prime Minister's Office has created a Government Innovation Unit (GIU), which, in addition to its broad developmental goals, offers small benefits and injects technology-driven productivity into the country. By now, the "Digital Bangladesh" program has enhanced the technological literacy of thousands of villages and delivered services that could never have reached such rural areas before. Furthermore, the GIU digitizes most transactions between the private sector and the government, creating a paper trail that makes it easier to track and punish corruption. Lastly, the large-scale deployment of technological know-how empowered Bangladesh to create its first ever universal, means-tested, social-safety program, putting Bangladesh far ahead of many its peers in the region.

Ultimately, good governance creates trust in the governmental system—by the people and for the people—and in the case of Bangladesh this trust has unified the aspirations of Bangladeshis of all stripes, thus forming a strong democratic core on which everyone can rely.

A Bangladeshi Culture

I had experienced the warmth of the Bangladeshi people, felt its economic achievements, and marveled at the strength of its civil society. But I still wondered if modernity in Bangladesh, as with many areas in developing countries, was just another process of Westernization.

We gained a peek into Bangladesh's unique cultural life during our leadership conference at North South University in Dhaka, the country's capital. Unlike our experiences with conferences in other cities, at this one, we discovered that our warm Bangladeshi colleagues had planned an "after-party" for us—a Bangladeshi-styled concert. The first student rock band chose Adele's newly released hit single, "Hello" as their opening song. Their soulful singer captured our hearts, but halfway through the song, an audience member's phone went off, with a prolonged ringtone playing Tchaikovsky's famous violin concerto. Already, both Britain and Russia were appearing as cultural influences.

Then, after two Hollywood songs, the band began to play traditional Bengali music. Suddenly, I realized that the songs at the beginning of their set had been chosen to honor us, their international audience. Now, after the switch to Bengali music, the mood of the hall changed. The students in the audience rose to their feet, their arms around each other as they sang and moved to the beat. I couldn't understand the lyrics, so my Bangladeshi friends translated as we went along.

As I enjoyed these fragments of a culture foreign to me, I couldn't help but notice something familiar in the art form. The pitch inflexions were local, the harmony was uniquely South Asian…but beneath the melody was a familiar beat cycle: this was pop music! Driving the rhythmic structure was a mixture of rock and classical styles, which explained the connection I had immediately felt with the music.

Bangladeshi culture, encompassing one hundred fifty million people, is not an artifact; instead, it retains a strong core identity while adapting to modern influences from all over the world. Like its people, Bangladeshi culture builds bridges rather than barriers.

Conclusion

I left Bangladesh deeply moved by a country that seemed filled with love, empathy, and care for others. As I departed from the Dhaka airport, I couldn't stop thinking about a conversation I'd had with a student and a Director of the Ministry of Foreign Affairs. When I commented to my fellow Trekkers that I had been impressed to see a student and a high-ranking official holding a personal conversation, my friend Sarika replied, "A lot of powerful people in Bangladesh are like that—busy but humble." Bangladeshi elites thus provide an example of the fact that national trust is built not from policies but from behavior. Commitment to fighting for a better future must be demonstrated through actions as well as on paper, and officials must spend time with the people they have vowed to serve.

I left Bangladesh ashamed that before my visit, I had to read about it in order to learn basic facts about the country. It is a nation awakening to its role in the global sphere. Its youth yearn for a better world as they embrace the country's rapid economic evolution of the last decade. And Bangladesh does not simply facilitate and benefit from the free flow of capital, it also has much to offer in its culture, music, and way of life.

Of course, the country still suffers from ethnic conflicts, poverty, and the tremendous difficulties of providing sanitation to its many citizens, among other challenges. But unlike many other developing countries, Bangladesh has been built on a strong foundation. Its commitment to female empowerment, its vibrant democracy, and its active and highly qualified public service make the country's success all but inevitable. While to outsiders, Bangladesh may look like a country primarily involved in a conflict with Pakistan, internally, Bangladeshis are slowly but surely helping their country to reach its fullest potential.

Part 3

Asia Leadership Fellowship 2016

| Chapter 5 |
The Purpose of Education

Lisa Lee

Ed.M, Harvard Graduate School of Education

● ● ●

I am an educator. I believe in the power of education. I believe in the power of knowledge. Most importantly, I believe in the potential of a single well-articulated thought to change the world. That's why I became a teacher. That's why I spent the summer piloting my curriculum in Asia with the Center for Asia Leadership Initiatives (CALI) in my quest to make students think, solve problems, design solutions, and become empowered agents of change.

In my view, what is most needed is a set of skills—critical thinking, problem solving, creativity, communication, and leadership—that produce in students the flexibility and adaptability to address the changing challenges of the 21st century. These have become known as 21st century skills, which have been a topic of discussion in many education circles.

We currently stand at the turn of a century, in which increasing globalization, technological progress, international conflict, and environmental degradation necessitate a generation of problem solvers, innovators, and leaders that our education system simply is not turning out. After graduating from the Harvard Graduate School of Education, I decided that my goal would be not only to equip students with the skills they need for a successful career, but to empower them to take action on the issues and problems they care about.

This is not to say that the value of knowledge, by itself, has declined. On the contrary: I believe that 21st century skills make use of knowledge in a way that is more powerful and effective than simple comprehension and short-term recall.

Becoming a Teacher

I have come a long way from my days on Wall Street as a securities trader before the Financial Crisis of 2008. After the fallout, I became a teacher, mostly by accident. My friend was running an after-school program in Chinatown, New York City, and asked me to substitute for a teacher who had just quit. I was thus thrown into a classroom with about twenty students, ranging in age from eight to eleven years old. They were all Chinese immigrants or children of recent immigrants, so they were struggling with the language as well as with cultural adjustments. As an after-school program, we were there to help fill in the gaps, provide help with homework, and offer enrichment that many of their parents or guardians were unable to give due to work or language barriers.

I didn't know it then, but the reason I was able to teach these students so effectively was that I could empathize with them. I grew up in the same neighborhood, with the same cultural and linguistic challenges. I understood these students; I knew that what they needed wasn't simply English or Math skills. With all that they faced at home, many of them had difficulty seeing the value of what they were learning. For me, as a result, teaching was less about feeding students facts and more about pushing them to keep thinking and trying to solve problems. The most satisfying moment for me as a teacher was when a student reached that "Aha!" moment, discovered the answer for herself, and thought, "Wow, I can do this!" or "Hey, I'm smart!" That was my year-end bonus. That is how I fell in love with teaching. And that was how I found my calling in life.

After I got certified to teach English, I decided to see if I could make a positive impact in Kazakhstan, where I volunteered to teach at an orphanage through the sponsorship of my church. I believe that whatever talents or gifts God gave me should be used to serve others. I felt I had a gift for teaching, and I wanted to reach the students who would most benefit, so I chose to go to Kazakhstan—where over 40 percent of the population is under the age of twenty-five—and work with youth there. In my two years there, I also taught at a university, worked at an international Montessori pre-school, and started an English club for university students.

The time I spent in Kazakhstan was formative both personally and professionally. It was the first time I had taught in a non-U.S. environment. While Asian education systems are typically stereotyped as being all about rote memorization and standardized exams, in Kazakhstan, which uses a largely post-Soviet model of education, I saw rote memorization without any accountability mechanism. There were no standardized tests to measure the progress of the students during primary or secondary schooling, only an exit examination that determined whether a student had completed secondary schooling and should be admitted to tertiary institutions.

While teaching English at the university level at one of the top technical universities in the country, I was given two hundred fifty technical vocabulary terms (RAM, motherboard, hard drive, etc.) to test my students on throughout the semester. The curriculum consisted of an *Oxford University Press English* workbook, from which I was to assign grammar exercises for every class. Most of my students could barely string a coherent sentence together, but I had to make them memorize the definition for "binary code." When I brought up the necessity of teaching students to use practical English skills like speaking, listening, and reading comprehension, as opposed to imposing vocabulary tests and grammar drills, I was told that the curriculum had been handed down from the Ministry of Education and that it was what we had to teach.

Then it hit me. In Kazakhstan's education system and many others, language proficiency did not mean the mastery of a set of skills to communicate but rather vocabulary memorization and a knowledge of grammar rules. And this is not atypical in other subjects in many education systems. Systems of this kind are what make teachers who really want to make a difference give up. It's frustrating to see so clearly what students need, but be told that we have to give them something else because that's what we have been given or that's what gets tested.

The problem begs a larger question: when will education move from a knowledge-based system to a system based on skills and competency?

Journey to Harvard

I knew that I didn't know enough to make the type of impact I felt students deserved, and so I explored various graduate programs in education. Eventually I applied to the International Education Policy Program at the Harvard Graduate School of Education (HGSE). I had several reasons for doing so:

- The school and program were focused on policy, as opposed to most teaching colleges, which are focused on pedagogy or administration.
- The program was international in scope, while the majority of the top education programs are focused on the U.S. I wanted to be in an international program because I wanted a greater perspective on what is being done in education around the world.
- There was a thriving entrepreneurial spirit at the school that encouraged innovation and creative problem solving. I wanted to be in an entrepreneurial environment and to find others to partner with in my venture.
- I wanted to learn, not just about education, but about the world and how to change it for the better. Harvard, unlike some other schools, is not just an institution of thought but one that prides itself in action. It has a long history of producing leaders that have impacted the world. If I wanted to do the same, then I had to learn from the best.
- I knew that what I wanted to do could not be done alone. I had to build an extensive network of connections with people who were not just in positions of influence but who also cared deeply

about what I cared about. And Harvard is well known for its vast and powerful network.
- Harvard ensures instant credibility. I knew that with a Harvard degree in International Education Policy, I could gain access and at least a hearing in almost any place in the world.
- Harvard is well resourced. I wanted access to as many thought leaders as possible. People all over the world come and share their thoughts at Harvard. The program would give me access to a wealth of resources, classes, and professors from other schools within the Harvard system, like the Kennedy School of Government and the Harvard Business School.
- Lastly, as I observed one of the standard courses in the program, I finally saw what I was longing for in a classroom: high-level critical analysis of policy, consistent and respectful engagement with ideas and disagreements, and, underlying each debate, the understanding that quality education should be a right for all students.

I didn't bother applying to other programs. I knew that I wanted to start my own educational venture, and HGSE provided an entrepreneurial environment that cultivated ideas, risk taking, and action. Once I was admitted, I knew that I made the right decision. I liked what I saw of the student population, particularly in my cohort in the International Education Policy program. People were down to earth; they had taught in other countries; they had seen challenging educational environments; they realized that the world is much bigger and its problems much more complex than what is highlighted by politicians—yet they still wanted to make a change. They cared about social justice and educational equity. I didn't want to be in an ivory tower, speculating on solutions to big educational problems. I wanted to be on the ground, trying out solutions—and I found myself in good company.

What Is the Future of Education?

When I visited an HGSE class during the application process, it happened to be an International Education Policy class, and the professor—who would later be my program advisor—was Fernando Reimers. The class lecture for that day was on 21st century skills—soft skills like communication, collaboration, creativity, critical thinking, problem solving, and leadership, as well as cross-cultural skills. The debate in the session focused on whether developing countries should focus on basic skills, such as language and math, or integrate 21st century skills into their curriculum. The discussion was rigorous, with strong proponents from each side. What I appreciated most was that the students came from so many different educational contexts, from Asia to Africa to the Middle East—and they all vigorously defended their positions. "How can we think to add all these soft skills when over half of our students aren't even literate? We must focus on teaching them the basics before we can move on to soft skills." Others argued that basic literacy was not enough, that even those who acquired basic skills did not have other necessary skills to succeed upon completing school.

21st Century Skills

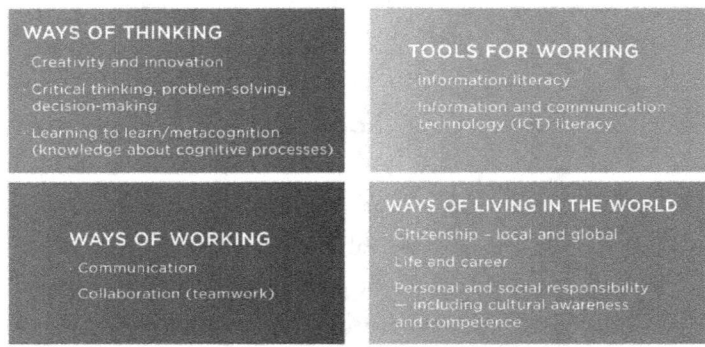

Source: http://www.atc21s.org/.

Defining 21st Century Skills

There are currently multiple definitions for 21st century skills, but instead of narrowly defining a particular set of competencies, I would rather provide a description of widely accepted common themes from competing definitions. For the purposes of this chapter and its intended audience, I will use a working description of 21st century skills drawn from the Asia Society Report published in 2012, *Teaching and Learning 21st Century Skills: Lessons from the Learning Sciences.* One constructive way of understanding the skills is to understand their common themes. A helpful visual aid has been created by the Assessment and Teaching of 21st Century Skills Consortium (AT21CS):

This was a project funded by Cisco, Intel, and Microsoft "to sponsor a research collaboration to accelerate global education reform by mobilizing the international educational, political and business communities to help transform the teaching, learning and measurement of 21st century skills. The Assessment and Teaching of 21st Century Skills (ATC21S) project is focused on defining those skills and developing ways to measure them."[1] The four categories—ways of thinking, ways of working, tools for working, and ways of living in the world—encompass a holistic set of skills, knowledge, values, ethics, and attitudes necessary for a student to succeed in the 21st century. Breaking 21st century skills into thematic categories in this way makes it easier to insert other skills not currently listed. Leadership, for example, can be categorized under Ways of Working or Ways of Living in the World.

A quick look at seven survival skills necessary to prepare students for the 21st century—as proposed by Tony Wagner, co-director of the Harvard Change Leadership Group, in his book *The Global Achievement Gap* (2008)—demonstrates how such skills can be categorized into the above four themes[2]:

1. Critical thinking and problem solving
2. Collaboration and leadership
3. Agility and adaptability
4. Initiative and entrepreneurialism
5. Effective oral and written communication
6. Accessing and analyzing information

---

1 Accessed 9/20/2016: http://www.atc21s.org/about.html.
2 Accessed 9/20/2016: https://asiasociety.org/files/book-globalcompetence.pdf.

7. Curiosity and imagination

These skills fall largely into two categories, Ways of Thinking and Ways of Working, and this is probably because the book is informed by a series of interviews with business leaders, as well as with non-profit and education leaders.

Because of the increasingly globalized nature of our world, I believe the explicit mention of global citizenship and competence is necessary in any discussion of 21st century skills. Global competence, as specified by The Asia Society and the U.S. Council of Chief State School Officers, means "the capacity and disposition to understand and act on issues of global significance."[3] Under this definition, students should be taught to:

1. Investigate the world beyond their immediate environment.
2. Recognize perspectives, others' and their own.
3. Communicate ideas effectively with diverse audiences.
4. Take action to improve conditions.[4]

In combining these definitions of 21st century skills, the broad working definition I will use in describing the curriculum I developed is as follows: 21st century skills are those that equip students with essential knowledge (e.g. information, technology, media literacy), the skills to apply that knowledge to real-world problems (e.g. critical thinking and problem solving), the ability to work with others toward

---

3 Ibid.
4 Ibid.

a solution (e.g. collaboration, communication), and the competence to make a meaningful impact (e.g. leadership, flexibility, adaptability).

The Debate over the Importance of 21st Century Skills

If the debate over the importance of 21st century skills were distilled to its essence, it would become a debate over the role of education itself. Is education solely about the transfer of factual knowledge? Or is education about developing certain skills in students? I don't think the two are mutually exclusive. Basic literacy, for example, associates certain letters or symbols with certain sounds—this is factual knowledge. Letter recognition by itself is simply recall. However, reading is a skill—it requires the linking of several symbols with their requisite sounds to form words that have associated meanings. These words are strung together in a structured manner to convey ideas. Skillful reading requires comprehension of ideas organized into themes. Critical thinking is a skill that evaluates how these ideas form and fit into one's perspective on the world. Teaching a child to recognize and read text without the ability to think critically about its meaning is a haphazard endeavor.

Yet, as we become ever more focused on measuring student outcomes based on standardized tests, which measure a narrow set of numeracy and literacy skills, many educators are concerned by the inability of students to grapple with the pressing social, moral, ethical, and political challenges of an increasingly interconnected and globalized world. Cyber bullying, global climate change, systemic racism and discrimination, civil war, political polarization, privacy concerns, economic inequality, and terrorism are just a few of the problems facing youth today. These problems and their effects are filtering down and impacting people at younger and younger ages. In one extreme, civil conflict has spawned the recruiting of child soldiers, while international terrorism seeks new recruits among malcontented youth. The lack of purpose, direction, agency, and meaningful skills makes these young people easy prey. On the other hand, when we consider many of the revolutions of history, we can see that they were often organized by proactive students.

I entered the Harvard Graduate School of Education with the intention to start my own educational venture, seeking a means of empowering young people to think critically and solve such problems. As much as I wanted students to be able to find jobs after completing their education, I knew that their skills and leadership would be needed not only in the workplace but in society as a whole.

The Role of Teachers

Before our academic year started at HGSE, during our first week of IPSIE (Intensive Preparation for the Study of International Education), one of our Teaching Fellows asked us this question: "What makes a good teacher?" There were several answers regarding training, skill sets, and various other traits, but when I was asked this question directly, I did not hesitate in my answer: "A good teacher makes you think." If I were to offer a more complete answer, I would say that a good teacher makes you think and apply knowledge in real situations. I have always believed this. It's how I saw my role in the classroom.

However, I grappled with this idea during my studies at HGSE and often found myself at odds with students in the Technology, Innovation, and Education program, who saw the role of teachers as obsolete, citing technology's ability to deliver information faster, more easily, and on a larger scale online. They preferred to call themselves facilitators—people who could be paid less and didn't require as much training. This idea was, of course, anathema to the many teachers who had gone through the arduous process of learning about lesson planning, classroom management, instruction, and grading. But the two different perspectives were based on two very different views of education. The technologists minimize the role of teachers because they see their job as delivering information and then checking to see if the information was received. I saw my job as teaching students to think and apply knowledge effectively. Of course, this process is difficult to measure, assess, or scale. But I felt confident that this was what I would learn at Harvard. I was looking for a systematic way to teach these skills to students, and once I began to look into possible methods, I realized why education systems are so slow to innovate: overhauling curricula, teacher training, and resource management for entire school districts is a laborious and time-consuming task—and it costs money.

The Demand for 21st Century Skills

Nevertheless, the demand for 21st century skills is increasing among employers. The World Economic Forum's Future of Jobs Report, released in January 2016, conducted a survey of all Chief Human Resource Officers across all industries and geographies to provide an outlook on the world job market. In it, the report named these skills in order of importance as the top ten needed for 2020 and

Top 10 skills

in 2020

1. Complex Problem Solving
2. Critical Thinking
3. Creativity
4. People Management
5. Coordinating with Others
6. Emotional Intelligence
7. Judgment and Decision Making
8. Service Orientation
9. Negotiation
10. Cognitive Flexibility

in 2015

1. Complex Problem Solving
2. Coordinating with Others
3. People Management
4. Critical Thinking
5. Negotiation
6. Quality Control
7. Service Orientation
8. Judgment and Decision Making
9. Active Listening
10. Creativity

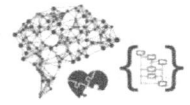

Source: Future of Jobs Report, World Economic Forum

Source World Economic Forum, 2016.

compares it with those skills predicted as necessary in 2015.[5]

The report goes on to state that we are currently in the midst of the Fourth Industrial Revolution, which is a digital revolution that will fuse technologies, blurring the lines between the physical, digital, and biological spheres.[6] The first industrial revolution was the creation of

---

5 Accessed 9/21/2016: https://www.weforum.org/agenda/2016/08/10-skills-you-need-to-thrive-tomorrow-and-the-universities-that-will-help-you-get-them/.
6 Schwab, Klaus. World Economic Forum website. Accessed 9/21/2016: https://www.weforum.org/agenda/2016/01/the-fourth-industrial-revolution-what-it-means-and-how-to-respond/.

Navigating the next industrial revolution

Revolution	Year	Information
1	1784	Steam, water, mechanical production equipment
2	1870	Division of labour, electricity, mass production
3	1969	Electronics, IT, automated production
4	?	Cyber-physical systems

machines; the second was mass production; the third was the automation of machines for production; and the fourth is the blending of physical systems with cyber or virtual systems. Physical systems like cars or homes can now be controlled virtually through your phone or computer.

The Fourth Revolution will be characterized by its velocity, scope, and systems impact, evolving exponentially and "disrupting almost every industry in every country. And the breadth and depth of these changes herald the transformation of entire systems of production, management, and governance."[7] The labor market disruption that it causes will probably result in greater unemployment, inequality, and discontent. It will also produce a slew of jobs and functions "in a near-simultaneous impact on employment and need for new skill

---

7 Ibid.

sets, requiring an urgent and concerted effort for adjustment."[8] Thus, the ability to adapt and learn quickly in a rapidly changing environment is a critical skill, one that is now more urgent than ever. The report predicts a total loss of 7.1 million jobs between 2015 and 2020, with two thirds of that loss concentrated in routine office and administrative roles.[9] Technical fields, such as computer, math, architecture, and engineering-related fields, will in contrast see an increase of two million jobs.[10]

Interestingly, two job types stood out in the report as ones that would be critical in 2020; they were the most frequently and consistently jobs cited across almost all industries and geographies: data analysts and specialized sales representatives.[11] Because of the increasing ubiquity of big data, analysts are needed to provide key insights for strategic management decisions. This requires critical thinking, analysis, metacognition, acute information literacy, and hard technical skills. Conversely, the field of sales requires what most consider "soft" skills, such as communication, initiative, entrepreneurialism, agility, and adaptability.

Based on the survey conducted by the Future of Jobs report, the World Economic Forum said the following on skills stability:

> On average, by 2020, more than a third of the desired core skill

---

8 Accessed 9/21/2016: http://reports.weforum.org/future-of-jobs-2016/drivers-of-change/.
9 Accessed 9/21/206 (p1): http://www3.weforum.org/docs/WEF_FOJ_Executive_Summary_Jobs.pdf.
10 Ibid.
11 Accessed 9/21/2016: http://www3.weforum.org/docs/WEF_FOJ_Executive_Summary_Jobs.pdf.

sets of most occupations will be comprised of skills that are not yet considered crucial to the job today, according to our respondents. Overall, social skills—such as persuasion, emotional intelligence and teaching others—will be in higher demand across industries than narrow technical skills, such as programming or equipment operation and control. In essence, technical skills will need to be supplemented with strong social and collaboration skills.[12]

While the Future of Jobs Report predicts the need for such skills, the American Management Association's 2012 Critical Skills Survey already cited that 74.6 percent of managers report that the 4 C's (Critical Thinking, Communication Skills, Collaboration and Team Building, and Creativity and Innovation) will become more important for their organizations in the next three to five years.[13] Of these managers, 61.4 percent indicated the pace of change in business as the main reason for the increasing importance of these skills. That was four years ago. These skills are becoming ever more important. And 59.1 percent of managers believe that it is easier to develop these skills in students and recent graduates than in existing employees.[14] The demand for these skills in the next three years means that college students should already be demonstrating these skills now, in order to be competitive in the job market—and that in turn means that they should be cultivating these skills even before that, in high school.

---

12 Accessed 9/21/2016 (p3): http://www3.weforum.org/docs/WEF_FOJ_Executive_Summary_Jobs.pdf.
13 Accessed 9/21/2016 (p5): http://www.amanet.org/uploaded/2012-Critical-Skills-Survey.pdf.
14 Ibid.

A Call to Action

Current workforce strategies to deal with the disruptive changes that will be brought on by the Fourth Industrial Revolution have been slow in taking effect. While 65 percent of respondents in the Future Jobs Report intend to invest in retraining current employees, at least 50 percent of all respondents cite insufficient understanding of the disruptive changes and resource constraints as significant barriers to change.[15] According to the report, the pace and scale of change may be outstripping current strategies:

> During previous industrial revolutions, it often took decades to build the training systems and labor market institutions needed to develop major new skill sets on a large scale. Given the upcoming pace and scale of disruption brought about by the Fourth Industrial Revolution, however, this is simply not an option.
>
> Without targeted action today to manage the near-term transition and build a workforce with futureproof skills, governments will have to cope with ever-growing unemployment and inequality, and businesses with a shrinking consumer base. Moreover, these efforts are necessary not just to mitigate the risks of the profound shifts underway but also to capitalize on the opportunities presented by the Fourth Industrial Revolution. The talent to manage, shape and lead the changes underway will be in short supply unless we take action today to develop it.

---

15 Accessed 9/21/2016 (p7): http://www3.weforum.org/docs/WEF_FOJ_Executive_Summary_Jobs.pdf.

For a talent revolution to take place, governments and businesses will need to profoundly change their approach to education, skills and employment, and their approach to working with each other. Businesses will need to put talent development and future workforce strategy front and center to their growth. Firms can no longer be passive consumers of ready-made human capital. They require a new mindset to meet their talent needs and to optimize social outcomes. Governments will need to re-consider fundamentally the education models of today. As the issue becomes more urgent, governments will need to show bolder leadership in putting through the curricula and labor market regulation changes that are already decades overdue in some economies.[16]

The World Economic Forum, through this report, recognizes that the challenges are too large to allow for a simply reliance on businesses to adapt. In order to meet the imminent economic turbulence, governments, businesses, and education institutions must work together to prepare for the Fourth Industrial Revolution. Those who are opportunistic and recognize what is needed to capitalize on the changes will probably come out ahead, much like the dot-com-era entrepreneurs who embraced the commercial shift from in-store to online and became millionaires as a result.

---

16 Accessed 9/21/2016 (p6): http://www3.weforum.org/docs/WEF_FOJ_Executive_Summary_Jobs.pdf.

Challenges to Teaching 21st Century Skills for Education Systems

Among the various strategies that businesses are pursuing to address the challenge of changing workforce skills, only 25 percent of respondents cited collaboration with educational institutions.[17] While disappointing, this is not surprising. *The Asia Society Report on Teaching and Learning 21st Century Skills: Lessons from the Learning Sciences* cites three main barriers to students learning 21st century skills.

First, the transmission model of learning is still the most widely used in compulsory education systems. Teachers worldwide are still giving facts to students and then testing them on those facts, without application or discussion.[18] Even those countries that recognize this as an outdated model have had difficulty transitioning out of it because education systems are notoriously difficult to change and the transmission model requires less disciplinary and pedagogical expertise than teaching 21st century skills.[19] Retraining existing teachers is a colossal undertaking and one that would require immense resources, funding, and political will, as well as cooperation.

Second, 21st century skills are not explicitly taught, either as a subject or as a requirement in most curricula.[20] While the report argues for the integration of 21st century learning through existing disciplinary studies as opposed to stand-alone courses, I disagree with this pro-

---

17 Ibid. p7.
18 http://asiasociety.org/files/rand-1012report.pdf (p7).
19 Ibid.
20 Ibid.

posal. Instead, I argue that short, intensive, and integrated programs focused on honing these skills are a more efficient and effective way for students to attain 21st century skills than waiting for each of their teachers to find a way to embed the skills into their individual curricula. As I will outline in my next chapter, it is important to teach these skills explicitly, dedicating time and resources to naming, cultivating, and practicing them, so that the students can enter the world with a heightened awareness of the importance of their abilities and find opportunities to exercise them.

Third, there is the difficulty of assessing 21st century skills.[21] Usually, the things that are taught are the things that can be assessed or tested. But how does one systematically grade a student on communication skills, or on leadership, teamwork, and citizenship? The difficulty of developing a widely accepted list of 21st century skills is superseded only by the difficulty of creating a rubric to assess them. In my curriculum, I address this issue by staying away from benchmarks or standards and instead approaching assessment in terms of the student's effectiveness and impact in exercising such skills, as well as the student's continuous improvement.

Despite these challenges, the report proposes that assessment may not actually be the biggest barrier to the 21st century model of teaching and learning. Instead, the key barrier may be building teacher capacity and an instructional curriculum, especially in countries that are only just starting to implement teacher reform. Therefore, the need for high-quality training and resources is crucial in taking the first steps toward innovating education.

---

21 Ibid.

The Asian Context

Asian countries care about education, and it shows, especially on test scores. Singapore, Taipei, Hong Kong, Seoul, and Shanghai have consistently topped the PISA (Programme for International Student Assessment), a skills and knowledge test of fifteen-year-olds across the world, administered by the OECD. However, as Development Asia points out, this is arguably the result of a "shadow system" of extra tutoring and cram schools that is pervasive in Asia.[22]

Entire ecosystems of external education have been built around the largely exam-based system found in Asian countries, and the system as a whole has contributed to a number of social problems. As one example, the academic stress of high-stakes national college entrance exams in places like China and Korea, as well as the oppressive nature of school bullying in Japan, has driven up suicide rates among youth between the ages of ten and nineteen. This summer, many of the Asian students I taught confirmed that this is a major problem among youth in their countries.

For some, the pressure comes from preparing for highly competitive entrance exams. To get into a prestigious national university, you have to get into a competitive high school; to succeed in that, you have to do well in middle school; and to get a leg up against the competition, you should really start in Grade 3—and so the cycle extends to embrace students' entire lives. For others, it's the sense of helplessness they feel in the endless monotony of school, tutoring,

---

22 Accessed 9/22/2016 (p9): https://www.adb.org/sites/default/files/publication/29072/devasia10.pdf.

and weekend test prep. For others still, it's the need they feel to do not just well but perfectly. In Korea, it's not uncommon for students to be in school and then *hagwon* (after-school tutoring clubs) from 7 a.m. to 10 or 11 p.m., six or seven days a week. Not surprisingly, Korea has one of the highest suicide rates in the world, at 29.1 deaths per one hundred thousand people, two and a half times the OECD average, with suicide the number one cause of death in 2014 among those aged ten to thirty-nine and academic stress as the main reason for student suicides.[23]

Against this backdrop, it is not difficult to see that spending so much time, effort, and focus on test taking leaves little room for creativity, innovation, or learning by discovery. A competitive exam-based education system induces learning for a test, as opposed to learning to solve problems.

21st Century Skills in Asia

Despite all this, Asian countries have recognized the importance of 21st century skills and have taken steps to integrate them into educational policy. *The Asia Society Report on Teaching and Learning 21st Century Skills: Lessons from the Learning Sciences* cites the following measures taken by various countries to address the need for teaching 21st century skills:

As with most innovations in education, the largest cities are the first to adapt and thus maintain their status as the epicenters of high-

---

23 Accessed 9/22/2016: http://www.koreaherald.com/view.php?ud= 20150830000310.

Table 1. How Education Systems Are Addressing 21st Century Skills

Hong Kong	Japan	China	Finland	Singapore	United States
Learning to Learn reform addresses applied learning and "other" learning experiences, including service and workplace learning[6]	Zest for Living education reform stresses the importance of experimentation, problem finding, and problem solving instead of rote memorization[7]	Greater emphasis on students' ability to communicate and work in teams, pose and solve problems, and learn to learn[8]	New focus on "citizen skills": (1) thinking skills, including problem solving and creative thinking; (2) ways of working and interacting; (3) crafts and expressive skills; (4) participation and initiative; and (5) self-awareness and personal responsibility[9]	New Framework for 21st Century Competencies and Student Outcomes is intended to better position students to take advantage of global opportunities[10]	Common Core State Standards Initiative redefines standards to make them "inclusive of rigorous content and applications of knowledge through higher-order skills, so that all students are prepared for the 21st century"[11]
2000	2006	2010	2010	2010	2010

Figure 2 Malaysian GDP per capita growth, 1980-2013. Source: World Economic Forum.

quality education. These cities turn out the highest achieving students and are often sought after as places for parents to send their children for schooling. Unsurprisingly, they also are some of the most expensive cities, populated by those in the highest income brackets, and so can shoulder the cost of such reforms more easily, since they are less reliant on government funding. Once these cities succeed in their reforms and have evidence that such measures are effective, the changes trickle down to other cities. Governments will then see the reforms as less risky and will be more willing to roll them out across the country. By the time such reforms are instituted broadly, the first cities will have already had them in place for five to ten years and will probably have reaped the benefits of higher-achieving students before the rest of the country has even caught up. This is the reason that education reform is so slow.

According to Ms. Vivien Stewart, Senior Advisor to the Asia Society, while all the major cities cited have taken steps to implement 21st century skills into their education systems, they have allowed for varying degrees of integration within their school systems. The following overview is provided by Stewart's report from the Global Cities Education Network meeting in Shanghai.

In Seoul, Korea, students consistently score in the highest percentiles on international examinations while concurrently reporting dramatically low levels of happiness and motivation.[24] Instead of systematically instituting structures for 21st century learning, the education ministry has instituted a free learning semester in which middle-school students can engage in extracurricular activities, community service, and career exploration. During this semester, no exams are given, so that students can develop interests without fear of falling behind in performance.

In Shanghai, another indirect approach to embedding 21st century skills into education has focused on teacher training to integrate critical thinking and project-based learning into the subjects they teach. Additionally, after-school activities, which often take place outside of school, have broader activities beyond the core subjects, in order to develop 21st century skills in the students.

In Hiroshima, education reform is more systematic, focusing on four areas: knowledge, skills, values, and ethics, as well as motivation and attitude.[25] Instead of establishing specialized programs to ad-

---

24 http://asiasociety.org/global-cities-education-network/preparing-students-21st-century.
25 Ibid.

dress these areas, teachers are expected to integrate these competencies across all their activities. Teachers will learn to do this through a cohort model of training seminars and a new model of project-based learning in schools.

Singapore presents the most comprehensive and explicit case of the integration of 21st century skills into its education system, providing its own framework for 21st century competencies and expected student outcomes26:

Framework for 21st Century Competencies and Student Outcomes

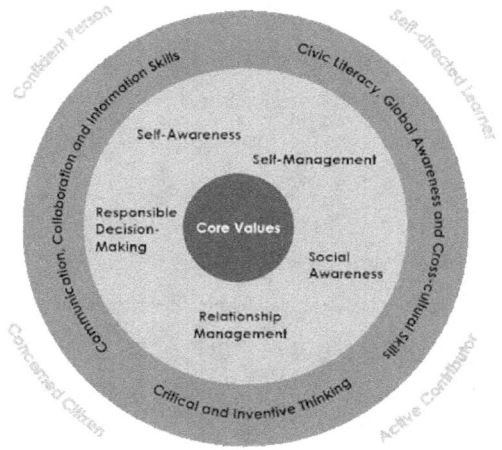

Source: Ministry of Education, Singapore.

---

26 https://www.moe.gov.sg/education/education-system/21st-century-competencies.

By creating a framework and explicitly naming the expected outcomes in this way, reform initiatives can be tightly monitored and held accountable with little variation across schools. According to the 2010 OECD Report, *Strong Performers and Successful Reformers in Education: Lessons from PISA for the United States*, Singapore holds human capital as its most precious asset and thus takes a long view on education and its approach to teaching students. Teachers are competitively paid, respected, and rewarded based on performance.[27] They undergo continuous professional development and performance reviews, and they have multiple opportunities to advance in their careers, including being selected to become school principal and working in the Education Ministry.[28] With a focus on inquiry-based learning, Singapore's schools integrate the use of technology, which is used for everything from posing questions to teachers and peers to producing knowledge via social media platforms like Twitter and Facebook.[29] Teachers create their own materials, form professional learning communities, provide feedback on lessons, and share best practices.[30] The culture seems pervasive at all levels of Singapore's education system. Research is constantly being gathered and shared on modern pedagogy, and the Education Ministry and the National Institute of Education regularly collect school data to measure how Singapore is doing relative to international benchmarks.

---

27 https://www.oecd.org/countries/singapore/46581101.pdf.
28 Ibid.
29 https://www.edutopia.org/education-everywhere-international-singapore-video.
30 Ibid.

Is It Enough?

Singapore is well known for its dedication to integrating 21st century skills into every level of education. As a city state with a small population of 5.7 million and a highly centralized and controlled government, it is nimble enough to set, execute, and monitor new educational policy measures, as well as to adapt and alter its policies when something is not working. Admirable though its efforts are, however, it is difficult to imagine replicating that same success in countries as large as, for example, China.

While several policy proposals have suggested professionalizing the teaching profession—equipping teachers with up-to-the-minute methods, integrating ICT in classrooms, and changing assessment measures—that all takes time. If, as the World Economic Forum predicts, the pace of change in business, technology, and the world is already outstripping our ability to adapt to it, what can be done for the students who languish in educational purgatory while governments and education ministries figure out how to implement and execute 21st century learning?

It was this burning question that drove me to develop my own curriculum, which empowers students to think critically about problems, create solutions, and execute their solutions in the real world. In the next chapter I will detail the philosophy, structure, and pedagogy underlying my curriculum, as well as the adaptations I made to the curriculum for my Asian audience.

The problems that pervade our society today cannot wait for education systems to catch up. As an educator, I would consider it a tragedy if I had to send my students into the world ill-prepared for the moral, ethical, economic, political, and social problems that await them.

One Way of Meeting the Challenge

My initial solution centered around the hypothesis that short, intensive periods of dedicated focus on learning, practicing, and applying 21st century skills to real-world problems would leave a strong impression on students. I believed that, if encouraged, they could transform their perspectives in the classroom and be trained to see and take later opportunities for their 21st century skills to be developed further.

My curriculum—tailored, in its initial pilot, to fit within a five-day leadership camp, in which the students were given time and space to learn without competing academic obligations—presented them with a pressing social problem to study and critically analyze. They worked in teams to complete design thinking exercises that led them to create a solution to the problem. Over the course of the five days, the students prototyped and tested their ideas, gathered feedback, made alterations, planned for execution, and finally presented their solutions in a pitch presentation before a panel of stakeholders or judges.

In the next chapter, I will give a detailed description of the program that I piloted with the Center for Asia Leadership Initiatives (CALI) and then offer my reflections on its impact on students in Asia. Using a combination of pedagogies that I learned and experienced at Harvard, I will analyze the merits of all the elements of my curriculum and describe my reasoning for integrating them into my system of teaching 21st century skills.

| Chapter 6 |
Developing a Method for Acquiring 21st Century Skills

Lisa Lee
Ed.M, Harvard Graduate School of Education

● ● ●

As a teacher, I believe 21st century skills are important because, beyond making sure that my students know how to read, write, and do math at the end of their schooling, I want to know that they will be well-adjusted, functioning contributors to society. Yet, a quick glance at the news is all that's needed to see—the dire moral, ethical, and social malaise that today's young generation is grappling with.

After spending two years working with youth in Kazakhstan, nothing disturbed me more than the helplessness that many of them felt about their futures. So, with another colleague, I started an English Club for university students, using English to talk about the many issues that concerned them. We offered discussions, role plays, team building, and volunteer activities. For the majority of them, it was the first time they felt directly engaged with the world around them. Many believed that, once they were set on a particular path, it was impossible to do anything else. This, combined with the fatalistic mentality that came from the country's Post-Soviet style of governance, rendered most of Kazakhstan's youth helpless and hopeless about the possibility of change. Their apathy stems partly from the way their education system is structured. Students study until Grade 10, when they then take a national exit exam and, based on the results, get placed into colleges, vocational schools, or continued study for university placement, which is fully funded by the government for four years. However, students must choose their course of study at university at this time, and they cannot deviate without starting over from year one. In Kazakhstan, you cannot be hired for a job in which you did not receive a degree. Thus, futures are determined at sixteen, when students take their exit exams. Structurally, this type of system leaves little flexibility for students to explore or learn about other subjects than their chosen major; it is the opposite of an interdisciplinary system.

Kazakhstan's education system, like many others, was not teaching its students the basic skills needed to think critically, solve problems, or, most importantly, take action in real contexts. None of these skills were in the curriculum. None of the teachers were trained to instill them in their students. The more affluent families who were aware of this problem would send their children to expensive international schools or to study abroad. After I began to engage with my students in interactive discussions and activities, I realized that there was something they desperately wanted but were not getting from their education: a sense of empowerment or agency over their own lives and their immediate environment. This discovery was what motivated me to apply to the Harvard Graduate School of Education. While there, I rigorously observed, studied, questioned, and brainstormed ways to teach these 21st century skills—skills like critical thinking, problem solving, collaboration, citizenship, and leadership. These are the abilities that most experts and researchers agree will be necessary to successfully navigate the 21st century.

The initial idea for my new curriculum sprang from my very first education hackathon at Harvard, which drew together students from across the Harvard campus who were trying to hack education. Our group of Education and Business School students formed around the idea of using the case method to teach critical thinking and problem solving skills. One of the members, Fred, came from China, where he said these skills are necessary, especially to teach leadership skills. Although he had never been a teacher himself, he had experienced learning through the case method at Harvard and was intent on bringing that transformative experience back to students in Asia. As we worked on the project over the course of the two days, I also experienced the transformative learning that came from working on a project, testing assumptions, getting feedback, and improving our idea before presenting it to a panel of judges.

We won Best Pitch at the hackathon, but I was the only one interested in pursuing it further. So, over the course of my studies, I took the idea of using case studies and combined it with other powerful learning experiences at Harvard to create an integrated learning curriculum that empowers students to take action with what they learn. The remainder of this chapter will describe the different pedagogies that I experienced at Harvard, my rationale for incorporating them into my curriculum, and my experience of trying to teach it to students in Asia during my pilot of the program.

Much of the time that I spent outside of class at Harvard was dedicated to networking, finding potential partners who were willing to test my curriculum, or developing my product at the Harvard Innovation Lab. I was hoping to pilot my program in the U.S. before taking it abroad. However, it was challenging to find schools open to trying something new, and I realized that I would probably have to start with out-of-school programs, which had more flexibility.

Toward the end of the semester, I was considering whether I should pursue my educational venture or get a full-time job after graduation. The prospects of bootstrapping my start-up from scratch were daunting. Then, one of my classmates serendipitously told me about the summer teaching fellowships with the Center for Asia Leadership Initiatives (CALI). When I had learned more about the vision and mission of the Center—to equip young people with leadership skills, a goal in line with the vision I had set for my program—I applied for the summer fellowship. After several rounds of interviews, I pitched my program to Mr. Hungsoo S. Kim, the President of CALI, who was gracious enough to let me pilot my curriculum in one of their youth programs.

The Prototype

My prototype program consisted of three modules: case studies to practice critical thinking and analytical skills; design thinking to practice problem solving skills, while cultivating innovation and creativity; and project-based learning, which centered all these activities around a specific project in a real-world context. These modules were seamlessly integrated so that students would be exposed to a skill, immediately apply it in a structured environment, and then have the freedom to experiment with it in their projects.

While I had to condense my curriculum to fit it into the five-day, intensive leadership programs of CALI, I was still able to maintain the basic structure of my program:

- **Case Study** – A social problem is presented as a case, and students discuss the different contributing factors and stakeholders in a particular problem. Case studies are also used to demonstrate what other problem solvers have done in similar situations.
- **Design Challenge** – Project-based learning, in which students are divided into teams and tasked with creating their own solutions through a series of guided design thinking exercises.
- **Testing and Feedback** - Students bring their ideas to the stakeholders for assessment and critique so that they can improve their solution, making it more realistic and practical.
- **Strategy and Execution** - Students plan how to implement their solution for maximum impact.
- **Presentation** – Students present their solutions to a wider audience and before a panel of judges for feedback.

A typical day opened with a case study of a problem that a leader had faced. For example, how a director of a water utility could bring water to all of Phnom Penh, Cambodia. Students assessed the problems he was facing, analyzed the strategies he took to address them, and then brainstormed what he should do next. This opened up the students' minds to consider different approaches for problem solving, which prepared them for design thinking, in which I demonstrated an exercise to help them generate ideas. They then practiced the exercise and asked questions, and I gave them some time to apply the exercise to their design challenge—for example, how to play football without seeing. Over the course of the week, they designed their own solution as a team and started prototyping and testing it by gathering feedback from others. Then I gave a lesson on all the factors they needed to consider in carrying out their solution. Students worked both in class and out of class. During my test runs with CALI, I found that giving them feedback during their workshopping time out of class was very helpful in pushing them to think of more innovative solutions. When circumstances permitted, I invited stakeholders to give feedback on their ideas. Finally, on the last day, the students gave five-minute pitches of their solutions to a panel of judges and stakeholders, who gave honest feedback.

The only aspect of the curriculum that was difficult to carry out during the five-day program was the Implementation Phase, in which the students implement their solutions and collect data on their impact. While I tried to integrate learning by doing as much as possible into my class time, there is no better teacher than the real world, when you go out and take action on the ideas that you have cultivated in the classroom. My goal was to expose these students to the possibilities for action in front of them and to equip them with enough skills to attempt action. One student reached out to me after the program because she felt inspired to carry out her project proposal at her school, but she ran into challenges from the school administration. She was encountering her first lesson in problem solving in the real world: you have to convince others that there is a problem, and that you have a solution they should try. A good dose of conviction and persistence is necessary in persevering through such challenges, and that is something that can be taught only through experience.

Because of the positive feedback that I received in the pilot workshops, I was able to improve and modify my program for a series of social innovation design challenges for students, for the remainder of the summer. With each new batch of students, I learned more about what Asian students struggle with, what works for them, what doesn't, and what it takes to motivate them to work toward solving difficult problems. Through my partnership with CALI, I was able to reach over five hundred students with my program, focusing on a host of challenging social issues. Some of the design challenges this summer included:

- How might we provide education for child refugees in Malaysia?
- How might young people promote understanding and better relations between Japan, Korea, and China?
- How might we help students adapt to new cultures?
- How might we improve healthcare and education in Malaysia?

I could not be prouder of the work that my students did this summer and the thoughtful solutions they created in just a few days or, in some cases, just a few hours. The students sometimes even surprised themselves with the solutions they designed and presented before a panel of judges. But the most satisfying part of the summer was when students emailed me afterward and told me that, because of the workshop, they were now going to pursue the project that they had created or to take action in some other way about the issues they care about.

Learning from the Best

I spent the majority of my Master's program taking classes that I thought sounded interesting and potentially useful in developing my own venture. I specifically did not want to take courses that would "specialize" me in some field of research or policy-making. The International Education Policy program at the Harvard Graduate School of Education was ideal in this respect because, although it has a few requirements, it provided the flexibility that I needed not just to learn but to experience different forms of pedagogy. What better way to learn how to teach than to be taught by some of the best professors in the world? I took courses with what I believed would be the most effective and innovative pedagogies and integrated them into my curriculum to teach 21st century skills to high school students.

Though I am proposing a new model for skill based education, I am in no way discounting other forms of pedagogy. In fact, because I value them so much, I have taken to integrating them into my own curriculum. Here I will detail some of the key takeaways regarding pedagogy that I gleaned from my time at Harvard, as well as why I believed they were valuable and how I incorporated them into my curriculum. In teaching my curriculum to students in Asia, I realized that I had to adapt my teaching methods to draw out these skills in Asian students. Therefore, after each section, I will share my reflections on how the pedagogies in my curriculum were received in Asia and how they had to be contextualized.

It is also important to note that these reflections are based on my personal experiences, teaching a self-selected group of students who signed up for these summer leadership camps. I recognize the importance of not mistaking the few for the whole. Nevertheless, I am sharing my experiences as a window into greater understanding of the task ahead of us—something we will certainly need if we are to equip our young people to meet the challenges of the 21st century.

The Lecture: Knowledge Is Not Dead

From the various classes I took, I came to understand many things about learning and teaching that I integrated into my curriculum prototype. One of my favorite classes, however, had nothing to do with education and fulfilled none of my requirements; I was simply interested in the topic, and the professor was extremely engaging. The class—"Why Are Countries Poor, Unequal, and Volatile?"—was taught at the Harvard Kennedy School of Government by Ricardo Hausman. It was an International Economic Development class that was based on Professor Hausman's own research and theory of economic development. He was not rehashing other economic theories, although we did review them; instead he offered his own way of thinking, which was completely new and fresh (at least to me). Moreover, the class offered just the right combination of content delivery, rigor, practice, and review needed for active engagement. As a teacher, I marveled at the way he intentionally constructed the curriculum so that it was scaffolded; the discipline in which he executed each class, delivering over sixty slides of content within seventy-five minutes; the breadth of knowledge he had of world economies; and the rigor with which he did his research and answered students' objections to his ideas. He lectured for seventy-five minutes straight, two to three times a week, and he kept his students engaged for an entire semester, a noble feat for any teacher.

I reference this course as a contrast to some other graduate courses that curated content for discussion instead of generating new content. While such curation also has its benefits, in some progressive education circles there has been some movement away from the lecture as a pedagogy, since pure knowledge can be delivered through other media besides a human being. Having taken such inspiring lecture courses, however, I disagree with this movement. New ideas must be delivered by human beings, especially the ones who have formulated the ideas in question. Learning and the refinement of ideas come from the interaction of ideas, people, and contexts. There is nothing more powerful than listening to people who have lived their ideas, failed, learned, and adjusted. This is why I believe that lectures can still be powerful when complemented with time for discussion, questioning, and the application of concepts.

Instead of considering lectures as "merely" content delivery, we need to value them as an efficient method for students to receive and absorb complex information for immediate application. Well-constructed lectures can be very effective when paired with concept application (homework or classwork). I think where we have gone wrong with the lecture is the propensity to feed information to our students and then instruct them to regurgitate it. A truly engaging lecturer considers student needs, frames the information so that it is useful, and then provides relevant examples in which to apply the knowledge. A lecturer should not simply deliver information without challenging students to do something with it.

Lectures in the Asian Context

Because students in Asia are so used to teachers delivering information that they need to know for the exam, I was careful not to lecture students for more than fifteen or twenty minutes continuously, for fear that they would disengage. However, when there are only eighty minutes both to understand the complexities of a problem and to start brainstorming ideas, it is necessary to provide students with the information they need directly, so that they can then apply it to the problem. For example, when I led the design challenge for education for child refugees in Malaysia, I needed to provide a lot of information on the context of the situation, so the students could understand what was within their parameters of control to create solutions. Because of the intensive nature of the five-day program, I could not wait for them to research and find all this information for themselves, though it would have been preferable. Additionally, I lectured mainly to explain why certain things should be considered while they were creating their solutions; I then immediately gave them an exercise so that they could apply it to their own projects. I found this to be the most effective way for students in Asia to use information from a lecture.

Project-Based Learning: Applying Concepts in the Real World

Project-based learning fills the void that is left by most lecture-based classes. In project-based learning, a student or group of students is given a project in which they must apply all of their learning in a particular field. An example project for an engineering class could be to build a robot or car engine using the concepts they have learned in class. Instead of homework assignments, students thus apply what they learn in class. I took a few Project-Based Learning courses, in which we had to develop either a program or a product to address various educational needs. These courses typically curated relevant content and assigned them as course reading, which we sometimes discussed in class, and guest speakers were invited to share their experiences. Occasionally, we did exercises to help us generate or refine ideas for our project. In these courses we were given a real problem to work on, stakeholders to interview, constraints, parameters, and a fixed timeframe. While I liked the practical aspect of these courses, however, I sometimes felt frustrated by the lack of guidance or structure, and I often wanted more rigorous application in the classes themselves.

I understand that some professors do not want to constrain their students by providing too many parameters or rubrics because they feel that the course should be not about the grade but about the learning. Yet it was often difficult for me to decipher what I was supposed to be learning in these classes, and as I would discover more acutely later, students who don't know why they are doing something often lose motivation to do anything.

Of course, at the graduate level, one shouldn't expect much handholding, and I noticed that many of my professors were wary of prescribing how one should think. Yet, while I understood the purpose of this, I often felt deprived of the benefit of the understanding that a professor would bring to an issue or problem. After all, I was at Harvard to learn and hear from the best. If I had been satisfied with my way of thinking, I wouldn't have spent all that money to go to graduate school. I understand the fear of just feeding answers to students, but, at the graduate level, I believe that those admitted have enough powers of independent thought to take information given by a professor and assess for themselves whether it is useful or pertinent.

Project-Based Learning in Asia

For my students in Asia, I posed a design challenge in which I expected them to create a solution. It was apparent that the students were used to a very prescribed way of learning and doing assignments. Project-based learning presents students with the freedom to come up with any answer that might possibly fit the problem. For students who have been trained to take tests and identify answers in specific formats, this kind of freedom is terrifying. I gave them basic parameters for their projects but found that they needed examples. When I did give examples, many of the students would simply copy the examples as if they were templates. Hence, creativity was squelched, not because the students didn't have it but because of their learned mentality of "giving the right answer" or giving the teacher what he or she wants. I had to be careful when using examples so that they didn't become prescriptive. Nevertheless, parameters are necessary and sometimes helpful for creativity, because they push students to think harder and more thoroughly about their ideas.

To leverage the full value of project-based learning, I had to be very explicit about how each lesson applied to their project and to challenge them to give me examples. I found this reinforcement crucial in motivating the students to try different things on their own. If given more time, I would have also asked students to submit written reflections on what they learned in the process, for such a process internalizes the learning. However, the greatest value that I believe project-based learning provides is a tangible end product for a student's time, efforts, learning, creativity, and problem solving. The project serves as evidence of a student's ability to work independently or in a team to solve a difficult challenge—and, for the student, it testifies to what is possible through applied skills and effort.

The Case Method: Critical Thinking in Context

Another approach to applying concepts to real-life situations is the case method. Students are given a case—a real scenario, usually in written form—in which the protagonist is faced with some critical decision. The professor engages students in a lively discussion in which all the facts are drawn out and assessed, and then he or she facilitates the discussion so that a few key points in the case are highlighted and underlying assumptions are probed and challenged. This is the most indirect way of teaching, but, when done properly, it is also the most effective way to facilitate self-learning and reflection.

Of all the pedagogies outlined, I believe that the case method is the most difficult to teach well. In sixty to ninety minutes, a professor needs to draw out everyone's thoughts, challenge biases and assumptions, introduce alternative ways of thinking, and drive students to think ever more critically—all without directly stating any imperatives. Teaching by case method is both an art and a science. I've sat through some poorly run case classes that felt more like conversations going nowhere and in which the professor was just fielding answers. I've also experienced case classes in which the professor wove together all the information into a beautiful tapestry, so that everyone felt they had contributed to the big picture.

The case method can be very powerful. It puts learning and learning outcomes into the hands of the students. When done well, this can be very empowering for the students and spurs active engagement and self-reflection outside the classroom. Unlike other pedagogies, it provides a framework and lens through which a student can look at problems in the real world.

However, a drawback of the case study method is that it relies heavily on the experiences of students and peer-to-peer learning. This makes sense at the graduate level, where the diversity of backgrounds and work experiences contribute to the robustness of the discussions. But it becomes problematic at the high school level, where those experiences tend to be limited. In this context, the case method is better used as a launching point from which to engage in guided problem solving. Since high school students have not been exposed to as much real-world experience, cases are a great way to introduce them to different approaches and perspectives, giving the students insight and inspiration.

The Case Method in Asia

In the Asian context, where students aren't regularly solicited for their opinions or perspectives, the case method can be a very difficult pedagogy to implement. The difficulty is compounded by the fact that many students find public speaking challenging in general. Students are afraid to give the "wrong answer," and, in my experience, they often wait for the instructor to provide the solution. When the students do give answers, they are often sung aloud in a chorus. Instead of lively discussion, an instructor must cold-call or break down questions to the most obvious answers, so that students are not afraid of appearing wrong in front of others. This is understandable when you look at the structure of many Asian education systems, which focus on getting the right answers on a slew of high-stakes written examinations. Students are conditioned from Grade 5 or earlier to identify the right answers and remember them when it's important.

One way I worked around this challenge in my pilot program was to allow students to discuss the problem in pairs or groups before sharing their solutions with the class. Occasionally I sat in on conversations, and if I heard something interesting, I would ask the student to share it with the class. This prepped the students and gave them the confidence to speak up. I stressed the importance of articulating one's thoughts, backing them up with evidence from the case, and offering alternative solutions. I explained that these are skills they will need in the workplace, in relationships, and in everyday negotiations. Without giving them a specific reason to train themselves in this important communication skill, few Asian students will push themselves out of their comfort zones to share their thoughts in class.

Design Thinking: Problem Solving through Applied Trial and Error

Design thinking has recently become a popular trend not just in consumer design, but also in social innovation and education. It is essentially a systematic way of problem solving through applied design exercises. The typical design thinking process consists of five different phases:

- Empathize with the user
- Define the problem
- Ideate Solutions
- Prototype Solutions
- Test the solutions and gather feedback

After you test your solution, you gather feedback so that you can improve and refine your solution, and then you go through the five phases all over again.

I was encouraged by an alumna to take a design thinking course after she learned that I was interested in starting my own venture. My first exposure to design thinking came through the Design Thinking Course at the Harvard Business School. I was surprised that the first few classes focused so heavily on the user for whom you are designing a solution. Later I realized that this is the genius of human centered design: it focuses on the person experiencing the problem in all the ways they experience it, from specific pain points to the larger context. Often, in problem solving, we are satisfied with simply finding a solution without giving a thought to the stakeholders or the implementers of the solution. This happens not just in consumer product design but in policy as well, making design thinking for social innovation a merited mission.

Design thinking is especially useful when you know the specific problem and the audience for whom you are designing. While I completed many design thinking exercises in my course, I wish I had more class time to apply those exercises to my own project. The main complaint about many design thinking exercises is that they are too short and leave students wanting more. The hope is that students will go home and use the exercises to tinker with their own projects in their free time, but, as I've come to learn as a teacher, many students get distracted by other assignments, obligations, and classes. Fully leveraging classroom time became a goal of mine during my workshops.

I integrated design thinking into my curriculum because it was an active, hands-on way to solve problems and breaks through the propensity of students to wait for answers. It compels them to engage in exercises by systematically taking them through timed thought exercises. Timing the exercises is beneficial because:

- the pressure of coming up with answers forces students to focus intently on the problem;
- the speed with which they have to come up with as many answers as possible prevents them from unduly rejecting their own ideas;
- after the first few obvious answers, the students must think more creatively to generate more ideas;
- and it allows quiet students to voice ideas that might otherwise get squelched in a group discussion, in which one person tends to dominate.

While my students sometimes felt rushed, they admitted that the pressure forced them to come up with more ideas and thus gave them more ideas to choose from. The generation of many ideas by each individual is at the core of design thinking, and unlike many group discussions, which tend to be dominated by a few individuals, design thinking allows each student to contribute and be heard.

Design Thinking in Asia

For almost all students in Asia, design thinking is a new and unorthodox way of thinking and learning. In my pilot program, few of them actively engaged in lessons where they had to brainstorm, ideate, or draw diagrams or pictures to explain their ideas. Because it is the nature of design thinking to come up with as many ideas as possible (i.e. quantity over quality), students needed a bit of adjustment time. They were used to sitting at their desks, listening intently to a teacher, and copying down copious notes. I could see from their faces that if I gave them five minutes to brainstorm, they would spend the first three or four minutes wondering what I was looking for or if their answers were "correct." Also, while most students enjoyed the active engagement and moving around that design thinking required, some preferred to sit and work quietly. I struggled most at the Trilateral Leadership Summit, which brought together fifty students from Japan, Korea, and China. All three countries have highly competitive, exam-based education systems, with the resulting cram schools. Perhaps because the students were from countries with strained international relations or felt uncomfortable speaking in English, it took a bit longer for them to warm up to each other and actively engage in working together to design solutions. In Malaysia, by contrast, students jumped at the chance to be active and had much more lively interactions, meaning that consequently they generated more ideas and more creative solutions.

Interestingly, a general characteristic that I observed in all of my students in Asia was their aversion to being rushed, sloppy, or messy. However, the design process is inherently a chaotic activity of generating ideas, trying them out, and throwing away ideas that don't work.

As much as I tried to emphasize the time constraints and the needlessness of writing in neat lines, I could not deter some students from taking out their rulers and drawing perfectly straight lines in their diagrams while they were "prototyping" in fifteen minutes or less. While the conscientiousness of Asian students is admirable, their difficulty in adapting their work processes to the situation at hand can become problematic in later life, especially in technologies industries where the pace of change may outstrip the time it takes to draw the perfect prototype.

Creating Safe Environments

This theme of perfection and getting the right answer was pervasive throughout the workshops I taught this summer. If we truly want our students to think and experiment, teachers need to create an environment of psychological safety, in which students are not shamed when they don't know the answer, give the wrong answer, or try something that doesn't work. When they do feel ashamed, students turn off their brains and no longer try to come up with solutions on their own. They just wait in silence until the teacher provides the answer, and this squelches the creativity so necessary for innovation. It is also highly disempowering: what it reinforces to a student is that there is only one right solution, and someone else has it—a teacher, a boss, the government, etc.

Psychological safety comes from building a relationship of trust between the teacher and the student. Most of the time, the teacher-student relationship is viewed as the teacher giving information, the student receiving, and the teacher checking to see whether the information has been absorbed. I like to view teaching as a coaching or mentoring relationship, in which my students and I embark on a learning journey together and collaborate to find ways of applying knowledge in the real world.

All teachers understand that we must look for certain answers in order to progress with a lesson. But, when a student provides a response that does not lead in that direction, instead of rejecting it and moving on, we should ask how her or she came up with the answer. This is deeper learning because it exposes how a student thinks, and, if the logical progression is faulty, it can be corrected. More often than not, however, it exposes the other students to a different perspective, which expands their creativity, innovation, and problem solving skills.

Final Reflections

Reflecting on our learning experiences was a common theme in all of my classes at Harvard. It wasn't unusual to spend the last class of the semester reviewing what we learned, providing feedback on what could have been done better in the course, and sharing what we had internalized from the semester. I have always been a reflective person, but now this consistent and regular process of review, assessment, and reflection became a systematic activity in which I appraised all my experiences. In practice this usually means that I pause what I'm doing, ask what I'm learning or if I'm being effective, and then change course if necessary. At the end, I glean lessons that can be internalized for the future.

This process was habitual for me while I was teaching my pilot program this summer. As much as I wanted to be right about the value I was delivering to students, I constantly sought feedback from students and teachers on the effectiveness of what I was teaching. If something wasn't working, I didn't give up on the exercise, I adapted it. If students were not answering my questions in class, I gave them post-its to write down their thoughts. If they didn't understand a certain exercise, I stopped and demonstrated it. It took me a few classes to realize that for many design thinking exercises, I was explaining the instructions in English, which was not the primary language for any of my students. After that I took care to put my instructions in Power Point presentations, to give demonstrations, and to check for understanding.

At the end of each long and intensive week, I collected rigorous feedback on lessons that were helpful or unhelpful and topics that were difficult to understand, as well as suggestions for improvement. This was critical to the improvement of both my teaching and my program. The most important insight I gained from these surveys was that less is more. In the beginning, I tried to cram as much content and activity into three hours as possible, and this often resulted in students rushing from one activity to another without understanding their purpose or how to apply them to their projects. I thought that by exposing the students to as much as possible, I would be providing them with more possibilities to choose from, but in fact that system often overwhelmed or confused them. This piece of feedback forced me to distill my lessons to the key exercises that I believed would most benefit my students. Framing the lesson, linking it to their projects, setting up the exercises, facilitating the application, and debriefing became the most important aspects of my lessons.

Another important insight from my summer was that it is both challenging and labor-intensive to teach relevant, customized, skills-based lessons that are transformative for students. I spent hours every night for weeks and months scouring resources for content that would be relevant to the students' work; I brainstormed six different ways to practice communication skills; I played out all the possible discussion scenarios for our case discussions. It is no wonder that I slept little during our workshops.

But the end result made all my efforts worthwhile. When the students presented their work, they surprised their peers and even themselves. After seeing their achievements, I know that what I teach is both important and valuable. At the same time, I recognize that many teachers don't have the time or energy to go through such a rigorous process. That's why I am creating an online platform to aid teachers in implementing these lessons in class, learning centers, or leadership camps. By providing the lesson plans, PowerPoint presentations, exercises, and online tools to track students as they execute their projects, teachers can focus on delivering these lessons and cultivating 21st century skills in students.

In the end, I am a teacher. I will always be a teacher. I don't necessarily believe students will learn these skills on their own or in a vacuum. One of my goals in creating this curriculum has been to make it easier for teachers to teach and develop 21st century skills in students. It is up to us as educators, policy-makers, parents, and advocates to make it our priority to instill values and ethics, cultivate independent thinking, and equip students with all the skills they need to become positive contributors to society.

Part 4

Asia Leadership Trek VII

| Chapter 7 |

Reflections on Kyrgyzstan after Ten Years of Absence

Umar Shavurov

MPA, Harvard Kennedy School of Government

●●●

It's 5 a.m. on June 8, 2016. I am in the departures section of the Manas International Airport in the outskirts of Bishkek, Kyrgyzstan, about to board a plane to Dubai *en route* back to Bogota, Colombia. The lounge is filled with people, mainly male and visibly Muslim: they wear beards and white dresses, and the women are covered by headscarves and occasional burkas. Their appearance is startling to me. I can't recognize these people as my own compatriots; there seems to be a gaping hole between their identity and mine. This is when I realize, for the first time since arriving some days before with the Asia Leadership Trek, that I have been away from my country—Kyrgyzstan—for way too long. To be precise, ten years. My feeling of disconnection at the airport made me stop and think about what had happened in Kyrgyzstan in the past decade and, reaching further back, since its independence. What could have made the people in this country, once regarded by many Western leaders as a *beacon of democracy in Central Asia*, to look for answers in another version of Islam, not traditionally practiced before? What are the many struggles—political, economic, and social—that face this country's population, and why, despite its adoption of a democratic political system, has it failed thus far to become a stable and prosperous nation?

The Rise of Islam in Kyrgyzstan[1]

A relative of mine told me of his recent experience with this issue in our village in South of Kyrgyzstan. He was approached by a group of activists from our village asking for a donation to build a second mosque. He asked them why they hadn't instead fundraise for another school in the village. The answer was quite straightforward: they had already received some funding for the mosque from sponsors in one of the Gulf countries, and they needed to come up with a local cash contribution. They also said that more people would benefit from the mosque since it would be built to please God. Meanwhile, the school was a difficult project: it required funding from the state and would probably not come to anything, since bribes would need to be paid. My relative, to his own dismay, yielded to peer pressure and ended up giving money for the mosque. His story reveals three facts about conditions in modern-day Kyrgyzstan: (1) Economic hardship and rampant corruption are driving people to seek answers

---

1 In this section I will tackle the very sensitive subject of religion and its role in modern-day Kyrgyzstan. This will undoubtedly elicit much criticism and potentially even accusations that I have lost my faith. To all such critics: this essay is an attempt to dissect intellectually the real problems facing the country, including the rise of extremist Islam, and to find ways of overcoming these predicaments for the people of Kyrgyzstan.

in religion, where, they believe, corruption has not entered because of the fear of God. (2) Generous sponsorship from other Muslim nations is encouraging the spread of Islam in the country. (3) People in Kyrgyzstan have lost their faith in the power and usefulness of education. This is especially intriguing since traditionally the people of Kyrgyzstan have had placed a great deal of importance in the education of their children. Yet madrassas—Islamic religious schools—now seem like a better option for the moral education of their offspring.

The role of religion in Kyrgyzstan since the country gained independence in 1991 has grown exponentially. In 1991, there were one hundred mosques; in 2016, approximately two thousand five hundred. There are now more mosques than public schools (there were two thousand two hundred schools in 2016).[2] The current version of Islam gaining strength in the country is new: the majority of Kyrgyzstanis have traditionally practiced a local religion combining Islam with pre-Islamic beliefs. It seems clear that the more recent and extreme brand of Islam has become an escape from the difficulties that so many people in the country face. I would argue, however, that it offers only a coping mechanism. The greatest challenge confronting Kyrgyzstan, which so far the country has failed to meet, is building a modern, prosperous, and democratic nation based on respect for the individual rights of its citizens.

Two revolutions, in 2005 and 2010, and two inter-ethnic conflicts, in 1990 and 2010, have compounded this challenge. Some might consider these outbursts as extreme forms of coping. Violence and force were used to gain power in order to combat the injustice of the

---

2   Data from meeting conversations with public figures.

ruling elites. These uprisings, however, did not right the wrongs of the ruling class; instead they legitimized the use of violence to gain power. Despite these setbacks, Kyrgyzstan has managed to preserve some basic elements of democracy: freedom of speech, more or less free and fair elections, and the right to assembly. Perhaps the strongest gain from the last quarter-century of independence has been the creation of a strong civil society. Yet these gains seem impressive only in comparison to the country's semi-democratic neighbors. So what yardstick should we use to measure Kyrgyzstan's level of democracy?

An Illiberal Democracy

If we use Western democracy as a standard of democracy, Kyrgyzstan falls far short. The liberal democracy of the West is characterized not only by free and fair elections but also by the rule of law, a separation of powers, and the protection of basic liberties of speech, assembly, religion, and property ownership. According to Fared Zakaria, a prominent Western scholar, these elements, together with a fundamental respect for the rule of law, form constitutional liberalism, which differs from basic democracy. Zakaria calls those democratic states that lack constitutional liberalism "illiberal democracies."[3] In 1997, when he wrote his seminal essay explaining the concept of liberal vs. illiberal democracies, 35 percent of states around the world

---

3   Fared Zakaria, well-known columnist and scholar in U.S., coined this term. The basic tenet, according to Zakaria, is that an illiberal democracy, also called a partial democracy, low-intensity democracy, empty democracy, or hybrid regime, is a governing system in which, although elections take place, citizens are cut off from knowledge about the activities of those who exercise real power because of a lack of civil liberties.

were illiberal democracies, according to his criteria. Kyrgyzstan was among them and, I would argue, remains one today. After independence, the leaders in Kyrgyzstan wrongly assumed that by simply imitating democratic institutions—specifically elections—and copying the constitutions of Western countries, they could create a democracy. A basic form of democracy. They told the public that through democracy the country would become more prosperous and stable. But the truth of the matter is that this did not happen. The country is less well off than it was before. There is a wider income disparity between the rich and poor, corruption has increased, the safety and security of citizens are often at risk, and primary and secondary education are declining. All in all, the situation does not look promising, to say the least.

Fared Zakaria argues that it is difficult to obtain a properly functioning political system, with a properly functioning market economy, by going from democracy to constitutional liberalism. Normally it's the other way around. Zakaria cites the experience of the West, where often the rule of law was established before the present form of elected government came into being. Unlike Western states, however, most new democracies, including Kyrgyzstan, have opted for the "shortcut." You can't blame them. It's easier to start with low-hanging fruit, imposing a democratic electoral system without committing to the other elements of constitutional liberalism.

Back in late '90s, my university's administration announced open elections for the student Parliament. The idea was to allow the students to participate in the decision-making process. In reality, the students who ran were promoted by the administration to help them legitimize their decision—but many people still took the process seriously and were inspired to make use of the democratic system. One of them, a good friend of mine, vehemently protested the university's lack of regard for students in not heating the classrooms during winter conditions of minus 20 degrees Celsius. He organized the students to boycott their classes until the heating was reinstated. This case demonstrates the potential of democracy to be both used well and abused, depending on the people operating the system. For the last quarter-century, Kyrgyzstan as a whole has experienced a similar push-and-pull process in deciding between democracy's form and content.

Many people became exhausted with the process of getting things done. Some call it "procedural" democracy, which requires the participation of many stakeholders to define the direction of the country through the institutions and procedures governing their day-to-day lives. Some Kyrgyzstanis feel disenchanted, arguing that the loudest voices have hijacked the country's political system for the benefit of their own interests. The ruling elites also have mastered the use of these loudest voices to manage the attribution of powers in the system. It has become a legitimizing factor. Such self-interest is evident in the numerous constitutional amendments in the past allowing the ruling elite to usurp power in the executive branch, neglect the judiciary, and convert the Parliament into a rubber stamp—though the country has also seen smaller, more active factions rise to the moment and restore the balance, effectively beheading the "dragon." Nevertheless, throughout this fluctuating process, the government has yet to exhibit a true acceptance of liberal democracy, with all its moral and ethical components, as the answer to the nation's problems.

The rising popularity of Islam indicates the Kyrgyzstanis' continuing attempt to find purpose. Democracy, which coincided with rise of capitalism and favored the well-connected and those willing to break the rules, has thus far not provided the answers. So religion has filled the void, acting instead of the state to regulate the relations of people not only in households but also slowly to dictate behavior in the economic and political realms. This is not abnormal for the population of the south, which has tended to be religious, but it is puzzling to see Islam's growing dominance in the north, which has historically been less open to Islam. Nomad culture, traditionally practice by the Kyrgyz, throughout centuries has helped people to demonstrated incredible resilience and ability to adapt to the new challenges. No more. Islam is becoming an attractive alternative in the light of economic hardships and growing void of lack of viable and legitimate secular, moral and ethical values. In part because I am from the south, I have never felt a tension between being a Muslim and having democratic aspirations. And if the Islam now prominent in Kyrgyzstan had been the version traditionally practiced in wider Central Asia, I would not view it as a problem. The new Islam, however, which is now thrusting itself forward, is more orthodox, akin to the version practiced in the Gulf countries. This Islam, unlike the traditional Kyrgyzstani version, strives to influence the political, economic, and social realms. Even more worrying, many current politicians are using the religion to score points and garner votes. This blend of religion and politics is surely to backfire. The harsh strictures of the current version of Islam may seem to provide a quick answer to rule of law that people badly yearn for but will take the country further away from liberal democracy. What is needed now is not simply a system that will get people to vote and hold elections, but one that will require day-to-day work of building of institutions, rules and procedures through democratic practices and respect for individual rights. Only in that way Kyrgyzstan may become a liberal democracy.

A Work in Progress

On August 31, 2016, Kyrgyzstan marked its twenty-fifth anniversary of independence. It was a significant milestone for a nation in a harsh region, surrounded by illiberal democracies. All of these states have the bells and whistles of a democratic system while missing the fundamental spirit of democracy. Elections are used simply to legitimize the ruling elite's mandates. The people serve the rulers rather than the other way around.

In 2015, Kyrgyzstan was able to digitize its voting process, which reduced the threat of election fraud. The Parliament that was voted in with this new system did not promise to be effective or efficient, free of corruption, or equipped with a new strategic vision, but at least it was voted in through a free and fair election. The incumbent President's party—the Social Democratic Party of Kyrgyzstan—was able to garner only a third of the votes, as compared to the presidential parties of the neighboring nations, which normally claim an astronomical 90 percent of voter support. Kyrgyzstan's elections are no longer dramatically different from those in the West. Yet it still lacks the institutions that uphold the rule of law, property rights, separate governmental powers, and free speech and assembly. As is evident in the people's growing frustration, merely entrusting the citizens with the vote is not enough. A functional, liberal democracy requires the constant oversight of public servants to make sure that their policies are transparent and that they are held accountable for their actions.

In Kyrgyzstan's current political system, no one is responsible for the consequences of their actions. The elected officials promise to steer the country in the right direction but in reality proffer favors to local constituencies in exchange for their support. The people, on the other hand, believe that by delegating their civic responsibilities to their elected leaders, they need not do anything to ensure a functional day-to-day democracy. If the country is to prosper, the people in leadership positions need to change the attitudes of the people, encouraging all Kyrgyzstani citizens to engage actively in the democratic process. The people collectively must grapple with the country's challenges and decide on its best course. If they decide that religion should be paramount in political life, let it be. But the decision must be tackled by the local communities before being handed over to their Members of Parliament. Active and informed participation is crucial for people in upholding the principles of liberal constitutionalism. "Outsourcing" decisions to the elected few will not lead the country out of its current path. Democracy must be a joint process.

If Kyrgyzstan does not embrace a liberal democracy, the consequences are bleak: an atrophied judiciary, a weak legislature, and a dangerously strong executive branch. It came as no surprise when a prominent MP, Omurbek Babanov, drew in his outline of a vision for Kyrgyzstan on the example of Singapore, referring to Singapore's early years of independence and its strong emphasis on the rule of law. Between 1991 and 2016, the Kyrgyzstani Constitution has been amended eight times. Often it has been tailored to ratify the vested interests of the ruling elite. All of its presidents—Akaev, Bakiev, and Atambaev, with sole exception of Otunbaeva—have made an attempt to usurp permanent power, believing in their own absolute sovereignty over the people. These attempted coups resulted in the centralization of power, both horizontally, by weakening the other branches, and vertically, by taking functions away from regional governments and municipalities. Under this scenario, in which the main source of law is constantly accosted and no institutions exist to uphold and protect it, liberal democracy never had a chance to demonstrate its power as guarantor of stability and prosperity.

The challenge the Kyrgyzstani people face now is to turn the tide and regain their faith in the democratic system. This means giving the democracy a second chance, so that it can be used to its fullest potential.

The Stigma of Cooperation

Kyrgyzstan is a landlocked country, bordered on the north and south by two larger and more powerful nations: Kazakhstan and China. Its position entails high costs in overland transportation, an immense problem that thus far no one has been able to solve. Ms. Roza Otunbaeva, an interim President of Kyrgyzstan in 2010, told us in our meeting with her what she believed to be the solution: "China is our Ocean." The Kyrgyzstani people seem not to have fully realized the potential of their proximity to this "ocean." The country's trade balance with China is negative, and the reason for that, in my view, is simple: the Kyrgyzstani people have not been able to coalesce around a unified idea and follow through on its realization. Collaboration and cooperation is crucial in building a strong and large-scale economy, if Kyrgyzstan is to become a serious competitor in the Chinese market—or any other market, for that matter. Individual farms and businesses will never provide the volume of products that a business would need to gain a foothold in China. Some may argue that, rather than focusing on volume, which may be difficult to achieve, Kyrgyzstan should focus on niche products. Former President Bakiev, who is now self-exiled in Belarus, hailed Kyrgyzstan as the organic greenhouse of China. In itself, this would not be a bad model, but in order to make it a reality the population of Kyrgyzstan still needs to communicate and unite in pursuing such a plan. Similarly, the country's industries must embark on meaningful collaborative projects if they are to become competitive forces in the market.

Despite these necessities, however, in today's Kyrgyzstan the word "cooperation" might as well be a bad word. After seventy-plus years of communism under Soviet rule, during which people were forced to collaborate against their will, the concept gained a negative stigma that still lingers today. Though there are exceptions, in general the Kyrgyzstani people would rather let their individual projects fail then come together and build a joint, larger project. But unless we acknowledge every part of our history, understanding its good elements and weeding out the bad, we will not move forward. The nomad culture followed traditionally by the Kyrgyz people emphasized a reliance on cooperation and a horizontal hierarchy: everyone shared the burden so that everyone could survive. In today's world, one can see through examples from all over the world that communication and collaboration lead to problem solving and innovation. Take, for instance, South Korea in the aftermath of World War II and the Korean War. After the devastation of these conflicts, people came together to find new solutions. Today, Korean goods are flooding the high-tech market not by force but by consumer choice; thanks to cooperative problem solving, Korea's products are one of the best.

The Kumtor Gold Mine in Kyrgyzstan offers another illustration of what can go wrong when people can't come together and implement effective procedures with adequate oversight. The mine is Kyrgyzstan's most significant source of revenue, providing 40 percent of the country's export share. Its fate dominated many of the meetings we held on the Trek. The subject is mired in corruption and legal wrangling by the ruling elite. At the core of the problem is the legitimacy of Canada's ownership of the mine. Many Kyrgyzstanis believe that the country is being robbed of its most valuable asset; they argue that the mine should be nationalized. Others believe that nationalization of the mine by an incompetent government will do nothing but hamstring the nation's most significant revenue generator. The issue is complicated further by the laws surrounding property rights and by agreements signed by previous governments. Numerous Parliamentary inquiries have proven wrong-doing on the part of both the investors and the government—but so far little justice has been served. The challenge here is to stop the extortion of ill-gotten rent in a way that preserves the country's share of the revenue and still ensures the mine's continued attractiveness to investors. It is a tough problem, and yet it would not exist in a normally functioning state, in which the rule of law was upheld by independent courts and the executive branch did not intervene. As things stand now, even if the investigation were conducted properly there would be no guarantee that the local courts would find a way to serve justice and satisfy both parties.

The inability to come together and cooperate with others is one of the main obstacles standing between Kyrgyzstan's current state of affairs and the greatness it could achieve. Though Kyrgyzstanis are typically a very service-oriented and hardworking people, they are unable to build a sound infrastructure or to overcome the challenges of being landlocked. Kyrgyzstan could export goods to both the West and the East, or it could become a hub for re-exporting goods, but in either case cooperation is necessary. Kyrgyzstanis would need to start working together on a large scale as well as in their local communities. Fortunately, the value of cooperation is already embedded in the Kyrgyzstani culture: there is, for example, the concept of *ashar,* in which an entire village helps to build one villager's house. But where money or profit is involved, the Kyrgyzstani people have come to think individualistically: the winner gets it all. Once Kyrgyzstan as a nation embraces the idea that a win-win scenario actually makes the pie bigger, then the country will be able to think productively about its own interests and the larger community; it will gain a bird's-eye view of nationwide projects and regions, finding joint solutions that benefit all. In short, what Kyrgyzstan needs is to implement *ashar* on a national level, ensuring that the population works together for the well-being of all.

Pluralism: The Winning Formula

Kyrgyzstan is peppered with different ethnic groups, religions, and political ideologies. This multiplicity has been its strength in past, and it remains valuable in present. Indeed, I would argue that, in the future, it will be the country's salvation. Only by maintaining this diversity of ideas and human capital can Kyrgyzstan save itself. It must capitalize on its varied resources in order to uplift its economy, diversify, and innovate.

The scars of two ethnic conflicts were still visible in Osh when the Trek visited the city. For me, the sights called up vivid memories from my life in 1990 during the country's first inter-ethnic conflict. My family and I barely survived the angry mob of Uzbeks who were hoping to take out their anger on Kyrgyz people. We tried to escape in our car—my dad, who looked Kyrgyz; my mom and I, who look like Uzbeks; and my aunt, who looks like an Altai person from Siberia. The Uzbeks pulled us over. Luckily, they let us go after my dad uttered a few Russian words in his authoritative voice. That moment remains etched in my memory and serves as a testament to the power of multi-ethnicity. Sadly, however, its value is becoming less and less prominent in the eyes of the Kyrgyzstani population.

On the eastern side at the bottom of the holy mountain near Osh—Sulaiman Too (in English, Solomon's Mountain)—there used to be a *makhalla*, a community of Uzbek inhabitants, who lived together in close-knit communities. No other ethnic groups were allowed in the *makhalla*. Since the ethnic clashes in 2010, however, the Uzbeks have decided to move to the southern outskirts of Osh; they now use their homes near the Sulaiman Too only for business purposes. It's safer that way. The roots of the conflict stem from two opposing narratives. The Uzbeks tend to claim that Osh—the population of which is currently 73 percent Kyrgyz and 14.3 percent Uzbek—was historically their city and that the Kyrgyz took it over in the arbitrary division of territories during the Stalin era, in the early 20th century.[4] The Kyrgyz, by contrast, tend to view the Uzbeks as

---

[4] See the official site of public census at national statistics committee: www.stat.kg.

mere "tenants" on Kyrgyz land. They believe that the Uzbeks should go back to their traditional homeland, Uzbekistan. The truth is that the Uzbeks and Kyrgyz have coexisted in Osh for centuries. But because the region lacks a just legal system that can offer justice to both sides, the dispute has created a fertile ground for violent clashes.

It was disheartening to hear from the locals in Osh that the Uzbeks have lost any hope of reconciliation with the city's Kyrgyz population and that they have started going to separate mosques to pray. Such a division only pushes the ground for possible compromise further away. According to some studies, in environments in which ethnic preferences are very strong, it is more difficult for democracies to flourish.[5] But there are possible solutions to the stalemate in Osh. Some argue that securing land and property rights would help to neutralize the two groups' discontents and would build confidence in the city's institutions and its population's common future. Such a feat is challenging in a region where fertile land is scarce and there is a high population density, but whether or not it is achieved, one thing remains certain: an inclusive political system will win in the long run, both politically and economically. When democracy is not grounded in constitutional liberalism, it often leads to hyper-nationalism and war-mongering, sometimes against an internal enemy. Instituting checks and balances for all groups, ensuring that those with incompatible interests stand equally before the law, might be the way out. Otherwise there will be no future for this nation.

The American political system is based on the pessimistic assump-

---

[5] See for example: Alvin Rabuska and Kenneth Shepsele, *Politics in Plural Societies, A Theory of Democratic Instability*, Columbus: Charles E. Merrill, pp. 62-92.

tion that people cannot be trusted with power. The French system, by contrast, places faith in the good nature of humans and their ability to control their own conduct. Kyrgyzstan seems to have opted for the former system, but I believe that it should have chosen to trust in the good nature of human beings. Democratic governments are created ostensibly to protect individuals from the tyranny of the majority, but it also takes the work of ordinary citizens to make sure the minorities are protected.

I felt optimistic when we met with the Youth of Osh, a prominent non-profit organization in the city. This organization is mobilizing youth of all ethnic backgrounds to work on peace-building through a range of projects: civic engagement, cultural programs, volunteering, media training, etc. Our meeting was designed to connect the community workers of Osh with the scholars on our Trek, so that by collaborating we could create valuable new ideas. We found that while the Youth of Osh are eager to transform the energy and passion of the city's young people into constructive projects, some tensions have still survived. Appearances remained important: in a room full of members of the organization, there was only one representative of the Uzbek ethnic group. Despite the great track record of the organization, there is still work to be done in integrating representatives of other groups into the joint work. I asked them if their membership included more Uzbeks than what we had seen, and the answer that followed was affirmative but came too fast. Their hasty answer suggested that they knew of this weakness and wanted to remedy it.

Conclusion

Kyrgyzstan has changed a lot in the time I have been away—and, equally, I have changed and see things now through a different lens. One thing is evident, though: I am part of this nation. And I recognize that Kyrgyzstan is grappling with very difficult challenges in its own way, with the resources available to it. My hope is to contribute in the search for the questions that will lead to effective answers. The key for resolving Kyrgyzstan's problems is for the Kyrgyzstani people to look deep inside ourselves and find in the collective narrative the real causes that stand between us and progress. If we find them together and take responsibility as one nation, we will be able to improve our predicament. This essay was a modest attempt to contribute to this cause. I am certain that eventually we will be able to meet this challenge and find stability and prosperity, thanks to the numerous people in Kyrgyzstan who care about our nation and want to make its future bright.

| Chapter 8 |

Tajikistan in Transition:
Observations at the Crossroads of East and West

Sarah Golkar
MALD, Tufts Fletcher School of Law and Diplomacy

• • •

"What are these?" I ask the shopkeeper in Persian, my father's mother tongue. I point to a mountain of small, glossy, round fruits of a curious, bright orange hue. The man pauses for a beat to size me up, not expecting to hear a woman in Western clothing addressing him in Persian, as opposed to Russian. He answers in mutually intelligible Tajiki: "They are a kind of sweet lemon, but more sour than an orange." My father has told me stories about these fruits: mouth-puckering summertime treats popular in Northern Iran and unavailable at the chain grocery stores in the American suburb where I grew up. The man looks at me quizzically. "Your accent…are you from Iran?" I smile. "My father is, but I am American." This pleases him; it pleases me too. It is the first time I've used Persian outside the Persian-speaking diaspora. His question bestows a modicum of legitimacy on my conflicted, hyphenated identity.

I've spent the last ten years studying the modern Middle East and contemporary Eurasia in some form or another—first as an undergraduate student at the University of Texas at Austin, then as a professional researcher in Washington, D.C., and finally as an International Affairs graduate student at The Fletcher School of Law and Diplomacy at Tufts University. Examining Eurasia has been a way of satisfying my intellectual curiosity, but it is also integral to my search for identity and belonging. I've been preoccupied for many years with the ways in which historical memory shapes perception for elite politicians, citizens, and a country's diaspora. Now, as part of Center for Asia Leadership Initiatives' (CALI) Asia Leadership Trek to Tajikistan, Kyrgyzstan, Kazakhstan, and Uzbekistan, I am eager to explore the ways in which past empires collide with modern republics and the political cultures that these dynamics create. To do this, we will meet with a range of both high level and working level government, business, and non-governmental organization (NGO) professionals across Central Asia.

I pay the man for the lemons and continue walking down the winding, makeshift corridor toward a row of tea sellers. The Shahmansur Bazaar, named after the last King of the Persian Muzaffarid dynasty, who was killed by Timurlane in the 14th century, is a bustling market situated in the heart of Dushanbe. Losing track of time, I sample ripe summer cherries, plums, and melons. I examine the differences among popular tea varieties: Indian, Persian, Georgian. It begins to rain, but shopkeepers remain in place. Perched in one corner of the market is a small circle of fair-skinned Korean women, selling spicy pickled kimchis. They are the last vestiges of Stalin's 1937 forced migration effort, which resettled the Russian Far East's Korean population to Central Asia over fears that Japan was using the enclave to spy on Moscow. In another section of the market, Tajik women sell large, thick roundels of bread that were baked by sticking the dough with a firm slap against the side of a large clay oven. Its aroma wafts throughout the market.

Tajikistan, a landlocked, mostly mountainous country in Central Asia bordering Afghanistan, China, Kyrgyzstan, and Uzbekistan, has always sat at the crossroads of east and west. I think about the extent to which these winding corridors have changed since the heyday of the Silk Road, when the region served as a thoroughfare for weary caravansary who stopped to rest before continuing their journey. Even today, Tajikistan is part of China's 'One Belt, One Road' initiative, a modern-day corollary to the Silk Road that aims to increase China's trade and diplomatic ties with South and Central Asia, as well as with European countries. I'm curious about how these increased trade ties with regional hegemons will affect Tajikistan's delicate domestic, political, and economic balance. Will it enable the country to continue its positive growth and development trajectory, which is now threatened by Russia's financial troubles and China's purported economic slowdown? Perhaps more importantly, how does Tajikistan view itself? Does it lean toward Russia, China, or the West, and what does all this mean for the future?

Memory Politics: Tajikistan's Civil War and Counter-Terrorism Response

Lines of baton-wielding, anti-riot police flank the sidewalk leading up to the entrance of the soccer stadium. Our local facilitator, Farouk, has invited us to watch the Tajikistan vs. Bangladesh game, and the nearly all-male game-goers are playfully shoving the crowd forward. Security officers mingle with machine gun-toting military personnel, who examine the crowds to look for instigators. There is no hiding our foreignness among the crowd. An officer approaches us. "Our guests," he says with a wide grin, as he motions for us to skip the line. I turn to Farouk. "Are there normally this many police at soccer games?" He nods. "There have been some terrorist attacks recently," he claims.

A review of press reporting, however, reveals that there have been only a handful of politically or religiously motivated attacks in Tajikistan in the past several years. If the military presence at the game is a response to terrorism, it a disproportionate one. After conversations with a range of Tajiki officials and citizens, I learn that the government does not draw clear distinctions between political unrest and religious extremism. Politicians in Tajikistan blame the country's alleged rise of extremism primarily on wayward youth and political and economic discontent—and this policy informs the government's firm, largely indiscriminate crackdown on dissidents for trumped-up terrorism charges, which often wrongly target vulnerable populations.[1] While the strategy may ensure stability in the short term, in the long-term, it risks isolating key constituencies and galvanizing opposition to political and security elites.

The government's aggressive approach stems in part from the memory of Tajikistan's Civil War, which lasted from 1992 to 1997 and coalesced around two warring factions. Ethnic Uzbek elites, with

---

1   Edward J. Lemon, "Daesh and Tajikistan: The Regime's (In)Security Policy," *The RUSI Journal* 160, no. 5 (September 3, 2015): 68–76, doi:10.1080/0307 1847.2015.1102550.

support from Russia and Uzbekistan sought to preserve Soviet power networks. Whereas, ethnic Tajik groups, including pro-democracy activists and the Islamic Renaissance Party (IRP), wanted to upset the old order.[2] The fighting between these factions left an estimated fifty thousand people dead, six hundred thousand internally displaced, and eighty thousand as refugees.[3] In 1998, the war-weary groups reached a negotiated agreement that allowed Islamist parties to participate formally in the political process; 30 percent of parliamentary seats were allotted to opposition groups. The state, however, has since implemented a ban on religious dress for women, and Islamist groups remain under close state supervision.

A week before we arrived in Tajikistan, the country's citizens approved a referendum to remove Presidential term limits and lower the age threshold for Presidential candidates from thirty-five to thirty. These reforms effectively solidified President Emomali Rahmon's grip on power and paved the way for his son—Rustam Emomali, twenty-nine—to carry on his legacy. Yet, after we had landed in Dushanbe, not one person made mention to us of this referendum or its implications for the country's future. When I asked people in the county how they felt about Mr. Emomali Rahmon, they responded that Tajikistan needed a strong leader to prevent a descent back into the chaos of the 1990s. Mr. Rahmon is revered with passion; his image is a ubiquitous sight in both public and private spaces. Rightly or wrongly, some Tajiks view the President as the key to maintaining peace and security in

---

2   Rob Kevlihan, "Insurgency in Central Asia: A Case Study of Tajikistan," *Small Wars & Insurgencies* 27, no. 3 (May 3, 2016): 417–39, doi:10.1080/09592318.2016.1151656. p. 420-421.
3   Ibid. 422.

an otherwise uncertain political environment.

Across the globe, a debate has unfolded about the merits of relying on strong, central leadership to navigate domestic instability and the chaos of the international system. Russia's President Vladimir Putin, China's President Xi Jinping, and Turkey's President Recep Tayyip Erdogan personify the kind of blunt-force, strong-armed, no-frills, "managed authoritarian" leadership that fear-mongering and isolationist political trends often bring to power. We are right to critique this brand of politics because, more often than not, it marginalizes minorities, widens inequalities, and tramples civil liberties and the freedom of speech. At the same time, however, power concentrated in the hands of a few creates a barrier of fear that can prevent a society from teetering over the edge into internecine violence. In Tajikistan, the memory of the 1992-97 civil war and the fear of a return to violence are ever-present in this debate. Nevertheless, the country's protectionist, authoritarian tendencies offer a risk of broader instability later on.

Comparing Islamism in Tajikistan and the Rest of Central Asia: Local, Not Global

Islam in Central Asia surged in popularity in the aftermath of the Soviet Union's collapse in 1991, bringing repressed religious networks and nationalist sentiments to the political fore. Although only a minority of Central Asia's Muslim population supports the concept of Sharia Law (a legal system based on Islam) according to Pew polling data, the strength and capacity of Salafi-Jihadist groups, who espouse strict interpretations of Islam, continue to rise.[4] Since the 1990s, political elites across Central Asia have sought to reconcile their propensity for secular governance, established during Soviet times, with the region's historical, cultural, and religious traditions rooted in Islam. Driven by their own perceptions of the religious threat, regimes across the region have chosen to deal with political Islam in varying ways—minimal political accommodation, a complete ban on religious life, and violent repression.

The tensions surrounding Islam in Central Asia center on the primary drivers of extremist ideologies and their spread, as well as the extent to which extremist groups pose a threat to local regimes and to external powers—Russia, the United States, and China. Without question, extremists pose a threat to internal stability in Central Asia. Whether or not these groups also present an existential threat to their respective capitals and their external backers is a matter of debate. The emergence of radical Islam has been closely linked to socio-economic factors and political repression, but they seldom pose a significant threat outside of Central Asia.

Political regimes have often systematically labeled and persecuted opponents as extremists for political purposes, which has fueled radicalization. While international support for extremist groups in Central Asia is an important factor in their spread, their relative strength is "a result of decidedly local politics."[5] Almost all Muslims in Cen-

---

4 1615 L. Street et al., "The World's Muslims: Religion, Politics and Society," *Pew Research Center's Religion & Public Life Project*, April 30, 2013, http://www.pewforum.org/2013/04/30/the-worlds-muslims-religion-politics-society-overview/.
Ahmed Rashid, *Jihad: The Rise of Militant Islam in Central Asia* (New Haven: Yale University Press, 2002). 228.
5 Eric Max McGlinchey, "The Making of Militants: The State and Islam in

tral Asia ascribe to either the Hanafi or Sufi schools of Sunni Islam, which—as "traditionally one of the most tolerant forms of religion," one that de-emphasizes political participation[6]—has put a limit on ties with Salafi-Jihadist groups. Thus, while Islam is on the rise in Central Asia, the type of Islam that predominates in the region is at odds with extremist interpretations of Islam such as that which the Islamic State espouses.

There are similarities in these trends across the region. More so than in other Central Asian Republics, Islam in Uzbekistan has become a dominant force in the country's religious life, and the state has reacted with repressive measures to limit its influence. Fearing the religiously fueled political chaos in neighboring Tajikistan, Uzbekistan's former President Karimov worked to ban the participation of Islamic groups in political life. Several groups, including Hizb ut-Tahrir and the Islamic Movement of Uzbekistan, which grew out of a shared desire to overthrow President Karimov, remain barred from political participation and from disseminating their views in the media.[7]

Like the other Central Asian Republics, Kazakhstan has experienced persistent economic and social inequalities that have provided a fertile recruiting ground for extremist groups, particularly the Islamic Revival Party (IRP).[8] President Nazarbayev has used his politi-

---

Central Asia," *Comparative Studies of South Asia, Africa and the Middle East* 25, no. 3 (2005): 554–66.

6 Ghoncheh Tazmini, "The Islamic Revival in Central Asia: A Potent Force or a Misconception?," *Central Asian Survey* 20, no. 1 (March 1, 2001): 68.
7 Ghoncheh Tazmini, "The Islamic Revival in Central Asia: A Potent Force or a Misconception?," *Central Asian Survey* 20, no. 1 (March 1, 2001): 74.
8 Eren Tatari and Renat Shaykhutdinov, "State Response to Religious Revivalism in Post-Soviet Central Asia," *European Journal of Economic and Political Studies* 3, no. 2 (2010). 100.

cal power to limit the spread of the IRP, which has taken root only among a minority of non-Kazakhs.[9] Mr. Nazarbayev, however, has opted for a relatively moderate approach to repressing the country's Islamic tendencies, establishing the country's own Muftiate to "reduce spillover effects of perceived fundamentalist activities in neighboring Uzbekistan."[10] He also formed a "Council of Ministers" that monitors the religious reach of both indigenous Islamic institutions and foreign actors; the Council has the power to intervene in cases where ideologies "foment discord" in the political arena.[11]

Kyrgyzstan has tended to use heavy-handed, indiscriminate force in countering violent extremism—practices that have been criticized by human rights groups. The government has been accused of falsifying terrorist charges for political opponents and torturing prisoners.[12] Poverty and extremist ideologies have led to the rise of terror groups like the Islamic Movement of Uzbekistan, which predominates in the southern, primarily Uzbek region of Kyrgyzstan,[13] and the harsh treatment and systematic repression of ethnic minorities have deepened grievances among core opposition constituencies.[14] Bishkek also

---

9 Rashid, *Jihad*. 102.
10 Ghoncheh Tazmini, "The Islamic Revival in Central Asia: A Potent Force or a Misconception?," *Central Asian Survey* 20, no. 1 (March 1, 2001): 73.
11 Ibid.
12 Mariya Y. Omelicheva, "Convergence of Counterterrorism Policies: A Case Study of Kyrgyzstan and Central Asia," *Studies in Conflict & Terrorism* 32, no. 10 (October 2, 2009): 893–908, doi:10.1080/10576100903182518. 902.
13 Mariya Y. Omelicheva, "Convergence of Counterterrorism Policies: A Case Study of Kyrgyzstan and Central Asia," *Studies in Conflict & Terrorism* 32, no. 10 (October 2, 2009): 897.
14 Dilip Hiro, *Inside Central Asia: A Political and Cultural History of Uzbekistan, Turkmenistan, Kazakhstan, Kyrgyzstan, Tajikistan, Turkey, and Iran*, 1st ed (New York, NY: Overlook Duckworth, 2009). 298.

faces threats from Jaysh al-Mahdi, an ethnic Kyrgyz Islamist extremist group that has carried out bombings, robberies, and targeted killings. Given the ethnic strife, economic opportunities, political representation, security measures, and governance and rule of law in these countries, it seems likely that militant Islamists will continue to pose a challenge to the region's domestic stability. The likelihood is increased by the heavy-handed governmental responses to domestic and cross-border terror attacks and suicide bombings in Kazakhstan, Kyrgyzstan, Uzbekistan, and Tajikistan between 2004 and 2015.[15]

Putting these recent trends into an international context, the Institute for Economics and Peace describes the Central Asian Republics as posing little to no overall terrorism threat as of 2015, when compared to the rest of the world. The assessment takes into account the number of foreign fighters from Central Asia traveling to other conflict zones, including the borderless wars in the Afghanistan-Pakistan region and the Iraq-Syria region. As of 2015, between seven hundred and two thousand individuals from Central Asia had traveled to Syria to join extremist groups operating there, though this represents only a fraction of the other foreign fighters—between 27,000 and 31,000—who have traveled to Iraq and Syria from an estimated eighty-six countries, according to the same report.[16]

Although it is difficult to pinpoint the exact number of Tajikistan nationals traveling to Syria, the Tajik government in mid-2015 con-

---

15 Jim Nichol, "Central Asia: Regional Developments and Implications for U.S. Interests*," *Current Politics and Economics of South, Southeastern, and Central Asia* 23, no. 1 (2014): 43–151.

16 The Soufan Group, "Foreign Fighters Update" April 6, 2016, http://soufangroup.com/wp-content/uploads/2015/12/TSG_ForeignFightersUpdate3.pdf.

firmed that at least one hundred Tajik nationals had died fighting in Syria. However, 80 percent of the cases in which Tajik citizens were recruited to the Islamic State involved Tajik migrants living and working in Russia, not Tajikistan.[17] In other words, the Tajik government's domestic crackdown, which discriminates against certain groups and risks alienating key constituents, may need to be redirected toward the diaspora to be most effective. On the domestic front, poverty and a lack of economic opportunities are more pressing issues.

Tajikistan's Vulnerable Economy, Overly Reliant on Foreign Investment

In 2016, Tajikistan ranked 135th among the world's poorest countries, based on its Gross Domestic Product (GDP) at purchasing power parity—that is, it ranked above Equatorial Guinea and below Benin, according to the International Monetary Fund's World Economic Outlook. In 2015, the country's GDP per capita stood at US$1,240, up from US$339.80 in 2005. Similarly, between 1999 and 2014, the number of people in Tajikistan living under the poverty line decreased from 80 percent to 31.3 percent, according to the World Bank. The clip at which Tajikistan has reduced its poverty rates is impressive; it ranks number ten in the world for poverty reduction in the last ten years. Such a jump demonstrates the progress that country has made in the last decade—a recurrent theme during our visit with business and government leaders in Dushanbe. Still, there is cause for concern about the country's vulnerable economy and much

---

17 Lemon, "Daesh and Tajikistan." P. 71.

room for improvement in its development and education.

Taxation

In a meeting with RSM Global's Head of Consulting and Assurance Services, Mr. Firuz Saidov, we discussed Tajikistan's economic troubles. RSM Global is a tax and audit consulting firm that operates around the world. Tax collection is a basic source of government revenue in any country, but we learned that this apparently simple task is fraught with serious challenges for Tajikistan. The country still uses antiquated accounting methods of tax collection, based on an outdated Soviet model. Only recently has it implemented an automated, electronic filing option for businesses. A strong culture of skirting taxes has persisted in the country since 1991, particularly in rural areas, which are difficult to access and problematic for enforcement. The tax code itself is complex and hard to understand, particularly for individuals not accustomed to filing taxes. The company's strategic goals in this arena include increasing the information flow and clarifying tax legislation for major industries. The firm also conducts financial audits for large and medium-sized businesses in Tajikistan. Such measures to bring about greater transparency, if successful, would increase government revenue and provide a boost to the country's GDP.

Energy Priorities

Until five years ago, Tajikistan experienced rolling blackouts. On average in 2010, the capital received only four hours of electricity per day. Today, at least in the capital, electricity is available nearly twenty-four hours a day, with only sporadic blackouts during the winter because of excess demand on the power grid. Harnessing Tajikistan's energy resources as a revenue stream is a strategic priority for the government. In a meeting with Ministry of Energy officials, we discussed their plans to develop this sector while promoting energy security and poverty relief. In particular, officials have been discussing an initiative to form an energy co-op with Pakistan, in order to capitalize on Tajikistan's excess energy production in the summer and to relieve its shortages in the winter. The country produces an extra 1,720 billion kilowatt hours in the summertime, with no way to store it, and exporting to Pakistan could bring in extra revenue. And with Chinese partnership, the construction of a four hundred megawatt thermal power plant will help to remedy Tajikistan's peak-demand shortages in the winter. As with its taxes, electricity bill collection remains a problem for the country, an additional burden as it seeks to rectify its supply-and-demand imbalance while developing the sector.

The recent initiatives are organized around discovering new energy sources, harnessing hydroelectric and geothermal power, developing transportation corridors, promoting food security, and rehabilitating the old Soviet power grid, which is currently inefficient and lacks the capacity to meet the country's growing demand for energy. At the same time, though, there are major obstacles to developing the energy sector. Tajikistan is a mountainous country with much impassible terrain, which makes it difficult to build sustainable power lines and energy transit corridors to rural and hard-to-reach areas. Basic services and public security are weak in these rural areas, and there is only limited funding from international aid groups for such services.

New Transmission Lines

Tajikistan has grown dependent on international aid and unilateral donors for larger-scale development projects. One such project is a joint venture, with US$800 million in soft loans from China, to develop high voltage transmission lines. China has provided both a relatively cheap currency and the associated technology. With the distant United States and Europe both strapped for cash and risk-averse, China has been critical to developing Central Asia as part of its "Silk Road Economic Belt" initiative, first unveiled in 2013. The initiative promised tens of billions of dollars in investment in upstream and downstream energy infrastructure across Turkmenistan, Uzbekistan, Kyrgyzstan, and Kazakhstan. It effectively secures Chinese access to Central Asian oil and gas products by completing a seven hundred mile gas pipeline from the Caspian Sea to the Chinese coast. Tajikistan is a core component of this broader strategy.

Regional Energy Consortium

Tajikistan's most important longer-term energy goal hinges on the successful implementation of the CASA-1000 project: to establish a transnational electricity grid and an associated consortium with Afghanistan, Pakistan, China, and Kyrgyzstan. The effort would allow Tajikistan to export ten billion kilowatt hours of energy per year and to import electricity when needed, while Afghanistan would become a key transit corridor for the power grid. The World Bank, European Investment Bank, the United States, and others have promised funding for the project, and while it is currently forestalled by some financing shortages, the World Bank is likely to close this gap.[18]

---

18 "Q&A: Central Asia-South Asia Electricity Transmission and Trade Project (CASA-1000)," *World Bank*, accessed October 5, 2016, http://www.

Russian Economic Spillover and China's Rise

The last major issue weighing on the minds of business and government officials in Dushanbe is the effect of Russia's economic downturn on Tajikistan's economy. A decline in oil prices and Western economic sanctions have resulted in a nearly 40 percent devaluation of the Russian Ruble. To prevent capital from leaving the country, Russia has restricted migration from neighboring countries, including Tajikistan. A little more than half of Tajikistan's GDP is based on remittances from migrants living abroad, and Russian remittances account for nearly 80 percent of that figure.[19] As a result, Tajikistan has sought to broaden its economic partnerships with other countries, including China, Japan, India, Iran, and Persian Gulf states. Last year, China overtook Russia as Tajikistan's number one trading partner, highlighting the important role that China is playing in Tajikistan and in Central Asia more broadly.

Geopolitical Trends in Central Asia

Departing from our hotel in Dushanbe for the airport, I notice a magazine in the lobby with a cover photo featuring the overlapping flags of China and Tajikistan. The magazine's title, *Payvand*, means "to link," a reference to the strategic partnership between the two countries. The number of Chinese businessmen we observed in Dushanbe is a testament to China's ability to make good on its promises. Ta-

---

worldbank.org/en/news/speech/2016/05/10/central-asia-south-asia-electricity-transmission-and-trade-project-casa-1000.
19 Lemon, "Daesh and Tajikistan."

jikistan believes China to be a natural partner, given the two nations' geographic proximity and historical trade ties; they perceive little risk in taking on debt that is owned primarily by one country.

Since the early 2000s, Russia and China have independently formed several redundant and competitive institutions in Central Asia, aimed at promoting security, stability, and cooperation on energy and economic priorities. Russia's interests in Central Asia stem from a desire to retain geopolitical influence, to protect ethnic Russians living in the post-Soviet space, and to secure access to oil and gas re-exports to the European market. While China's relationship with Central Asia is similarly grounded in security and energy concerns, the Chinese government claims that it lacks a geopolitical agenda.[20] Nonetheless, some have called the Central Asia interaction between Russia and China a new "Great Game," and while the overlapping interests have occasionally caused friction, the two sides have been able to develop a status quo that seems to thwart broader conflict.

Analysts have pointed to the 2008 economic crisis as a catalyst for Chinese multilateral and bilateral expansion into Central Asia, at a time when Russia was deeply affected by the global financial downturn. Russia, because of plummeting European demand for natural gas in 2009, was forced to cease its imports from Turkmenistan, prompting Ashgabat to turn to Chinese financiers to weather the storm. In the years since 2008, China has increased its Central Asian import capacity to eighty-five billion cubic meters per year. The Chinese National Petroleum Company single-handedly financed the Central Asia–China pipeline expansion, which effectively broke

---

20 Ibid.

Russia's stranglehold on Central Asian gas exports to a single market in Europe.[21] The Chinese government is cognizant of Russia's stake in the Central Asian energy market, and, at least for now, Chinese leaders are avoiding manipulating the energy politics to Russia's detriment. Both nations seem capable of reading one another, and neither is priming for a conflict over Central Asian energy and security issues. Nevertheless, Chinese encroachment in the economic and security spheres may present problems relations down the road.[22]

Tajikistan at a Geopolitical Crossroads, Promoting a Façade of Independence

As Russian influence in Central Asia wanes, and as China fills that power vacuum, Tajikistan's government will be confronted with an important question: how should the country prioritize political stability and economic growth while balancing relationships with regional hegemons? I asked one Tajiki government official if the country saw itself as leaning more toward China these days to compensate for Russia's investment shortfalls. "We don't look for alternates," he responded. "We want to be independent."

In 2015, Chinese investment in Tajikistan reached nearly US$300 million; Russia's, meanwhile, has declined to US$35 million.[23] At a time when Chinese foreign investment is increasing as Russia's is sharply declining, does Tajikistan have a choice? What are the benefits

---

21 Ibid.
22 Lo, "Frontiers New and Old."
23 "Tajikistan, Turkmenistan Submit to Chinese Capture," EurasiaNet, June 24, 2016, http://www.eurasianet.org/node/79401.

and drawbacks of relying on Chinese investment as a core enabler of Tajikistan's development strategy? China, in the past, has pushed for territorial concessions in exchange for economic benefits.[24] Becoming further enmeshed in Chinese economic deals that Tajikistan cannot reciprocate could compromise the country's sovereignty and its own broader political stability. Even now, anti-Chinese sentiments among everyday Tajik citizens are rising.

At the same time, Russia remains a powerful political player in the region. The Russian language is still the lingua franca between Central Asian countries, ethnic Russians are still a sizeable minority across the region, and most official signs are rendered in both languages. Even as concern over Chinese meddling in Tajikistan and other Central Asian countries grows, there are important ways in which Russian cultural and political power stand as a bulwark against soft power influence by a third country.

I board my outbound flight wishing I'd had more time to spend in Tajikistan talking to and interacting with a broader range of perspectives. The trip across the region will raise more questions for me than it will provide answers. For example, Tajikistan's politics are the polar opposite of what I will find in Kyrgyzstan, a relatively open, democratic country that has struggled with instability and remains beset by volatile power transitions. This juxtaposition highlights the varying ways in which countries grapple with balancing political openness with stability. Does creating space for civil society to organize necessarily bring about chaos? What are the risks of stifling dissent? As the

---

24 "Tajikistan: China's Advance Causing Increasing Unease among Tajiks," EurasiaNet, February 14, 2011, http://www.eurasianet.org/node/62894.

Tajik government continues to silence opposition and public debate in the name of combating extremism, the country's leaders may be preserving order in the near-term, but they risk a backlash from internal and external critics in the longer-term.

| Chapter 9 |

Kazakhstan:
A Country That Punches Above Its Weight

Katarina Sabova
MBA, Columbia Business School

• • •

I often retroactively recognize patterns in my life: certain signs point to something coming over time, yet I am able to understand them only in hindsight. The story of my fascination with Kazakhstan is a good example of that phenomenon.

Sign #1: Back in the sixth grade of elementary school, in my native Slovakia, I took pride in being unbeatable in world geography. I would gamble for candies with my classmates, betting them that I knew the national flags, country populations, and capitals of every country in the world. One day, I lost. A friend, equipped with the latest edition of a book on world geography, gleefully pointed out that I had gotten the capital of Kazakhstan wrong. "It's not Almaty, it's A-S-T-A-N-A." I couldn't believe it: my friend must have misread the name—after all, it still started with the letter A. I took our quarrel to the geography teacher only to have him confirm my friend's claim: Kazakhstan had indeed changed its capital about two years before to the newly built Astana. I lost a chocolate bar and my know-it-all reputation (And despite re-checking all my geography facts in the following days, I never managed to rebuild it).

Sign #2: Fast-forward twelve years to 2013. I had become a consultant with McKinsey & Company and was being trained to solve pressing business problems for our clients. However, part of me still longed for those big questions about the world economy and the countries that shape it. Then I stumbled upon a dream opportunity at work: our Russian senior partner was looking for consultants to join him on a project called "Kazakhstan 2050," a high-profile study that would design a vision for a country that has multiplied its GDP eight times (!) within the preceding decade.[1] One of my colleagues happened to be working on an oil and gas project in Astana at that time and regularly appeared in my Facebook feed with pictures from glamorous parties and weekend sightseeing in a city that looked like a combination of New York-style skyscrapers and Disney World's monuments—not images that one would expect given the stereotype of emerging post-Soviet countries. Of course, I was extremely keen to join the team designing the future of such an amazing place. Unfortunately, however, it didn't work out: my years of training in international business rather than macroeconomics, combined with my lack of fluency in Russian, meant that I was not their candidate of choice.

Sign #3: In the spring of 2016, my good friend, Emilka came to celebrate her thirtieth birthday in my newly adopted hometown of New York, where I have been studying for an MBA at the Columbia

---

1 GDP 2003: $30.8 billion; GDP 2013: $243.8 billion. Source: World Bank data.

Business School. Emilka would not stop talking about her upcoming trip to Central Asia with the Center for Asia Leadership Initiatives (CALI). The mix of meeting political, social, and business leaders, and organizing "giving back" conferences for Asia's talented youth seemed very intriguing, especially with fresh memories of my most recent spring break: I had spent two fantastic weeks island-hopping through the Philippines. Nevertheless, I didn't feel I had really gotten to know the archipelago beyond its tourist-friendly, "beachy" façade. Now, I was ready to explore a new region in depth. A few days later, I made it onto the list of the Trek's participants, and the only things standing between me and Kazakhstan were a lengthy online visa application and a few trips to the Embassy.

I come from a country that can be very bitter about its portrayal in American pop culture. "EuroTrip," a 2004 movie that inspired an entire generation of rising freshmen to plan ambitious, seven-countries-in-ten-days trips across the Old Continent, depicted Slovakia as a place where you can open your own hotel with a nickel of investment (Google "eurotrip bratislava hotel" to see that infamous yet hilarious scene). And this international disgrace pales into an amusing embarrassment in the light of what Sacha Baron Cohen and his film "Borat: Cultural Learnings of America for Make Benefit Glorious Nation of Kazakhstan" have done to Kazakhstan's reputation. Before the trip, we were warned that any reference to this film would be a sign of bad taste and "Western" ignorance and that—if we couldn't resist—it should be made only among close friends.

A booming economy, a twenty-year-young capital, a crazy guy in a neon-green swimsuit, the Russian influence, vast oil and gas reserves, visionary leadership—with this cocktail of memories, preconceived ideas, and expectations swirling through my head, I landed in Almaty, the commercial center of Kazakhstan, a country that punches above its weight—as I would soon learn firsthand. It is important to admit here that I have had a chance to only visit two major cities, Astana and Almaty, and this article expresses the impression I gained based on these two avenues.

Meet the Family First

A long time ago, my grandmother gave me wise dating advice, which I would like to apply here, though in a slightly different context: "When you are trying to get to know a person, meet their family and their closest friends; no one becomes who they are in isolation." In order to get to know Kazakhstan, you need to understand the workings of Central Asia, which has complex relationships with the outside world and also among the countries within its boundaries.

The region was a focus for geopolitical strategists even before geopolitical strategy became a formal science. Sir Halford Mackinder, the founding father of geopolitics, introduced The Heartland Theory in 1904, stating that whoever ruled the Heartland—Central Asia along with some parts of Russia and Iran—basically controlled the world. One of the peculiarities of "the Heartland" is that it is practically inaccessible to any naval power: all its major rivers feed into inland seas (the Caspian) or into frozen parts of the world's ocean (the Arctic). When I realized the strategic importance of this often overlooked region, I decided to share it with my roommate, a designer with no obvious interest in geopolitics. Yet, he didn't seem at all surprised: "Of course," he replied to my remark. "Have you ever played the board game Risk? Whoever gets to hold Asia rules the game. And the best way how to get it is to start from its center." This conversation made me realize that there are many ways besides academic articles to gain a good sense of geopolitics.

The other catchy label given to Central Asia by a leading geostrategist is the "Eurasian Balkans," a phrase coined by a security advisor to U.S. Presidents, Zbigniew Brzezinski, in his 1997 book, *The Grand Chessboard*. I could understand this nickname too. Crisscrossing Central Asia on the Trek over the course of three weeks, I couldn't help but think of the countries there as if they were one big family. Russia would be an all-encompassing mother (or father), finally realizing that the children have grown up and that it is time to let them decide their own destinies. Kyrgyzstan and Tajikistan, different in their political and cultural make-up[2] but sharing the commonality of being small mountainous countries, would be young, non-identical, outdoors-loving twins. Tajikistan would seem almost like an adopted child: intrinsically it belongs more to its southern Persian neighbors, but it fits in well with the Central Asian family because of its shared history and Cyrillic script. Kyrgyzstan, in the meantime, would be the progressive child, sadly, prone to occasional uncontrollable fits in the form of its series of revolutions. Uzbekistan and Turkmenistan would be two introverted but resourceful teenagers—and that would be all we know about them, since they keep everything very private. And lastly, Kazakhstan would be the eldest and the largest son: ambitious, gregarious, eager to show off its independence, yet still unable

---

2   Kyrgyzstan is democratic, a U.S. ally that uses a Turkic-family language. Tajikistan is still dictatorial and is heavy influenced by Persian culture and language.

to move out from its former guardian's backyard.

Westernized Elements: A Cable Car, European Royalty, and the Language Debate

The first stop in our visit to Kazakhstan was Almaty. Its Kok-Tobe park beautifully embodies the former capital's rising middle class. Kok-Tobe, Kazakh for "Green Hill," is the highest point of the city, peaking at a respectable 3,600 ft (1100m).[3] It houses a lively entertainment park with a beer garden, arcades, a Beatles memorial, and a little zoo with fairly exotic animals. On summer weekends, the park is packed with families and children, couples on dates, and groups of friends enjoying the sunny weather.

The conventional way to get up on the hill is to take a cable car from the Hotel Kazakhstan. This car is quite impressive in itself, not least because of the bird's-eye view it offers of the city and its mountainous surroundings. A one-way ride on the car costs US$10 per person, with no discounts for locals or families. When we arrived, the ticket desk was serving a continuous stream of people seeking weekend recreation, and I realized that there must be a class of people in Almaty who do not shy away from spending money for entertainment, just as decently well-off people would do back home in Slovakia, which is a member of the Organization for Economic Co-operation and Development (OECD), the club of the thirty or so wealthiest nations in the world.

Moreover, the cable car is a state-of-the-art mode of transporta-

---

3 http://www.almaty-kazakhstan.net/attractions/entertainment/kok-tobe/.

tion. While waiting in line, which was coordinated by two men who efficiently ushered the passengers into spacious hanging boxes, each capable of carrying eight people, I thought of the Alpine cable cars that bring merry skiers up onto the slopes in the Swiss Alps. Once in our capsule, I realized that it was actually identical to its European counterparts. All the safety instruction labels were written in four languages—English, German, French, and Italian—with no trace of language customization to the local market. Above the busy streets of Almaty, the passengers may well forget where they are; their immediate surroundings encourage them to feel as if they are hovering over the wealthiest parts of Europe.

Kazakhstan's status as equal to the *crème de la crème* of Europe was accentuated by a tabloid story a few years ago in which Britain's Prince Harry reportedly took his girlfriend for a ski trip to a luxurious resort in the mountains just outside of Almaty. Indeed, the Kazakh people like to consider themselves as part of (extended) Europe. During the conference that we organized for the local students in Almaty, one participant, a student of International Relations, made a clever argument: "The European Union keeps haggling with Turkey about its quasi-accession; Turkey is considered to be a viable candidate, at least in terms of its geographic location. However, Kazakhstan is more European in that matter than Turkey; 10 percent of our land mass lies on the European continent, i.e. behind the Ural Mountains, whereas in the case of Turkey it is only 3 percent!" I was impressed by both his acumen and his ability to turn dry facts into negotiation bullets for the International Relations arena.

The issue of a national language has also spent a great deal of time in the limelight in Kazakhstan's public debates over the past twenty years. The main reason for this is that Kazakhstan is the only country in Central Asia that still keeps Russian, in addition to the native Kazakh, as its official language. The idea of transitioning from Cyrillic to Latin script has been around since the declaration of independence in 1991, since it is believed that the change would make the country more accessible to foreigners. The proposal even made it onto the list of initiatives in the "Kazakhstan 2050" project,[4] although the exact timeline of its implementation hasn't been fully fleshed out yet.[5] The tension between Kazakhstan's ties with Russia on one side and its Westernized elements and global ambitions on the other was noticeable everywhere during our visit—from the stickers in transportation vehicles to casual chats with locals to boardroom discussions with the state's elite.

In and About Astana: A New Futuristic Capital on the Steppe

Out of dozens of meetings with high officials, businessmen, and NGOs, all packed into three weeks of touring four out of five Central Asian countries, I remember one with special vividness. It could be because this appointment could be recorded only in my mind: no electronic devices, mobile phones, or cameras were allowed in the pompous Ministry of Foreign Affairs in Kazakhstan's capital, Astana. The building's majestic architecture, with white pillars and tinted windows, inspired respect from afar. Our group of twelve students,

---

4 http://kazakhstan2050.com/patriotism/.
5 https://nuwritersguild.wordpress.com/2015/03/04/kazakhstan-plans-switch-to-latin-alphabet/.

from nine different countries, was heading to a meeting with the Deputy Minister of Foreign Affairs and Special Representative for the European Union, Mr. Roman Vassilenko.

Mr. Vassilenko's enthusiasm and pride in his motherland resembled the feelings of the other government officials we met during our time in Kazakhstan. "We are a country that punches above its weight," he declared. "Our population is ten times smaller than that of Russia, our neighbor to the north, and one hundred times smaller than China's to the east." Indeed, Kazakhstan has tucked a string of major international accomplishments under its belt in the past year. In late 2015, the country joined the World Trade Organization as its 161st member, an outcome of two decades of negotiations, which hinged on questions surrounding agricultural subsidies and the harmonization of the trade agreements resulting from Kazakhstan's membership in the Eurasian Customs Union.[6] At the time of the Trek, the upcoming elections of the temporary members for the United Nations Security Council were the top priority in Kazakh diplomacy. Multi-party, behind-closed-doors negotiations were in full swing. Thus, thirty minutes into our session with him, Mr. Vassilenko had to excuse himself in order to join the U.S. Ambassador for a meeting next door. Our delegation benefited greatly from the timing of our visit: toward the end of our session, neat gift bags were brought into the room and we all received Kazakhstan-branded goodie packs, containing among other things tasteful printed ties for the men and elegant silk scarves for the women. We learned that these gifts were

---

6 The Union was established in 2010 and consists of five member states: Armenia, Belarus, Kazakhstan, Kyrgyzstan, and Russia.

often used in the run-up to elections in order to promote Kazakhstan among its potential supporters. After our visit, Kazakhstan succeeded in being elected and will serve on the Council for the next two years, alongside Ethiopia, representing the interests of the Africa and Asia-Pacific Group.

In between our high caliber meetings with government officials and university leaders, we also found time to explore the capital. Founded in 1997, it was named pragmatically "Capital" in the Kazakh language, and commemorates its City Day on July 6. Not coincidentally, this is the day when the country's leader, President Nursultan Nazarbayev, celebrates his birthday. There is a range of possible reasons—from the semi-official to some quite conspiratorial—for why the country spent more than USD10 billion in order to move its administrative center to the middle of the arid steppe. The official reasons offered by the government are multiple. First, the southern area of Kazakhstan is prone to earthquakes, and keeping the country's capital in an area exposed to natural disasters might endanger the country's stability. Furthermore, Almaty, nestled in the mountains, could easily become polluted by the increasing number of cars in the streets (which, in fact, has already happened; when landing in Almaty, our plane had to cut through a dense cloud of smog before the city became visible). A more symbolic explanation emphasizes the new start of state administration: only young, driven, and ambitious public servants were willing to move 1,200km to the north, leaving the state planning bureaucracy behind in Almaty. Non-official theories point out that after the proclamation of Kazakh independence in 1992, a substantial Russian minority remained in the country, especially in the capital and the northern regions. The choice of Astana, strategically located north of the geographic midpoint of the country, both decreased the amount of ethnic Russians living in the capital and cut the distance between the capital and the Russian-dominated far-flung northern territories.

The first structure built in the new, fledgling capital was the Bayterek, a monument and an observation tower in one, symbolically ninety-seven meters tall to commemorate the city's birth year of 1997. High speed elevators take a mix of domestic and foreign tourists up to the viewing platform. The tower, not even twenty years old, feels as if it has witnessed more than two decades of history. A few of the security windows are decorated with webs of cracks in the glass, hinting at the unfortunate deaths of high flying birds. Even more interestingly, I started feeling slightly nauseated when my friend, a former U.S. Air Force pilot, told me that he was experiencing vertigo for the first time in his life. The metal structure was gently swaying in the winds of the open wilderness. How stable was this shiny, promising symbol of capitalism and of a bright future for Kazakhstan?

National Identity: Multiculturalism, Hospitality, and a Global Role

I have heard on multiple occasions that Kazakhstan was multicultural before multiculturalism became "trendy." The origin of this phenomenon dates back to the Stalin era, when millions of people, often those seen by the Soviet regime as potential political troublemakers, were deported to remote areas of the U.S.S.R.. Not surprisingly, the vast Kazakh territory became one of the top destinations. More recently, after the country gained its independence in 1991, its ethnic composition changed dramatically again. While in 1989, the percentages of Kazakhs and Russians in the population were more or less equal, with 40 percent and 38 percent respectively, by 1999, when the first census since 1991 was organized, the share of people claiming Kazakh ethnicity jumped up to 53 percent and the share of Russians fell to only 30 percent. The remaining 20 percent stayed split among one hundred thirty other nationalities, with Ukrainians, Uzbeks, and Germans representing the largest ethnical minorities.[7]

The idea of the peaceful and supportive co-existence of people of different ethnicities in Kazakhstan is profoundly rooted in the nation's folklore. The Central State Museum of Kazakhstan in Almaty proudly displays various national costumes, kitchenware, jewelry, and books in its Third Exposition Hall, showcasing each ethnicity in a different exhibit. The narrative of the multi-ethnic state is supported also by the etymology of the country's name. While the "-stan" ending, typical for Central Asia, means "home" or "land" in ancient Persian, which explains the proliferation of the suffix within the region, the word "Kazakh" means "free man" in the native tongue, also called Kazakh, a Turkic language. Thus, the country's name has a double meaning, well aligned with its objective to keep its diverse citizen living in peace and harmony.

A story I was told by our local guide nicely portrays this sentiment. It is called 'The Legend of White Pebbles.' During the Soviet era, the spouses and children of political enemies used to be sent to a specialized Gulag, The Akmola Camp for the Wives of Traitors to the Motherland. Day-to-day life in this camp involved hard work

---

7   http://www.kazakhembus.com/content/ethnic-diversity.

and a constant lack of food. One day, when the women were working in the barren fields of Kazakh steppe, the local people came out and observed them from a safe distance. The Gulag guards became alert. What could have brought the villagers into this secluded farmland? Soon they found an answer: the villagers wanted to express their disdain for these detainees, who had committed crimes against the state's ideology, and began to throw white pebbles at the women working in the field. The guards didn't chase the villagers away—they thought the stone-throwing was an acceptable and harmless way to humiliate the traitors' wives. Eventually, the villagers' visits developed into a ritual; a couple of times a week a group would come out and irritate the field workers by throwing little stones at them. The guards didn't realize for years that the villagers weren't actually stoning the detainees—they were feeding them. The white pebbles were pieces of a traditional Nomadic cheese made of dried fermented milk, called *kurut*. The women would collect the pebbles and eat them secretly once they were back in the camp. The legend vividly illustrates Kazakh hospitality, even towards total strangers.

Another anecdote explains that because of cruel continental winters, when the temperature drops down to minus 50 degrees Celsius[8], and the long distances that people had to travel in order to reach another settlement, the local people would always offer shelter and comfort to guests before asking them any questions. In other words, the Kazakh hospitality developed as a necessary survival tactic amid the harsh demands of nature.

The Kazakh tradition of hospitality, combined with the coun-

---

8   Minus 58 degrees Fahrenheit.

try's global ambitions, has led to a strong interest in hosting world-class events. Almaty was an official candidate for hosting the Winter Olympics in 2022, with the slogan "Keeping It Real." The city's commitment to winter sports is apparent when one enjoys the spectacular views from the top floor of the local Ritz-Carlton hotel: the impressive ski-jumping complex, Sunkar rises up to the clouds right next to the city's commercial and shopping area in the south. However, despite offering tall mountain ranges and an abundance of natural snow in the winter, the city lost the bid by a narrow margin to Beijing, which thus earned the privilege of becoming the first city to host both the Winter and Summer Olympics.

Kazakhstan did not mourn for too long. Its focus shifted quickly to intensive preparation for Expo 2017, a prestigious international exposition that takes place every two to three years and, next year, will be hosted by Astana. The Kazakh government hopes that this world-renowned fair and its preparation will provide a new boost to its new capital's development. At first, the Expo's overarching topic didn't seem to match its location: an exposition titled "Future Energy" hosted by a country that has fueled its recent prosperity exclusively by exporting conventional hydrocarbons? I came to understand this paradox only months later, when I brought it up during a class discussion with my Macroeconomics professor, Andrew Scott, at the London Business School, where I spent a semester abroad. Exporting oil and natural gas has enabled Kazakhstan to develop a part of the energy industry's supply chain. It has also made the country's wealth dependent solely on one source of income, which can turn out quite unpleasantly, as we saw in early 2016, when the global market price of oil plummeted by more than 70 percent from a two-year high.

Venturing into adjacent fields within the energy industry is thus a natural move toward diversifying the national economy while utilizing its existing expertise.

During our time in Astana, our group had a chance to visit the construction site for the exhibition, less than a year before the Expo's official opening day—June 10, 2017. Ten thousand workers were busy on the site, which spread over one hundred seventy-four hectares of land. The design of the complex reminded me of a daisy, its seven petals offering premises for the exhibition sites and a large globe at the center serving as the main stage for the event.

I was left wondering how this large infrastructure would be used after the three-month Expo was over but Kazakhstan's forward-looking government officials have thought about this question already, as we learned during a meeting with the leaders of the Astana International Financial Centre. Their plan is to establish a global financial hub governed by Anglo-Saxon common law and courts, independent of local jurisdiction. The hub will provide professional and financial services for businesses seeking investments in Central Asia and beyond, and it will also solve another growing challenge for Kazakhstan: how to provide its increasingly educated workforce with adequate job opportunities. The government sends thousands of its brightest and smartest abroad every year, enabling them to obtain degrees from the world's best educational institutions—and sure enough, our meeting with the leaders of the Astana International Financial Centre felt very similar to a soirée in a high-end New York gentlemen's club, complete with friendly banter over whether Caltech, Harvard, or Yale is the best.

The financiers are thinking about multiple elements that need to come together in order for the new global hub to be a success. One of the executives told us that they are coordinating with the national carrier, Astana Air, which is planning to enhance Astana's global connectivity in the years to come. Direct flights to Tokyo's Naruto Airport are scheduled to start in 2017; negotiations with New York City's JFK Airport are well underway, targeting the launch of direct flights in 2019; and even non-stop flights to Tel Aviv are on the map, albeit with an unspecified timeline. The airlines' plans for route expansion demonstrate that Kazakhstan is implementing its national, "multi-vector" foreign policy in its practical, day-to-day life as well.

Shooting for the Stars

Coming to Kazakhstan, I was eager to see firsthand how the country has dealt with its Communist legacy, in part because I wanted to compare it with my own homeland of Slovakia, which underwent a similar Communist experiment in the second half of the 20th century. I was skeptical as to whether a country could truly prosper and develop a functioning market economy while its political leadership remained unchallenged for twenty-five years. Unexpectedly, however, I left with an impression that this is indeed possible. Every country has its own unique path toward progress, and we all "play with the cards we have in our hands." Central and Eastern Europe have benefited from its geographical proximity and cultural ties to Western Europe, which enabled those regions to attract foreign investments and to access new markets, eventually becoming part of the European Union. Kazakhstan's starting position was different, but it rode the wave of natural resources exploration and reinvested the proceeds to build up its infrastructure. Neither of these paths is superior to the other; they both stem from the opportunities that the regions had on hand.

Kazakhstan is home to Baikonur Cosmodrome, the place from which humankind rose to stars in 1961, with Soviet cosmonaut Yuri Gagarin leading the way. President Nazarbayev confidently stated in one of his recent speeches that he believed the 21st century would "become a star century for the Kazakh nation." I am keeping my fingers crossed for the success of this ambitious stellar mission.

Chapter 10

Uzbekistan's Future at a Crossroads:

The Historic Political Leadership Challenges and Opportunities Facing a Proud Nation

Justin Hartley

MPA, Harvard Kennedy School of Government

●●●

I sat on the tarmac and looked out of my window seat. We were about to depart Astana, Kazakhstan on Uzbekistan Airways. I was pleasantly surprised by the sight of a clean, modern-looking wing. The freshly painted sky-blue engine, with its yellow and green swan-like logo, made an impressive contrast.

It was surreal to be heading to Uzbekistan, a country that to me evokes intense allure and mystique. As we pierced through the clouds and reached our altitude, the engines and wings glistened in the morning sun. The passenger cabin was equally appealing and the smartly dressed crew confirmed the contemporary, inviting, and warm image I had formed from the exterior of the plane. I felt optimistic and excited as we headed to Tashkent, the nation's capital.

While I could not profess to have in-depth knowledge of the country I was about to visit, I knew that it has the curious distinction of being one of only two double-landlocked countries in the world.

In other words, an Uzbek citizen would have to pass through at least two countries to arrive at an ocean. Indeed, no fewer than five countries surround Uzbekistan. (The other double-landlocked country is Liechtenstein, which is surrounded by just two.) The statistic made me ponder what logistical and political scenarios might arise from geographic proximity to so many unstable regions. My personal experience could not have been more different: I grew up in Australia, an island nation and a safe and prosperous country.

As we flew, I contemplated what life would be like in Uzbekistan and whether or not the people would welcome our presence. I must admit that one esoteric, humorous "fact" entered my head, from the movie character Borat (played by British comedian Sacha Baron Cohen), who refers to "those evil nitwits" in Uzbekistan. Though "Borat" is a spoof, I still wondered if there was some accuracy to the character's remark. After all, it is said that there is a little truth in every joke. Why was Uzbekistan such a rival for Kazakhstan? The gibe piqued my curiosity, even more so since I had just left Kazakhstan's capital of Astana and had been surprised and impressed by that beautiful city. I wondered would Tashkent be the same?

Nearly seven hours later, the plane descended through ever-thickening cloud cover and the skies grew darker. My heart was noticeably thumping. Our touchdown was bumpy and used every available inch of the runway. When the brakes had taken control, the passengers launched into rapturous applause. Their resounding cheers at both appreciation for the Captain's efforts and relief at surviving the flight were infectious. I found myself joining in.

Standing before an immigration officer, I took out my passport along with the two immigration forms distributed to us on the plane.

These forms asked us for extensive personal information, including the exact amount of U.S. dollars and local currency that we were bringing into the country. For each person in our group, the immigration experience was "every person for himself or herself." We had half expected some difficulty upon entry, so we were pleased to emerge with the group intact. As we congregated outside the terminal entrance, we shared our stories like school children returning from summer break. Only two members had had their luggage searched, and we all felt a palpable sense of elation.

Then we noticed, across the inner terminal road, a throng of middle-aged men. Their dark hair and weathered, tanned faces gazed in our direction. Most held a cigarette and they were as curious about us as we were about them, but their grim expressions quelled our laughter.

Our transportation into the city—a pale blue mini-bus with white lace curtains across its windows—sat in the car park. The back looked far too small to accommodate our sizeable rucksacks and suitcases. To my amazement, however, the driver managed to fit all the bags in with remarkable efficiency, as if he were completing a simple jigsaw puzzle.

The city of Tashkent lies in the foothills of the West Tian Shan Mountains. Positioned along the Silk Road, Tashkent was settled as an oasis on the Chirchik River. Early in its history, it came under Sogdian and Turkic influence, and in the 8th century AD Islam was introduced. In 1219, Genghis Khan destroyed the city altogether, but Tashkent rebounded, eventually becoming a profitable city. The Russian Empire conquered the city in 1865—a harbinger of major growth and demographic changes. Industrialization arrived in the

1920s and 1930s. Fifty years ago, in 1966, a major earthquake, measuring 7.5 on the Richter scale, demolished much of the old city. Over the next four years, around one hundred thousand new homes were built, helping to re-house the three hundred thousand residents made homeless by the quake. Twenty-five years later, Tashkent, along with the rest of the world, witnessed the collapse of the Soviet Union. At that time the city was renowned for its achievements in science and engineering and was the fourth largest city in the U.S.S.R., behind Moscow, St. Petersburg, and Kiev.

Since then, the city has changed economically, culturally, and architecturally, becoming the most cosmopolitan city in Uzbekistan. According to Geohive (2016) in 2004, Tashkent had an estimated 2.35 million inhabitants while Gulliway (2016) states that approximately 63 percent are Uzbeks and 20 percent are Russians. InterNations (2016) reports that Tashkent was named the Cultural Capital of the Islamic World by Moscow News in 2004 and this is not a surprise to me, as the city boasts many historic mosques and significant Islamic sites.

Our hotel was an imposing concrete block of uninspiring design. It did not appear to have been renovated since the Soviet Union's collapse. Roughly two dozen men, some policemen, loitered in the lobby. In the main they were quite young and I was taken by how exhausted they all looked.

One of Uzbekistan's contentious economic policies became apparent to us upon check in: the treatment of foreign exchange. Foreign currency is not encouraged, and the Uzbek government is careful to ensure that there is no net export of US dollars. We were quoted an official rate (according to the hotel) of roughly three thousand Uzbekistani Som (UZS) to US$1. However, we were also told on the quiet by non-hotel staff that there was a thriving black market operating too, offering, astonishingly, around 6,000 UZS to US$1. I had never encountered such a discrepancy in currency quotations, but I balked at the notion of dabbling in the black market. We obtained our currency from the hotel, and as the money piled up on the desk in stacks, the thick wads of notes gave us all a false sense of wealth. They rendered my wallet useless—indeed, several wallets would not have been sufficient to accommodate this pile of weathered-looking notes. I felt a little silly.

Later we discovered that it was a common sight to see the counter in the hotel lobby covered with stacks of paper bills, each several inches high. There was even a special counting machine to dispense notes to guests. The hotel staff said that the objective was to deliver "approximately" the correct exchange currency back in return.

As I lay on the bed in my room, I pondered the leadership style that had allowed this situation to reach such an extreme. President Karimov was the only "post-Russia" leader that Uzbekistan had known. At the age of seventy-eight, he had already well exceeded the average life expectancy of an Uzbek male. Numerous rumors circulated in Uzbekistan surrounding his health, and it was not unusual for Uzbek citizens to speculate on his imminent demise. But what would such an event mean for the future prosperity and stability of Uzbekistan, and how would the country respond to a new ruler?

As it turned out, I did not have to wonder about this turn of events for long. Just a few months after our trip, Mr. Karimov passed away. This was a historic moment and a crucial time in the nation's history. Since Uzbekistan's independence in 1991, Mr. Karimov had acted as a master tactician, adept at using his political skill to maintain Uzbekistan's relative stability. While the outcome of this approach was largely positive, his methods caused much debate—but there is no doubt that Mr. Karimov served as a calming influence within the more widely troubled Central Asian region. Uzbekistan is this region's most populous country as well as its geographic hub, surrounded by Afghanistan and all four of the Central Asian "Stan" states. Mr. Karimov's legitimacy as Uzbekistan's unchallenged ruler led a political longevity that was nothing short of remarkable. To put it into perspective, at the time of his death more than 40 percent of the country's nearly thirty million people were under the age of twenty-five (Index Mundi, 2016), meaning that many Uzbek citizens had never known any other leader. Mr. Karimov is therefore rightly regarded as the father of the nation, and his legacy will most likely grow with time. His political shrewdness, rebuttal of international opinion, and willingness to oppress would-be-challengers were all key to his skilled handling of many different Uzbek powerbrokers—prominent figures and powerful interests who constantly jostled for ascendance in the economic, political, and commercial realms of the country.

The rampant speculation that arose in the aftermath of Mr. Karimov's death on the timing and cause of his demise provides useful insights into the future challenges that the Uzbekistan government will face. According to Turghunov (2016), a "long and detailed medical report on "Patient Islam Karimov" was read out on state television on the evening of September 2 and published on the government portal, *gov.uz*, after the official announcement had been made". Many believed that the announcement was made to suppress rumors of a possible coup within the President's inner circle. *The Moscow Times*

(August 29, 2016) reported that within the country, the independent website *FerganaNews* was one of the first to publish reports of the President's death, stating that Mr. Karimov died mid-afternoon on August 29, 2016. Interestingly, these reports were immediately denied by both the Uzbek government and Mr. Karimov's family. Their tune changed only on the evening of September 2, when a cabinet officially announced Mr. Karimov's death, but by then several foreign leaders had already publicly expressed their condolences. Various specialists reputedly treated the President in his final hours, including Professor Alexander Potapov, the Director of Russia's NN Burdenko Neurosurgery Institute, and another Russian specialist, Professor Leo Bokeria. However, Russia's Deputy Prime Minister, Ms. Olga Golodets, declared that Russia "had not received any official requests to treat the Uzbek president." (True Edition, September, 2016).

The Uzbek constitution stipulates that upon the death or incapacity of the President, power passes to the head of the Senate until an election can be held. Consequently, Mr. Nigmatilla Yuldashev, Chairman of the Senate, was appointed acting President between September 2-8, 2016. On September 8, Mr. Shavkat Mirziyoyev, the country's Prime Minister, was then appointed by the Supreme Assembly as interim President of Uzbekistan. Mr. Mirziyoyev is favored to continue as the next elected President, and several indicators point to the likelihood of this outcome: he was part of Mr. Karimov's inner circle; he is in good standing with both Mr. Karimov's wife, Mrs. Tatyana Karimov, and National Security Council chairman, Mr. Rustam Inoyatov; he headed the organizing committee for the President's funeral; and, both he and his first deputy, Mr. Rustam Azimov, were pall-bearers during the funeral ceremony. He also made a speech at the ceremony as chairman of the funeral commission. Although Mr. Nigmatilla Yuldashev was constitutionally designated Mr. Karimov's successor, Mr. Yuldashev himself proposed that Mr. Mirziyoyev take over the post of Interim President, in light of Mr. Mirziyoyev's "many years of experience." As a result, a joint session of both houses of the Uzbek Parliament ratified Mr. Mirziyoyev's appointment.

On September 16, the electoral commission announced that Mirziyoyev would stand as the Liberal Democratic Party candidate in the December 2016 Presidential election. He will be a clear favorite, but will the upcoming elections be fair? In the past, Mr. Karimov always dominated the country's elections, gaining virtually unparalleled support. Among the four candidates who contended in the most recent election, Mr. Karimov achieved 90.39 percent of the vote. This suggests two possibilities: either the Uzbek people felt dizzying levels of happiness with his leadership, or the election process was corrupted in some way.

Will Mr. Mirziyoyev, as Uzbekistan's potential next leader, follow in Mr. Karimov's footsteps? As Turghunov (September, 2016) notes, apart from being the country's longest-serving prime minister, he is known for having "a fist rather than a brain," though he has denied past allegations that he has mistreated subordinates and even beaten them up, saying in 1998 that it was "not his style to beat someone." He is also reported to have close links with Russian oligarchs and is in charge of the country's key agricultural sector, including the cotton industry, an industry heavily criticized for using both child and forced labor. Overall, Mr. Mirziyoyev's background suggests that as President he would forge a more cordial and tighter relationship with Russia than Mr. Karimov did—Mr. Mirziyoyev has already worked closely with Russia's President Putin, when he was Prime Minister between 2007 and 2011.

Nevertheless, as Uzbekistan enters the post-Karimov era, many believe that the real power already lies elsewhere. Some say it belongs with Mr. Rustam Inoyatov. As *Reuters* (September, 2016) stated, the seventy-two-year-old has run the powerful SNB security service for twenty-one years and is widely seen as Uzbekistan's main kingmaker. He is also regarded as the main instigator in the sidelining of Mr. Karimov's once-powerful daughter, Gulnara. Others are watching the long-standing head of the presidential administration, Mr. Zelimkhan Haydarov, though it is probable that he will continue to exert his influence in a role more behind the scenes.

Whoever does take the helm will enter the world stage with the obligation of maintaining intricate international relations, for Mr. Karimov was a shrewd diplomatic figure, adroitly navigating big powers and competing regional interests. Perhaps most impressively, he resisted Moscow's attempts to integrate Uzbekistan into its security and economic blocs. After Mr. Karimov's death was announced, Mr. Putin was quick to offer his condolences, saying on the Kremlin's website, "It is difficult to overestimate the contribution of Islam Karimov to the establishment of relations of strategic partnership between our countries." Browne (2016). Interestingly, however, most of the state leaders from the former Soviet Union, including Mr. Putin himself and the Kazakh President, Mr. Nursultan Nazarbayev, did not attend his funeral, a small indicator that Mr. Karimov was successful in his resistance against their political domination.

Other countries, including global powers, China and the U.S., simply sent representatives, and while President Obama has spoken of a new era for Uzbekistan, Mr. Karimov's death may prove to produce a new era of challenges for the U.S. too. In 1991, after achieving independence, Uzbekistan sought out relationships with the West but it was only after the 9/11 terror attacks that the U.S. sought cooperation with countries near to Afghanistan to assist efforts in fighting against al Qaeda and the Taliban. Mr. Karimov backed the U.S.-led intervention in Afghanistan, for the Taliban and al Qaeda were Uzbekistan's enemies too. The new U.S.-Uzbekistan partnership extended to Mr. Karimov sanctioning American use of Uzbekistan's airspace and offering the Karshi-Khanabad airbase to support U.S. operations in Afghanistan. However, relations between the two countries broke down in 2005, when the George W. Bush administration condemned the Uzbek security forces' crackdown on protesters in the city of Andijan. As a result, Mr. Karimov expelled all U.S. personnel from Uzbek territory.

During Mr. Karimov's reign, Uzbekistan faced a series of terrorist threats, most prominently the Islamic Movement of Uzbekistan (IMU). In 2000, the U.S. regarded IMU as a foreign terrorist group, and indeed it has since allied itself with al Qaeda and the Taliban. The IMU carried out a series of car bombings in Tashkent in 1999, though the group has largely confined its operations to the Afghanistan-Pakistan border region. Nevertheless, the group reputedly wants to overthrow the Uzbek government, and it recently declared allegiance to ISIS. Mr. Karimov's death could provide a window of opportunity for them to expand further into Uzbekistan. Other links between Uzbekistan and terrorism also exist: one of the terrorists who carried out the June ISIS-linked attack on the Istanbul international airport, killing more than forty people, was an Uzbek citizen, and, worryingly, the security consulting company, Soufan Group has reported that several hundred Uzbeks have traveled to Iraq and Syria as foreign fighters. All of these incidents both indicate and perhaps increase the distance between Uzbekistan and the West.

But Uzbekistan is still one of the more independent former Soviet states in Central Asia. While some countries in the region have opted to join Russian-led organizations and would-be rivals to the European Union and NATO, such as the Eurasian Economic Union and the Collective Security Treaty organization, Uzbekistan has not. Russia maintains military installations in three of Uzbekistan's neighbors—Kazakhstan, Tajikistan, and Kyrgyzstan—but not in Uzbekistan itself. Browne (2016) notes that Ms. Olga Oliker, from the Center for Strategic and International Studies, said on *CNN* that Mr. Karimov "wanted to make sure the Russians didn't get too much influence in the region." Uzbekistan was also able to purge Russian agents from its military and security institutions, which helped to cement the country's independence. During her *CNN* interview, Ms. Oliker noted that Mr. Putin is undoubtedly hoping for a more pro-Russian Uzbek leader but that the new leader may opt to go the other way, liberalizing the economy and other elements of society in a bid to attract Western investment and support. This turn of events will be especially likely if Mr. Mirziyoyev is elected.

Economically, Uzbekistan is heavily dependent on foreign energy, and in recent years, China in particular has increased its presence in Uzbekistan and the Central Asian region, with major investments in energy as well as infrastructure. Uzbekistan also relies on its cotton exports, as well as on remittances from millions of workers abroad, particularly Russia. Fortunately, the Uzbek government has enjoyed a strong fiscal performance in recent years, enabling the government to increase public investment and cut both corporate and personal income tax rates. Civil servants' wages have increased, as have those for employees of small businesses, and this in turn has created a stimulus for the domestic economy. Another victory for the Uzbek economy was that, in 2014, the public debt was extinguished entirely. Altogether, these developments have contributed to economic growth of around 8 percent per annum, a return that most countries would be pleased with (Trading Economics, 2016).

The World Bank has posited that future growth in the Uzbekistan economy is dependent on continued financial sector reforms. One major area requiring such attention is the cash and foreign-currency exchange. However, there is one large caveat in all of this analysis. Much of the discussion of Uzbekistan, including released "official data" is open to debate, for, while Uzbekistan has elements of independence, it is still by and large a closed and oppressive country in comparison with Western democracies. Notwithstanding its impressive economic growth, the true nature of the country's political climate and economic health are exceedingly difficult for outsiders to ascertain with any degree of accuracy.

Despite these difficulties, there are some encouraging and reliable signs of a stronger Uzbek economy and quality of life. For instance, according to the World Bank (2016) back in 2001, 27.5 percent of the population was living in poverty, but this number was nearly halved by 2013, decreasing to 14.1 percent. Uzbekistan joined the World Bank in 1992 and since then has reportedly initiated twenty-seven projects financed by the International Bank for Reconstruction and Development (IBRD) and the International Development Association (IDA). The commitment to Uzbekistan from the IBRD, as of September 2015, was just under US$2 billion. Principally, the funding has focused on improving the quality of life for Uzbekistan citizens in healthcare, education, agriculture, clean water, energy, and transport. In healthcare, Uzbek citizens now enjoy greater accessibility, affordability, and efficiency in the healthcare system, as well as better training for their medical professionals, developments that have increased the average life expectancy of the country to increase substantially. Similarly, public spending on education is high, with student-teacher ratios approaching those in richer countries.

Meanwhile, the World Bank Group – Uzbekistan Partnership: Country Program Snapshot (April, 2016) provides an enlightening report on the state of Uzbekistan's agricultural, energy, economic and transportation sectors, to name a few. Under the Rural Enterprise Restructuring Project, the agriculture sector, which currently employs 27 percent of the country's citizens, is expected to contribute strongly to Uzbekistan's economic growth, through various forms of diversification, including food processing, manufacturing, and distribution. There are 265 cities, towns, and settlements in Uzbekistan and 11,844 villages, including 903 that are largely inaccessible. Despite these intimidating statistics, however, clean water is becoming increasingly affordable, reaching a vast majority of people in the country. The Uzbek power network forms part of the Central Asian Power System (CAPS) and ranks only 145th among 189 countries in the supply of electricity to its people. However, the country has rich energy resources, including natural gas and coal reserves, which may transform its energy industry in the near future. The dominant mode of transportation within Uzbekistan is road travel, which accounts for 90 percent of the total market share in transportation. Uzbekistan's tonnage is approximately twice as much as Kazakhstan's, and, as a double land-locked country, it plays a central role in connecting the region. Major corridors that run through Uzbekistan connect China to the East, Europe, and the Caucasus to the West, Russia to the south, and the Middle East and South Asia to the north. Railways also contribute substantially to passenger and freight transport.

Though it has gained strength from these many positive developments, the biggest tests now facing Uzbekistan are its first leadership succession since independence and a slowing world economy. The government's resistance to change has kept it from launching truly effective economic and political reforms, a failure that has resulted in high unemployment—and this problem will only get worse as more young Uzbeks reach working age. With limited opportunities at home, millions of Uzbeks have gone abroad in search of work. Russia has absorbed most of these migrants, but the slowing Russian economy means that there are fewer opportunities there for Uzbeks. Moreover, China's economic slowdown could have real impacts in Uzbekistan, for China is a major investor in the state-dominated Uzbek economy and a leading trade partner. As Stronski (2016) notes, low prices for Uzbekistan's main exports—natural gas, cotton, and gold—are exacerbating an already bleak economic picture.

As far as security is concerned, it is believed that the Uzbek military is the strongest and most capable in the region, and various reports indicate that the government has invested heavily in the military and in national security, a move that would make sense given Uzbekistan's central location in an unstable region (The Economist, 2012). But, again, reliable data on the security and military capabilities of Uzbekistan is scarce. Whatever the truth of the matter, the new president will have to accommodate the interests of the security services as well as many other powerful groups.

But what about our experience on the Trek and our time "on the ground" in Uzbekistan? Our visit was short, and we spent most of our time within Tashkent itself, though we also drove several hours north to the World Heritage Site of Samarkand.

Tashkent is a city that combines pre-Cold War conservatism and starkness with modern expressionism, freedom, and color. It contains numerous buildings that could stand proudly in any global city. One of the highlights of our trip was going to one of the city's largest traditional restaurants. We arrived at 9 p.m. among a busy throng of locals breaking their Ramadan fast. Several hundred hungry Uzbek faces watched us as we went inside. The restaurant was packed and people spilled out onto the street and over to the adjoining ice creamery. Inside, the staff hurriedly prepared an oversized, eight-seated table for our group of four. I felt self-conscious and a little special: everyone knew that we were the only non-locals, and we were observed even by the curious young children in the glassed-in play room overlooking the restaurant. I have never seen such a cleverly integrated play area in the West. The food just kept coming; most memorable were delicious kebabs of chicken and beef.

After our meal, a local—the friend of a friend of one of the Trekkers—took us around in his unofficial taxi. I noticed a little pair of black boxing gloves swinging in front of my face. The sweet science is a major sport in Uzbekistan, which won the most medals in boxing at the 2016 Rio Summer Olympics. In the thirteen weight classifications, Uzbekistan's contestants won three gold, two silver, and two bronze. More than half of the country's gold medals overall came from boxing (Rio2016, 2016).

It had been a long day, and I was feeling fatigued. Our guide suggested a 200-meter walk, and we bid farewell to the taxi and proceeded. After ten minutes, it became apparent that what we had thought was an estimate of the walk's length actually meant something else entirely, which had been lost in translation. Our two-hour walking tour became even longer, and while my eyes and ears continued to delight in the city, my feet were staunch critics. Eager to see the renowned Metro network left over from the Soviet days, we raced to catch the last train.

During our walking tour, we saw not only many of Tashkent's highlights but also a Security Building complete with copious monitor cameras. As we crossed the road in the darkness, we caught sight of a police car with two figures seated inside, their eyes fixed on us. This happened several times during our stay, once near the hotel when it was pitch black outside. On that occasion, our inadequate iPhone lights revealed the unsettling image of two armed men in the car, filling us with a sense of unease and vulnerability. Our local guide later told us that he had been apprehended not long before in a spot-check one evening and interrogated by the police after they had discovered that he was not carrying his passport. Daringly, he managed to flee from the interrogation before they had secured his name. His story made me realize that, in a city of friendly people and a seemingly relaxed capitalist lifestyle, lurked a strong undercurrent of "Big Brother."

A more uplifting highlight of our stroll was visiting a small square with rides, games, and ice cream, as well as large screens set up for locals to watch the European football championships. Although it was already past 10 p.m., the public space felt inviting, vibrant, and safe. The locals were exceedingly friendly, however the contrast continued, for only a short time later, we passed two military guards brandishing semi-automatic weapons. Countless security cameras monitored our progress as we passed several signs that read, "No photography." The local warned us with half-smiles to take that friendly warning "seriously," and we did.

As we crossed another dimly lit road, a spark flashed from the darkness: it appeared that someone was lighting a cigarette. Again, we saw two military officials waiting and watching us from within a parked vehicle—keeping order in the blackness like great white sharks circling a harbor at night. Heads cocked, their gazed followed us. The experience of strolling by beautiful sites under the steely gaze of the military police perfectly sums up our experience of visiting Uzbekistan as a whole. The locals we met are eager to participate as free members of the global community, but their lifestyle is limited by the regime's arguably oppressive approach and policies.

Finally, our journey to Samarkand was a most extraordinary experience. I sat in the front seat of our mini-bus, next to the Russian driver. The van's suspension was minimal, and its inadequacy was most readily apparent at the front of the bus, as I soon discovered. When our speed increased to "comfortably above the limit," we hit a pothole and I was lifted off my seat entirely before the seatbelt jerked me back against the squeaky seat. This happened several times and drew great guffaws from my fellow Trekkers, who were sitting more sensibly in the back. From the driver, my movements drew only the occasional wry smile; he had clearly completed this drive many times before.

All fifteen passengers eventually drifted off to sleep, until the driver and I were the only ones awake. I was thankful that the laughter had subsided. The driver spoke no English, so we sat in companionable silence. As time went on, rain pelted down and the roads became more treacherous. I prayed the bus would hold firm, and it did. The villages we passed and people I saw along the roadside reminded me of traveling across India. It was a tough life, but every now and then, a group of children would wave or pose for us, flashing their teeth in radiant smiles. In the West, we would have been concerned about young children playing unsupervised near a road, let alone the major national highway. Yet, here they did so with seemingly reckless abandon and experience beyond their years.

At last, we arrived at our destination. Samarkand is one of the most ancient cities of the world, its foundations dating back two thousand five hundred years. It was conquered by the warriors of Alexander the Great, the army of the Arab Caliphate, and the Mongol hordes of Genghis Khan. Today it is famous for its craftsmen and scientists. Ancient sights abound and we visited magnificent mosques and squares that would by themselves have more than justified our visit to Uzbekistan. It is easily one of the most amazing cities I have ever visited, and I could write many pages about its fascinating treasures. Suffice to say that for those wanting to see some of the most magnificent buildings on the planet, Samarkand is a must for any serious traveler and person interested in world history.

All too soon, however, we had to return to Tashkent and then to the airport for our departing flight. Our journey had been both enjoyable and enlightening. I had been deeply impressed by the rich history and resources of Uzbekistan and by the friendliness and resilience of its people, though I had also felt unnerved by the ubiquitous police presence. Now, after Mr. Karimov's death, the country has reached a momentous crossroads. It will be up to the new government to display fortitude and political courage to break the shackles of oppression and to embrace much-needed reforms. Uzbekistan has much potential but only a collaborative leadership approach will open up this amazing country, benefiting the world as a whole but most importantly, Uzbekistan itself and its wonderful people.

References

Browne, R., (September 3, 2016) "US loses partner in terror war with death of Uzbekistan's leader," Retrieved from: http://edition.cnn.com/2016/09/02/politics/islam-karimov-death-us-uzbekistan-relations/index.html.

The Economist (September 29, 2012) " Dammed if they do," Retrieved from http://www.economist.com/node/21563764.

Geohive (2016) "Uzbekistan: General Information," Retrieved from http://www.geohive.com/cntry/uzbekistan.aspx.

Gulliway (2016) "Tashkent," Retrieved from: http://en.gulliway.org/public/wiki/asia/central-asia/uzbekistan/toshkent-shahri/.

Index Mundi (July, 2016) "Uzbekistan Demographics Profile 2016," Retrieved from: http://www.indexmundi.com/uzbekistan/demographics_profile.html.

InterNations (2016), "Living in Tashkent," Retrieved from: https://www.internations.org/about-internations/.

Litvinova, D., and Davies, K. (August 29, 2016) The Moscow Times "Islam Karimov Rumored Dead, "Uzbekistan Ponders Future," https://themoscowtimes.com/articles/uzbekistan-on-life-support-country-motionless-as-karimov-hospitalized-55147.

Reuters (September 2, 2016) "Likely Key Players in a Post Karimov Uzbekistan," Retrieved from: http://www.reuters.com/article/us-uzbekistan-president-kingmakers-factb-idUSKCN118139.

Rio2016 (2016) "Uzbekistan Medals," Retrieved from: https://www.rio2016.com/en/uzbekistan.

Stronski, P.,(March 21, 2016), "Uzbekistan at Twenty Five: What Next?" Retrieved from: http://carnegieendowment.org/2016/03/21/uzbekistan-at-twenty-five-what-next-pub-63083.

Tour Under Blue Domes of "Marakanda" (Dec. 2016) Retrieved from http://www.asiatravel-discoveries.com/uzbekistan/cities-of-uzbekistan/tashkent.

Trading Economics (2016), "Uzbekistan GDP Annual Growth Rate," Retrieved from: http://www.tradingeconomics.com/uzbekistan/gdp-growth-annual.

True Edition (September 4, 2016) "Patient Islam Karimov," Retrieved from: http://trueedition.com/world/patient-islam-karmov/.

Turghunov, P., (September, 2016) "Islam Karimov: Uzbekistan faces questions after leader's death," Retrieved from: http://www.bbc.com/news/world-asia-37271514.

World Bank (April, 2016) "World Bank Group – Uzbekistan Partnership: Country Program Snapshot," Retrieved from: http://pubdocs.worldbank.org/en/721071461603894085/Uzbekistan-Snapshot-s2016-en.pdf.

World Bank (December, 2016) "Uzbekistan," Retrieved from: http://www.worldbank.org/en/country/uzbekistan/overview#3.

Part 5

:

Afterword

| Chapter 11 |
Revisiting the Asia Leadership Trek's Origins and Objectives

Hungsoo S. Kim, Editor
MPA, Harvard Kennedy School of Government

●●●

Dear Prospective Trekkers, welcome to the Asia Leadership Trek 2016 info session! The Committee, under the support of the Asia Center, will be organizing a socioeconomic and political tour, this time around to eight destinations in five countries, in January, with the theme of 'Thriving Asia: When is Asia Set to Become World's Powerhouse?' This Trek will provide firsthand insight through an experiential journey, in which all of you will directly investigate political, economic, industry, and societal issues through engagement with relevant leaders and organizations on the field. The highlight of this program, unlike the Treks offered by other programs at Harvard, Tufts and MIT, is that you will have the opportunity to serve local communities. Through your mentorship, inspirational stories on leadership, discussions on best practices, and capacity-building workshops on the topics of change leadership and social-profit initiatives, based on the latest research and cutting-edge ideas taught to global leaders like you at Harvard, you will have the chance to contribute to local communities, helping them face and solve their challenges...

It was a chilly late afternoon on Monday, September 14, 2015, in Room 301 of the Taubman Building at the Harvard Kennedy School of Government. Facing the people I would later meet as Trekkers on yet another fascinating journey to Asia, at the turn of 2016, I sensed high hopes and passion throughout the room.

To the organizers' amazement, the application turnout for the eighth Trek was unprecedentedly high. More than seventy applicants from Harvard University, Massachusetts Institute of Technology (MIT), and the Fletcher School at Tufts University (the Trek in the summer of 2016 also included participants from the Graduate School of Business at Stanford University and Business School at Columbia University) had signed up to embark on a journey to explore, learn, and serve in Asia. It was astonishing to see the high level of interest despite the fact that we had not made any official announcement throughout Harvard and other institutions, except for the Harvard Kennedy School (HKS). I presumed they got to know about it by word of mouth. However, many factors contributed to the Asia Leadership Trek's popularity.

The first factor was intellectual exposure and growth. Many Trekkers have never traveled to Asia before. They were eager to understand the political and policy dimensions of the continent: how political structures influenced businesses, and how pedagogical differences shaped educational systems and then economic growth. The Trek was a chance to walk the streets, to sit in restaurants and learn to use chopsticks, to talk to professors and business people, to immerse oneself to different systems, and to grow as the end result.

The Asia Leadership Trek is rich in learning opportunities. In Shanghai, China, the Trekkers sought to understand the country's initiatives toward diversified and innovative economy, as well as its struggles with uncertainties looming amidst its slowing economic growth. In Singapore, we delved into business leaders' motivations for attempting to make another leap forward in an already mature economy. In Malaysia, we explored how this emerging economy was making efforts to spur growth while preventing a middle-income trap, as well as striving to find an effective system of governance. In Phnom Penh and Siem Reap, Cambodia, we witnessed public leaders integrating diverse sectors of society to aid the nation's institutional and economic recovery and development. Lastly, in Dhaka, Bangladesh, we examined how leaders were committed to envisioning the future of its state and what elements were most needed for effective public leadership.

In the first Asia Entrepreneurship Trek in Tokyo, Japan, we discovered how the government was making incessant efforts to instill an entrepreneurial spirit and foster innovative entrepreneurship in the young to reinvigorate a once-vibrant economy. Taipei, Taiwan, on the other hand, presented how the country, continues to uphold its competitive edge over mainland China, in terms of products and services, as well as entrepreneurship practices amidst political and social uncertainties. It managed to accomplish this feat by reinventing an ecosystem to survive challenges facing the country. Meanwhile, Seoul, Korea illustrated how speed and efficiency-driven research, development, and operations were vital to ensure success in both process and outcome.

Another batch of Trekkers, in the summer, visited four nations, namely Tajikistan, Kyrgyzstan, Kazakhstan, and Uzbekistan, the Central Asia Trek or the Asia Leadership Trek VII. The journey showed each country's progress, ten years after their liberation from the former Soviet Union. These countries offered huge potential, economically, and geopolitically, amidst the backdrop of rich history. However, they also faced overwhelming challenges that involve maintaining social harmony and equilibrium, secularism and democracy, regional security and stability from trans-border terrorism, and more importantly territorial integrity, on top of economic growth that was the linchpin of their success. Leaders across the board gave us a fresh firsthand account of how they were grappling with deeply ingrained challenges, like the ones above, as well as emerging ones they have never encountered before—finding a balance between developing soft power strengths, commitment to democracy, the rule of law and human rights which were crucial for its sustainable development and security, and unveiling the region's potential in its pursuit of various economic and geopolitical interests.

The second appealing element in the Asia Leadership Trek was its service opportunity. The Trek's participants came from Harvard, MIT, Tufts, Stanford, and Columbia, a privileged group of highly talented individuals who study at world-renowned institutions. As privileged they were, one thought I had in mind was to offer the Trek as a platform for these accomplished individuals to exercise their 'Noblesse Oblige' by giving opportunities to serve by sharing their knowledge and skills they have acquired at their institutions with the people that they will meet out in Asia. The exchange of stories, ideas, and best practices among the seventy-eight scholars from Boston, New York, and San Francisco, and the current and future leaders of Asia on three combined Treks was, in my hope, to help to inspire a new generation in the region who were eager to bring about meaningful social change. At the same time, such an exchange enriched the understanding of the Trekkers themselves.

The third essential ingredient in the Asia Leadership Trek was the opportunity to learn from each other. The seventy-eight Trekkers on the three Treks who were enrolled in many different institutions across Harvard and other renowned institutions as mentioned above, also represented many different nations, and came from a diverse range of careers, backgrounds, and interests. The group met several times as a whole, or in small teams even before the Treks began, planning on delivering workshops, preparing for talks, and learning from each other. On the three Treks, friendships were forged during formal and informal meetings, conversations at the breakfast table, in buses, or on planes. Mingling with each other before, during, and after the Treks sparked new interests and ideas, revealed synergies between different fields, opened up new career opportunities, and ultimately created a set of friendships that spanned across countries and communities.

Thus, the Asia Leadership Trek offered a unique blend of exposure, service, and friendship. So far, about two hundred seventy Trekkers have participated in the program and they often share their stories with us on how the Treks have continued to impact their lives. Some have shifted their focus to Asia, while others have discovered their ambitions through the experience. Several have pursued social-profit endeavors in Asia, with funding by organizations that they visited in Asia.

New opportunities within the Asia Trek arise often, thanks to the continuous support from past Trekkers. Some now serve as country or regional directors for us in their respective countries. They offer advice, guidance, and valuable logistical help whenever a Trek comes their way. Some have sent us proposals for an extension of the Trek to countries not visited in the past. For example, one proposal suggested four or five countries in the Middle East; another suggested Turkey, Armenia, Georgia, and Iran while a third proposal suggested Pakistan, Afghanistan, and Iraq (though doubtful whether we can go there at the moment). Within the past three years, we visited fifty-eight cities in twenty-two countries mostly in Northeast, Southeast, South, and Central Asia with an exception of few countries, such as Pakistan and North Korea. I am determined to continue extending the Trek and making these proposals a reality, hopefully reaching to all forty-eight nations that comprise today's Asia by 2022. We will see whether we are able to achieve this goal by then.

Several past Trekkers from non-Asian countries have sought my help in launching similar programs for other continents, such as the Latin America Leadership Trek and the Africa Leadership Trek. I am thrilled with these requests and I applaud their efforts to expand the Trek model to other continents.

As the Asia Leadership Trek continues to grow, the leaders of our team hope that many more people will benefit from the program, whether as Trekkers, leaders in Asia we meet, or as participants at our conferences. I believe that everyone will find something valuable in our activities. It is my hope that, after the Trek, all the participants will gain renewed hope and motivation for greater success in their respective fields and will have a better understanding of Asia.

How It All Began

I grew up in the Philippines as the child of Korean humanitarian workers, from 1988 to 1998. It was a humble upbringing: we lived in one of the crudest homes in our neighborhood, at times with no electricity or running water due to severe drought. I helped my parents care for people in dire need of attention, providing food, shelter, education, and health care. I still vividly remember memories of the locals' desperation at that time. Young children and old men slept on thin, filthy mattresses on the streets. A great number of children did not attend school and had never been immunized. Seeing the plight of people living under an ineffective regime, I developed a strong conviction of the need for effective and courageous leadership in society. The conviction sparked my search for a way to fulfill what I saw as a public responsibility—finding a type of leadership that was appropriate and effective for countries like the Philippines.

Three life experiences that followed, provided the direction for my search for what I currently do today for the communities in Asia. The first one came after college. I was given an opportunity to work as a political advisor at the United Nations in New York under the South Korean Mission to the United Nations. Besides gaining firsthand exposure to diverse international security matters pressing our world, I had the chance to meet with the former Secretary General of the United Nations, Mr. Ban Ki Moon, at that time, a special secretary to the President of the General Assembly of the United Nations. My personal encounter with him was in early 2003, in Seoul, when I approached him to request for a reference letter for my application to a graduate studies program in Seoul. In that short meeting, he counseled me to find my "true north" in a specific field of work, to define my role in the world and to reach out to as many people as possible. The last words he said before ending the meeting was that I should "think big, consider people first, be pragmatic and down to earth, and have integrity at all times." This personal encounter with such an inspiring and influential man piqued my curiosity about what makes a successful leader, the qualities that enable effective leadership, and the vision for a public cause that helps to form them.

The second influential experience that shaped my ambition was my involvement in entrepreneurship. I began my entrepreneurial journey as an attempt to compensate for my humble background by accumulating wealth through business. However, it later turned into a venture that provided business opportunities to low-income families in Korea. Initially, I co-founded a small company called SBT Franchise, Inc., a Western-style fast-food chain, that became one of Korea's leading franchises at that time. The company grew at a phenomenal rate: beginning with a loan of about US$85,000, in just two and a half years, it expanded to become a medium-sized enterprise generating millions of dollars, with about two hundred seventy stores nationwide and employment for over six hundred people. This experience taught me the power of commerce to improve lives and livelihoods. Although it began solely as a for-profit undertaking, we soon shifted its focus to be non-profit-driven. After realizing that many of our franchisees were using their businesses to rise from failure, we developed a set of low cost-to-start franchises for low-income business people. When I began to personally meet some of these people, I realized that there were many more of them than I had imagined—people who were very hard working, yet suffering from various setbacks, that wanted to rise from failures in every sphere. I became determined to do more substantive work for these people and I sought a clear set of agendas that could offer essential help for people striving to rebuild their lives. For this purpose, SBT Franchise, Inc. had also established and supported a variety of non-profit organizations including Impact Korea and Feet Works, community welfare programs in Korea and the Philippines. Thanks to these ventures, I have gained a deeper understanding of the people that I wish to aid. I have also realized the power of business to improve people's lives and to contribute to national economies. Social entrepreneurship is important not only on the individual level but on the national scale as well.

My third formative experience came in March 2012, when I went on the Korea Trek, an expedition arranged by a group of Korean students at the HKS, including myself. On this trip, I realized that my country's educational system was not properly preparing students for business in the 21st century. At a meeting with Korea's leading company, Hanwha, a business executive explained, "The public is not happy with us companies for not hiring enough new graduates, but we cannot hire individuals who are not fully well-prepared. Even the smartest kids lack a certain foundation of skills and experiences which we can tap into immediately. We have to train them for at least one and a half years before they can create a net value for our company. The sad fact is that the Korean school system just does not prepare them for the 21st century." When I asked, "What do you mean by a 'foundation of skills'?" he replied, "I mean skills that require something far beyond memorizing. Korean students excel at copying notes and regurgitating facts, yet they have not been trained to work in groups, to express their ideas, and to articulate what they want to convey—skills that you actually need in the workplace. And companies here are good at copying the best models, but not at creating innovations. As a nation, we're at a point where, if we want to take the next step, we have to lead in creating new things." Nearly all the executives, presidential aides, journalists, and academics we met echoed these sentiments. They all agreed that Korea's education must evolve in order for the nation to continue to compete economically.

I realized, however, that this problem was not unique to Korea. On the Southeast Asia Trek—which comprised of seven countries in the region, took place two months after I had returned from the Korea Trek, I learned that increasing access to education was bringing many parts of Asia out of poverty, just as it had for Korea. But outdated education systems were often seen as the obstacle holding nations back once they have reached the status of post-industrial societies. It was no surprise that the debate over this dilemma was loudest in Korea, Japan, Taiwan, Hong Kong, and Singapore—advanced economies that credited education as the savior of their past but the chief challenge of their future. I returned from my travels asking myself this question: what model of education does Asia need for the 21st century?

These experiences, as well as my own entrepreneurial ventures, led me to contemplate how I could contribute to Asia's development and, on a personal level, how I wanted my next forty years to be. After nearly a year and a half spent researching, developing, prototyping, and testing a model, I finally decided that I could make a meaningful, substantive, and long-lasting impact through efforts in the education and leadership fronts—the former aiming for a change in the pedagogical approach favored in Korea and many other Asian countries while the latter targeting to identify and cultivate a capable and ethical method of political and social leadership for the Asian continent. Throughout my four years at the HKS and the Harvard Asia Center, I was sustained by the hope of carrying out this endeavor.

Developing the Trek

My two years at the HKS were extremely worthwhile. Among many other experiences that I greatly value, the opportunity to establish the Asia Leadership Trek stands out as the one that most inspired me. Its development at this time had much to do with my realization of the relative dearth of programs that focus on Asia, for students at the HKS, as well as a shortage of opportunities for experiential learning. Despite the fact that there were programs similar to the Trek being run at the HKS, many of which involved travel and site visits, they did not have an extensive geographical scope, deep emersion, and firsthand learning through dialogues with thought leaders, nor rich opportunities to give back to the community that I had hoped for. The lack of opportunities cemented my determination to create a program of knowledge exchange between Asian countries and the prestigious universities in Cambridge, Massachusetts.

The ideas I had in mind were growing clearer; however, implementation was another story. For the program to run effectively, I needed to find people who shared my ideals and a business model with a well-defined objective, framework, and rationale. My initial move, beginning in my first semester, was to explore and understand my new environment, familiarizing myself with the curriculum, coursework, lecturers, and new friends. I also introduced myself to professors in different schools across Harvard, MIT, and Tufts University. Conversing with them on matters ranging from my coursework to my plans such as the Asia Leadership Trek was extremely helpful in solidifying my aims. They referred me to various resources, arranged meetings with experts in the area, and offered advice that helped me move in the right direction. Later, some offered to give lectures and workshops to the Trekkers and even graciously permitted the Trekkers to use their materials in our conferences in Asia. I also spent an enormous amount of time reading, writing, thinking, and holding discussions about Asia and the multi-country leadership tour I was envisioning. Ultimately, the initial research and reflection provided the conceptual structure for the Asia Leadership program.

The most rewarding experiences, however, were the dynamic and fruitful exchanges I had with my fellow classmates at the HKS. These students, who came from all kinds of backgrounds and represented approximately a hundred nations, helped me immeasurably in broadening my knowledge of the world and deepening my understanding of leadership, its practice, and its impact. Their stories of success and failure in striving for social change and the lessons they learned in the course of their leadership journeys gave me much food for thought and motivated me to find concrete ways to serve communities in Asia.

Pondering on everything my classmates and professors had taught me, I developed three main features that I wanted to incorporate into the Trek. Firstly, I needed to find people who were highly committed to the public cause, who were eager to solve social problems and improve global communities. I hoped to find other people who felt, as I did, a call of duty to leave a positive legacy of change in the world.

Secondly, I decided that the true exercise of leadership meant not only generating potential solutions for pressing problems, identifying opportunities, and maximizing their impact—but also being able to turn downsides into upsides, so as to improve communities from within rather than imposing external values on them. Lastly, I came to believe that, important as it is to have powerful ideas and strong guiding principles, it is even more crucial to implement real-world actions and solutions. According to the people I had spoken with, meaningful social change can be attained only when passion and idealism are put into action.

So, on the one hand, I hoped that the Trek would offer a comprehensive yet deepened learning experience to aspiring leaders, including both the Trekkers and the people we would meet in Asia. And on the other, I wished to disseminate the world-leading best practices produced at renowned institutions like Harvard and MIT, to share these transformative tools that could profoundly benefit Asian leaders and ultimately, the whole of Asia. The latter process would involve much more than seeing and learning; we needed to train the leaders of tomorrow by equipping them with the best possible skills and the most innovative ways of thinking, in order for them to become strong, capable, and ethical agents of change.

Together with John Lim, a trusted friend from primary school, now the Managing Director of CALI Boston, along with few others from the HKS, we took a leap of faith in initiating the ALT. Shortly before, John and I had several meetings with two of Harvard's renowned scholars, Professor Marshall Ganz from the Harvard Kennedy School and Professor David Garvin from the Harvard Business School. These professors provided us with the basic framework for the Asia Leadership Trek, comprising three key elements that would shape the program: "knowing, doing, and being." Becoming a leader requires all three of these actions. "Knowing" means gaining familiarity with best practices through the acquisition of knowledge—typically through primary to tertiary education. "Doing" means putting that knowledge to use in a way that improves existing practices—designing, performing, creating, and effecting positive change. "Being" means developing one's internal self—learning and understanding what kind of a person one can and should be; it refers to our ways of thinking, our demeanors, our characters, and the way we see ourselves in respect to others.

My next step was to utilize both the human and academic resources at the HKS. Given that the HKS attracts many of the world's most exceptional public leaders, both current and future, I knew that it offered an amazing pool of resources for the Trek such as candidates themselves to this program and extensive networking they have across the globe. Connecting such people to Asia will become more and more important as Asia exerts its growing influence on world politics and the global marketplace. I felt that it was imperative for the HKS community to be exposed to Asia and to connect with its many countries, in order to gain an understanding of its immense resources, power, and potential. The Trek would be an ideal vehicle for achieving these objectives: a group comprising professors, researchers, and students would travel to different cities and countries in Asia to meet with leaders from various fields. Nothing could be more worthwhile than bringing these two groups together to share ideas and expertise, and jointly tap into new opportunities. For Asian communities, maximizing the use of the value-add they bring, resolving their current challenges, and identifying their opportunities all require learning from leaders who bring different perspectives, insights, and skills. For the Trekkers, Asia represents a growing, and multi-faceted global force in which countless dynamic opportunities exist but have yet to be fully discovered. Today, Asia is among the best places in the world to introduce innovative and potentially world-altering ideas.

To make the Trek as valuable as possible, we needed to schedule meetings with key decision makers, thought leaders, and trend-setting or leading organizations in each country, ranging from people in the government and politics to those in the corporate and non-profit worlds; they would provide up-to-the-minute accounts of the present state of their countries, explaining the strengths to be exploited and the variety of potential challenges to be faced. As far as I could see, this firsthand exposure to influential individuals was the most effective, cost-efficient, and rewarding method of experiential learning.

Equally important was the aim to impact communities in Asia by offering new inspiration and hope through stories, mentorships, workshops, and discussions. In my interactions with students at Harvard, MIT, and Tufts, I had seen extraordinary value in their drive, knowledge, and insight, all of which would be immensely helpful in Asia. Their stories of leadership experiences, diverse achievements and interests, and unique perspectives would be of enormous worth to Asia's current and future leaders, and I saw endless potential in bringing them to the many different communities in Asia. To facilitate the exchange of knowledge and practices, our organizing team, including myself, would arrange half-day to full-day conferences throughout the Trek, in each country we visited, so that the Trekkers could give talks, hold information sessions, and exchange ideas with our Asian counterparts.

In practice, these conferences were even more enriching than I had hoped. The Trekkers' contributions mainly consisted of brief TED-style talks, panel discussions, career mentoring and networking sessions, workshops, and professional development seminars (Please refer to Appendix IV: Program Details for full list of topics). The TED-style talks were opportunities to share personal stories that offered powerful life and leadership lessons. Topics included "Disruptive Innovation," "Authenticity and Leadership," and "Women in Leadership." Our hour-long panel discussions included a moderator and four to six panelists who shared ground-breaking ideas, strong guiding expertise, and valuable leadership advice. The panels provided an arena for discussion and debate on leadership, innovation, politics, and education. There was also a forum to engage and inspire young students and professionals. Usually, the final twenty minutes were devoted to free-flowing question-and-answer sessions. Panel topics included "Perspectives on Leadership," "From Good Intentions to Leading Social Change," "Innovation and Leadership," "Careers in the 21st Century," "Success vs. Significance," and "The Meaning of Social Entrepreneurship in Any Profession."

In the career mentoring sessions, the Trekkers shared their work experiences and offered guidance in choosing career paths. They took on the role of career counselors, helping young Asian students and professionals to gain insight into their own career prospects. These sessions were also designed to help Trekkers connect with other young professionals and discuss issues in their fields. Topics ranged from preparing to get into top U.S. universities, job searches and successful employment to balanced work lives and effective teamwork. The career fields that were discussed included management consulting, academia, finance, politics, social entrepreneurship, media, international organizations, foreign service, and medicine.

The professional development seminars offered down-to-earth guidelines and instruction on topics such as building resumes, managing LinkedIn, giving an elevator pitch, writing a business plan, dressing for success, applying for schools in the U.S., writing a statement of purpose, storytelling, interview skills, writing good essays, writing a policy memo, becoming an effective and powerful twitterer, launching your own website using WordPress, doing a camera interview, using social media, and scaling up your organization. All of these activities were designed to impart valuable hands-on skills and to equally focus on practical applications. The main objective was to ensure that attendees could use the skills they had learned right after they walked out of the seminar rooms.

One of the reasons that contributed to the success of the Trek's conferences was that the Trekkers already possessed a wealth of experience in their fields. Equally important was the thorough planning beforehand. Fully prepared on how to design and run informative leadership sessions, the Trekkers held eighty to one hundred sixty-minute workshops modeled after the most Asia-relevant courses at Harvard, MIT, and the Fletcher School. These workshops were divided into four categories: Leadership and Decision-Making, Public Speaking and Strategic Communications, Innovation and Practical Skills, and Special Topics. The workshop topics included themes such as "Social Change Starts with Good Intentions," "How to Run and Manage a Campaign," "Addressing Cognitive Biases in Decision-Making," "Building Bridges through Inter-Cultural and Ethnic Dialogue," "Entrepreneurship in the Developing World," and "Financing Entrepreneurial Ventures," amongst other.

Over the course of the Trek, since its official beginning in January 2014, we have carried out more than seventy half-day to one-day conferences, about ten three-day forums, and thirty five-day leadership schools, in over twenty countries across Asia. Reflection papers, assessment surveys, and live-stream debriefing sessions demonstrated the ways in which these programs inspired, educated, and motivated the attendees to face the problems they see in their communities today. Approximately twenty-two thousand individuals, from middle to high school students and educators to start-up entrepreneurs, government officials, and corporate employees, have benefited from these endeavors. In many cases, our program has led to concrete changes, both big and small, as the Trekkers became empowered to support our Asian counterparts in tackling the challenges around them. In return, many of the hundreds of participants who have attended our leadership conferences in Asia were motivated to turn their ideas for change into action, some seeking ways to improve their societies through start-ups or social-profit works while others deciding to work for institutional and global policy changes.

My greatest hope is that our work through the Asia Leadership Trek will lead to a ripple effect that continues to spark social change and emboldens new leaders within and throughout Asia. The program represents an extraordinary group effort that demonstrates the collaboration we emphasize as one of our central tenets. I have been endlessly impressed by my colleagues' humility, their eagerness to learn, and by their willingness to promote the Trek. It is also important to state that we could not have achieved this feat without the unique resources provided by the HKS. The people, environment, and high expectations from the institution helped to turn the Asia Leadership Trek into reality.

I am now fully committed to my long-term plan of designing and promoting leadership programs that connect Asian countries with students and thinkers from all over the world. I am humbled and thrilled to have witnessed how well the model has worked thus far, and I look forward to seeing what else is in store for the Asia Leadership Trek.

| Chapter 12 |
The Legacy of the Asia Leadership Trek

Hungsoo S. Kim, Editor
MPA, Harvard Kennedy School of Government

• • •

Shortly after we officially got the Asia Leadership Trek off the ground, three other programs came into existence. They are the Acumen Case Center, Acumen Publishing (formerly known as CALI Press), and the Asia Leadership Institute which have expanded alongside the Trek in the past two years. These initiatives have their roots embedded in the Treks; they were inspired by ideas coming from a myriad of meetings and events that were held in Asia. The Asia Leadership Institute and Acumen Publishing were established in the summer of 2014. The Acumen Case Center, an educational pedagogy training and content development of CALI, came into existence much later in January, 2016. Although this arm is still a work in progress, it has successfully launched its very first training program entitled "Case Method Teaching: A Way Forward for Effective Pedagogy," last summer in Malaysia, attracting more than forty educators, researchers, and school administrators from nine countries. All of these programs will help to empower individuals, organizations, and governmental bodies in Asia to play a more active and meaningful leadership role in their communities. Here is a summary of the direction, moving forward.

The Asia Leadership Trek

The Asia Leadership Trek (ALT) will continue, first and foremost, to host socioeconomic, political, and cultural study tours, combined with public service programs to multiple cities in Asia. It will continue to emphasize the ways in which participants can serve local communities in Asia through mentorship, inspirational stories on leadership, discussions of best practices, and capacity-building workshops on leadership and social-profit initiatives, namely entrepreneurship, innovation in education, and social responsibility. Overall, the ALT will strive to remain the transformative and rewarding program that many past Trekkers have found it to be.

In terms of geographical scope, I hope that the ALT will eventually cover every one of the countries within the perimeter of Asia, including countries in the Middle East and the Persian region. Having said that, my goal by 2022 is to take my Trekkers to every single nation of all forty-eight countries in Asia, spanning from Japan to India and Jordan. So far, we have almost reached the midpoint. We have managed to visit twenty-two countries, so we have another twenty-six more to go.

I also hope that at least one Trekker from each of the world's two-hundred twenty nations will participate in the program. To date, we have participants representing more than fifty-five countries. We will continue to keep our doors open to participants from other parts of the world. By the winter of 2017, we would have expanded the ALT's scope considerably, visiting several countries in the Middle East. Hopefully, the Trek will cover Iran, Turkey, Georgia, Azerbaijan, and Armenia in the summer of 2018.

Thus far, only a limited number of people have been able to participate in a single Trek, and only a small amount of Treks have been organized each year. Over the past year, beginning March 2016, we began to expand both of these numbers, running four Treks in 2016 and diversifying the nature of its Trek, and even opening the doors to public participation to increase its outreach and impact.

In March 2016, we organized the first Asia Entrepreneurship Trek to explore Asia's silicon valleys and education hubs in three countries – Japan, Taiwan, and Korea. Attended by Harvard scholars from all around the world, it offered participants the opportunity to learn about innovative entrepreneurship, and discover the latest trends and insights from prominent business leaders throughout the Trek. The Trek served as an avenue for participants to explore the "trendiest" industries (Hi-Tech, Fintech, and Biotech) and ways to translate innovative ideas into corporate business models. Participants also learned about the financial aspects of entrepreneurship and networked with inspiring individuals from various backgrounds which enabled them to expand their mindsets and cultural self-awareness. We look forward to the next Asia Entrepreneurship Trek which will include both en-trepreneurs and scholars from both Harvard and Asia.

Another ambitious program called the Global Leadership Trek was successfully held in August 2016. It consisted of a seventeen-day leadership program that took place in Washington, D.C., New York, and Boston. It included a nine-day experiential study tour to examine pressing issues and cutting-edge ideas through firsthand engagement with prominent social and corporate leaders and organizations in the U.S. Targeted at college and university students, the program, this time, offered eight youth Fellows from four countries with the opportunity to expand their horizon, and acquire invaluable knowledge and insights on problem solving strategies, apart from gaining an enjoyable overseas experience, and learning about U.S. history, business, politics, culture, and society.

On another note, we will be putting together a new program called the Global Education Trek this year in 2017. This first-of-its-kind educational pedagogy and policy study tour will bring leaders in education from two different continents, namely Asia and North America, to Singapore, Seoul, Korea, and Boston and New York, U.S. Through an experiential journey to these four educational hubs, participants will get the opportunity to learn from the best of each other by engaging with relevant thought leaders and organizations on the field, and to better understand major educational issues affecting our world today. This Trek aims to not only build bridges between the two communities but also inspire participants to become agents of change to make a difference in their respective communities that they serve. I hope that many of the readers who are passionate about education and creating change in the world would take the opportunity to come and join us in this enriching program.

The Asia Leadership Institute

The Asia Leadership Institute (ALI) offers leadership training, specialized education, and academic and cultural experiences designed on the framework of "knowing, doing, and being." Having discovered what an impact sharing and learning can have through the conferences we hosted during the Asia Leadership Treks, we launched the ALI in February 2014 with the aim of giving students, professionals, and government workers an access to innovative leadership training methods and specialized education. Most of the programs are one to two-weeks long and have the capacity to train fifty to two hundred individuals at one time.

To date, we have run about ninety conferences and programs in thirty-nine cities across twenty-two countries, and trained more than twenty-four thousand bright individuals. What makes the ALI programs unique is that they incorporate methods of teaching and learning profoundly different from Asia's conventional form of education. Eschewing structured, hierarchical, rote-memory, and regurgitation-based learning, the programs instead use active learning models—engagement, simulation, experience, and dialogue—and in doing so, provide learning spaces that allow their participants to become highly competent individuals who are committed to making a positive impact in their societies.

The ALI aims to address two problems that have been increasing in Asia: (1) an absence of effective social and political leadership, whereby leaders today fail to see leadership as a collaborative journey that involves them and their constituents, at times, engaging in difficult conversations and actions that require tough decisions, commitment, and losses for the greater cause and real progress of its community; (2) a relative lack of commitment by our current generation to face the opportunity and responsibility to meet the complex challenges of our times, by initiating and participating in the work of managing the process of creative problem solving that produces meaningful outcomes—all of which are critical in today's world if we are to see real change on a global scale. In Asia especially, leadership and governance often exhibit alarming weak points. Despite the immense dynamism and potential of Asia, the continent suffers from a deficiency of leaders who can help their followers make reasonable choices and mobilize them to innovate for a brighter future. With this in mind, we undertook the initiative to help train both current and future leaders in Asia for Asia who were both ethical and capable of exercising effective leadership in times of complexity and uncertainty.

For this vision to bear fruit, we have developed and introduced about twenty-five programs that run, as noted earlier, under the framework of (a) knowing—acquiring highly relevant knowledge and skills needed in today's world, (b) doing—the doing of knowledge or making use of what we know into creating values that our society greatly needs, and (c) being—understanding who we are as leaders with questions asking what we could do for our nation and community. The programs were created in the context of enabling participants to reflect, develop, and practice leadership across these three realms; personal, community, and global. The ALI programs consist of: (a) Global Change Agents Program, (b) Leadership in Development Program, and (c) Leadership Summer School Program.

	Global Change Agents	Leadership Summer School *Summer Only – July to August*	Leadership in Development
Seniors	M1: Disciplined Leadership – Ethics, Power and Decision-Making [3 Days] M2: Adaptive Leadership – Leading Change for Organizational Renewal [3 Days] M3: Perspective Leadership – Character, Courage and Commitment [3 Days] M4: Global Leadership – ALT & GET [2-4 Weeks]		
Managers		Harvard's Way of Developing a Talent: Harnessing Strengths and Passion to Sustain Leadership Presence [5 Days]	P1: Negotiation & Mediation Strategies for Managers [1 Day] P2: Leadership Best Practices—Managing Career Accelerators and Derailers [1 Day] P3: Maximizing Your Leadership Potentials—EQ, SQ, RQ and Happiness at Work [1 Day] P4: Transforming Workplace through High Impact Teams [1 Day] P5: Developing a Powerful Gender Partnership—Shared Values, Goals and Actions [1 Day]
Youth		P1: Asia Leadership Youth Camp: Building the 21st Century Core Competencies [6 Days] P2: Global Leadership Trek [2 Weeks] P3: Asian Union Leaders Summit Cultivating Emerging Leaders Across Borders [5 Days]	P1: Mega-Trends of the 21st Century and Talents Required [3 1-Days] P2: Becoming a Professional Thinker [3 1-Days] P3: Enhancing Your Effectiveness in Communication [3 1-Days] P4: Unleashing Creative & Innovative Capacities [3 1-Days] P5: Cultivating the Entrepreneurial Mindset [3 1-Days] P6: Asia Leadership Conference [1 Day]

A. Global Change Agents Program

Targeting established thought leaders, opinion makers, and decision makers across the board, the Global Change Agents Program is a three-day leadership workshop that entails eighty-minute Plenary Sessions which encourage actual cases and in-depth discussions to promote moral competence and practical ethical judgement; eighty-minute Case Discussion exercises to discuss the course materials for an enriching experience, and to debate on the types of moral competence that professionals require to work effectively; eighty-minute Workshops that enable participants to practice making bold but calculated risk through simulations and role-play exercises; and forty-minute Seminars that give participants an opportunity to reflect on the day's learning and to discuss action plans moving forward.

We completed three major programs in August and October 2016. The five-day **Personal Leadership: Ethics, Power, and Decision Making** and **Case Method Teaching: A Way Forward for Effective Pedagogy**, programs were conducted in August with Professor Kenneth Winston and Professor Mathias Risse from the Harvard Kennedy School. The "Personal Leadership" program helped working professionals strategically address leadership challenges involving ethics, decision making, and exercising of power and influence; and gain insights and develop competencies for leadership as change agents in the workplace. Meanwhile, the "Case Method Teaching" program exposed participants to the Case Method, a signature pedagogical approach to learning, employed at the Harvard Business, Medical, and Kennedy Schools. Both programs used fourteen Harvard case studies to help sixty-five participants learn the importance of adhering to the highest standards of personal and professional conduct. The three-day **Adaptive Leadership: Leading Change for Organizational Renewal** program was held in October to offer fifty-five senior leaders from across industries the platform to discover how to become effective change agents in a dynamic, shifting, and interdependent world by crossing boundaries that divide groups to mobilize diverse stakeholders to participate in the creative work of making progress, and generate responses and breakthrough solutions. Another program bound to take place in mid-2017 is **Perspective Leadership: Character, Courage, and Commitment** in which participants are to learn how to adopt fresh perspectives, initiate new ways of working together, implement bold new actions, and continue to deliver results in the face of new and often overwhelming moments of uncertainty and complexity.

B. Leadership Summer School Program

Established in July 2014, the program consists of a week-long leadership school in which the participants, under the guidance of seven to ten Teaching Fellows from Harvard and Stanford University, undergo an intensive mentality shift and leadership skills training. The program aims to achieve two goals. The first is to increase the participants' capacity to adapt to a variety of conflicting pressures and to communicate effectively in diverse settings; the participants practice adaptive learning, acute diagnosing, and self-deployment through the case method of instruction and case-in-point teaching, as well as strengthening their skills in negotiation, persuasion, and problem solving through structured exercises. The second goal is to develop the participants' ability to adopt new perspectives on leadership practices, and to increase their entrepreneurial and creative thinking skills through the design thinking method of instruction, structured exercises, and simulations that produce shared values and outcomes.

These programs were modeled after most high on-demand courses by students across the Harvard community, and were custom designed to offer as a set of programs best catered towards the needs and demands of the communities in Asia. They include, among others, communication, global change agency, negotiation strategies, transformational leadership, design thinking and innovation, ethics, power and influence, decision making, effective advocacy, and cross-cultural communication.

Our current programs include the following:

1. Harvard's Way of Developing a Talent: Harnessing Strengths and Passion to Sustain Leadership Presence

Targeting mid-career and junior executives across industries, the five-day leadership program exposes working professionals to various leadership paradigms to better understand what real leadership looks like through plenary and interactive workshops. The program involves two eighty-minute Plenary Sessions to foster in-depth discussions on effective communications and to learn ways to implement persuasion approaches to a particular interest; two eighty-minute Workshops (a total of six topics are given as choices) to develop leadership knowledge, skills, and goals, and build entrepreneurial thinking via creative hands-on ideation; sixty-minute Professional Development sessions (six choices of topics) to advance participants' capacities in verbal, written, and professional areas by providing them with knowledge, best practices, and skill sets that will help them in their personal, academic, and professional lives; a forty-minute Special Seminar for participants to reflect on the day's learning; and Coaching Sessions to be guided in career and life choices.

2. Asia Leadership Youth Camp: Building 21st CenturyCore Competencies

The six-day leadership program allows high school and university students discover their real 'me' and to understand their personal brand and carve their own path. The program includes two eighty-minute Plenary Sessions to foster in-depth discussions on effective communications and to learn ways to implement persuasion approaches to a particular interest; two eighty-minute Workshops to develop leadership knowledge, skills, and goals (Leadership Workshop - three choices of topics), and build entrepreneurial thinking via creative hands-on ideation (Innovation Workshop - three choices of topics); a sixty-minute Professional Development session (six choices of topics); a sixty-minute Career Mentoring session (six choices of topics) to enhance participants' capacities in verbal, written, and professional areas by providing them with knowledge, best practices, and skill sets that will help them in their personal, academic, and professional lives; and four hours of Community Service practicum.

3. Asian Union Leaders Summit: Cultivating Emerging Leaders Across Borders

The five-day leadership program is designed to take high school and university students in Asia on a journey to learn ways to confront and resolve issues, and take a step forward in shaping a promising and thriving future for everyone. It introduces the theory and practices of negotiations, representation, and legislative procedures. The Simulation enables its participants, supposedly to assemble two from all forty-eight countries in Asia, to understand the qualities that make a leader and what can be done to foster a healthy agenda-focused representation comity in the complex world of transnational politics.

Some of the concepts that the program focuses on are:
(a) regional and national representation—in the Simulation, each participant represents his or her own country, bearing in mind that each country is a responsible member of the Asian community at large;
(b) fair and interested representation—each participant belongs to another agenda-based committee of his or her choice, out of seven possible transnational agenda;
(c) power, influence, and persuasion—the participants learn to promote their bills by creating factions within the committees;
(d) practical reasoning—the participants take part in committee hearings to test and reinvent their proposals;
(e) ethics and decision making—the delegates carefully assess their stakeholders' national and regional interest, then vote for or against, and defend bills;
(f) constructive collaboration—the participants draft bills in small groups after intense debate and discussion; and
(g) responsible leadership—at the end of the Simulation, there is a plenary session, which concludes with a final draft in place that

could result in benefiting the Asian community across board. The first program is bound to take place in mid-2017.

4. Trilateral Leadership Summit

It is an international program designed for Chinese, Japanese, and Korean high school students who are interested to learn how to tackle emerging leadership challenges the Northeast Asia region is facing. Just having completed its third phase in Incheon, Korea the past summer, the Summit consists of special lectures and a simulation exercise that replicated—with hypothetically expanded activities—the activities of the Trilateral Cooperation Secretariat created by the three nations in Northeast Asia in September 2011.

The opportunities for global leadership by these countries in Northeast Asia are growing, and as a region, it has the potential to be immensely prosperous. However, it also faces drastic challenges, due to the geopolitical uncertainties surrounding its historical and territorial issues. Our Summit convenes young representatives from China, Japan, and Korea for discussions, simulations, and skill-building workshops, thus increasing the chances for future leadership initiatives in the region, while at the same time offering a platform for inter-country dialogue, networking, awareness raising, and the development of collaborative skills and perspectives. The frameworks and concepts used in the program are based on courses at the Harvard graduate schools including Adaptive and Multi-Context Leadership, Negotiation and Mediation, Cross-Cultural Communication, Systems Thinking, and Overcoming Immunity to Change, conveyed through activities such as speech competitions, tripartite law making simulations, outdoor field work, and panel discussion sessions.

The Summit is held on a rotational basis in all the major cities of the three countries. In November 2014, the first Trilateral Leadership Summit was held in Seoul, Korea; followed by the second Summit in Sendai, Japan, in August 2015; and the third one in Incheon, Korea, in August 2016. The fourth is bound to take place in Incheon, Korea or Tokyo, Japan in August 2017.

C. Leadership in Development Program

This program caters to young professionals and managers across industries, as well as college and university students who wish to acquire 21st century core competencies and mindsets that are crucial to navigating the volatile and fast-moving world. Through the program, participants will get the opportunity to partake in four eighty-minute Plenary Sessions that encourages them to engage in theory and practice through real-life simulation cases, peer coaching, and open dialogues to develop leadership skills that are essential for personal and professional development; and thirty-minute Debrief and Discussion exercises to discuss the course materials and debate on the kinds of strategies required to strengthen their leadership competencies.

The one-day programs for working professionals include:

1. Negotiations & Mediation Strategies for Managers
The workshop engages participants to explore their strengths and weaknesses in negotiating a deal. Participants will learn the best practices and strategies to achieve optimal results in the workplace.

2. Leadership Best Practices: Managing Career Accelerators and Derailers

Offers participants an avenue to learn and equip themselves with best practices and right skill sets to address opportunities and challenges in today's ever-evolving world.

3. Transforming Workplace through High-Impact Teams

Provides participants with new knowledge, tools, and techniques to achieve high level performance and outcomes in the workplace as a team.

4. Maximizing Your Leadership Potentials: EQ, SQ, and RQ

Allows participants to acquire a sense of self-awareness and social awareness, and develop strong relationship and self-management practices as part of their leadership journey.

5. Developing a Powerful Gender Partnership: Shared Values, Goals, and Action

Created to help women leaders identify where their value-add can be fully utilized in the workplace. The 'personal' element aims to help participants develop their core competencies while the 'organizational' component discusses best practices to achieve an effective gender partnership.

Meanwhile, the Center is offering five three-day programs for college and university students:

6. Mega-Trends of the 21st Century and Talents Required

Participants will learn about six mega-trends of the 21st century that impact the way we work, live, and play. Through the workshop, participants will discover best practices and strategies to tackle complex problems in the modern world.

7. Becoming a Professional Thinker

The fast-moving globalized world offers opportunities as well as challenges. The workshop helps participants to develop higher-order cognitive skills that provide both on-the-ground and birds-eye perspectives that would assist in identifying opportunities and turning downsides to upsides as means to invent a new future that is purposeful and intentional.

8. Enhancing Your Effectiveness in Communications

Designed to aspire youth to master the art of exercising effective influence through outstanding communication skills. The workshop exposes participants to ways of communicating clearly, persuasively, and thoughtfully to diverse audiences in order to achieve engagement and participation.

9. Unleashing Creative & Innovative Capacities

The workshop enables participants to learn core competency skills such as creative thinking, practical reasoning, constructive collaborations, and communication skills to resolve multi-disciplinary and open-ended problems in today's challenging world.

10. Cultivating the Entrepreneurial Mindset
It introduces participants to the idea of intrapreneurship: an entrepreneurial process of innovating within an organization in order to stay relevant in the competitive world.

At ALI, we are committed to developing the most effective leadership prototype for Asia. Currently, the continent boasts many great business leaders, yet innovative ideas and endeavors are often left stranded. We envision an Asian Facebook, Google, McKinsey, and Pfizer—but in today's Asia, these types of ventures often do not get the opportunity to realize their full potential due to ineffective and corrupt political leadership. Shockingly, according to Transparency International, 64 percent of Asian countries score from the mid to high-range level of corruption, and only four of the twenty-eight countries in the Asia-Pacific group fall in the low corruption range. Identifying potential future leaders, equipping them with ethical and forward-looking modes of thought, and training them in adaptive and innovative practices will require patience, time, and continuous efforts. But with ALI's dedication in grooming leaders of tomorrow, I am confident that we can see substantive progress in achieving this ambitious goal.

The Acumen Case Center

Our third main initiative is the Acumen Case Center (ACC), a research think tank based in Kuala Lumpur, Malaysia. Thanks to Professor Katherine Merseth from the Harvard Graduate School of Education, Professor Arthur Kleinman from Harvard University

Asia Center, and Professor David Garvin from Harvard Business School, two years before its establishment, I had conducted extensive research, developed innovative education prototypes, and designed actionable models that can be used to reform the transmission-heavy, rote-learning, and regurgitation-based model of education prevalent in many classrooms in Asia.

Based on the framework of "knowing, doing, and being," the ACC aims to train educators, administrators, policy-makers, and even students who are passionate about education in Asia. It also investigates local and global issues, with the goal of formulating case studies and practical programs that will help to resolve them. Today, the ACC focuses on Asia's antiquated and to some extent, dysfunctional education system, assisting educational institutions to re-establish its authority and credibility as a place of learning and development, equipping next generation leaders with knowledge, skills, and mentality that are crucial in the 21st century. Such an approach would mean learning new pedagogical methods to teaching so that students could acquire eight important skills necessary for success in the 21st century: four "ways of doing"—practical reasoning creativity, communication, and collaboration—and four "ways of being"—reflection, empathy, citizenship, and adaptation. The ACC currently uses two central methods of teaching and learning: the case method, and the Harkness conference-table method to convey these skills.

As part of our initial attempt to embark on such endeavors, we organized the "Case Method: A Way Forward for Effective Pedagogy" program in August 2016 which was mentioned earlier. We are committed to carrying out more programs such as this to meet the learning needs of leaders who are keen to strengthen their analytical thinking skills as they face the challenges of 21st century leadership in various areas including education.

To facilitate the ACC's strategy and efforts, Acumen Publishing (AP), its publishing arm, was established in February 2014. Besides developing contents for teaching and learning, AP provides an avenue to Trekkers, Fellows, scholars, and visiting experts to formulate groundbreaking ideas, offer strong guiding expertise, and disseminate insightful analyses to various individuals and organizations in Asia and beyond. This is conducted through online and print publications including books, newsletters, blogs, and editorials.

AP is currently working toward publishing its own material. To date, it has published four paperbacks, with this volume being the seventh in all, and third of its ALT ten-book series. AP aims to publish at least one book annually based on personal essays from the Asia Leadership Trek, with two or more paperbacks on leadership-related topics in Asia. The next two years' projects include *Women & Leadership in Asia*, *Unleashing the Power of Influence*, *Becoming a Professional Thinker*, and *Cases on Asian Leadership Practices*.

For *Women & Leadership in Asia*, I have selected one influential female leader from each of the eighteen countries that the ALT has visited so far, analyzing their leadership styles, triumphs, and failures in order to shed light on challenges facing Asian women leaders. The book offers insights on how women in positions of power have overcome obstacles to advance their career and sends a message of hope and inspiration to aspiring women leaders in Asia and the rest of the world.

Meanwhile *Unleashing the Power of Influence* introduces shared practices from Harvard on ways to bring effective discussion schemes that produce meaningful progress, and discusses conditions and competencies that foster a healthy culture of productivity and collaborative innovation. This promotes creative thinking to help us solve problems at home and in the workplace. Catered primarily toward the Asian audience, it discusses the why, what, and how of collaboration—the rationale, design requirements, and insights—necessary for a discussion mechanism to generate real work.

Becoming a Professional Thinker discusses key skills and attributes needed to meet the expectations of our ever-changing world. Again, catered to educators in Asia, the book explains that despite the high level of academic achievement, particularly in Asia's advanced economies, students are ill-prepared to take on challenges of the 21st century. The problem with Asia's exam-based approach to learning is that it is founded solely on knowledge accumulation. Besides a foundation of "knowing," education should adopt the concepts of "learning by doing" which develops creative skills and "learning by being" which enhances life skills. Examining where Asia is now and where it needs to go, this book illustrates the skills and knowledge that can be gained from "learning by doing and being": practical reasoning, creativity, communication, collaboration, reflection, empathy, citizenship, and adaptation. This book then introduces how the case method of learning can help to address this issue. It shows how this kind of educational module can be applied in East Asia and the types of activities that 21st century individuals should be engaging in. Implementing change is not a task that can be accomplished easily. There are systemic and individual challenges such as policy reform, cultural barriers, as well as teachers and students' beliefs about learning, to name a few. Nevertheless, this book provides a call to action and gives readers a glimpse into the vision that we must endeavor to contribute to the development of our schools and communities.

The final book, *Cases on Asian Leadership Practices* is a compilation of cases on creativity and innovation, namely learning how to think and ask good questions, developing creative thinking skills, and building high-impact teams that can be widely used as a manual for training purposes for our program participants.

Conclusion

Ultimately, the Asia Leadership Trek, Asia Leadership Institute, and Acumen Case Center aim to bring innovative and adaptive leadership techniques to Asia, while learning from current systems as well as individuals who strive for progress and change in Asia. All three initiatives are committed to tackling complex leadership challenges in the political, entrepreneurial, educational, and social realms, emphasizing cooperation and the exchange of knowledge and best practices that invent new future through progress and breakthrough results. It is my hope that all three initiatives will continue to offer fresh perspectives to up-and-coming and established leaders in Asia, and expose them to current global trends and an array of learning tools that will help them fulfil everyone's shared aspiration, value, and outcomes. I strongly believe that all our communities will greatly benefit from our endeavors and as we continue to chart new ways for the betterment of the society at large.

Editor's Acknowledgments

•••

I would like to acknowledge the help of all the people involved in the Asia Leadership Trek 2016, Asia Entrepreneurship Trek and Asia Leadership Trek VII, and those who have had a hand in the publication of this book.

Thank you to all the Trekkers, with whom I spent a memorable time traveling and learning in a once-in-a-lifetime journey throughout Asia: Aaron Jay Kleiman, Adam George Malaty-Uhr, Annie Yu Kleiman, Benjamin Goh Chun Wei, Carolyn Elizabeth Fallert, Chow Shenn Kuan, Clare Claro, Daniel Junghyun Kim, Dominique Liana Russo, Elsa Babette Kania, Eunhae Grace Oh, Faustino John Henry Lim, Hazel Yek Kai Jeng, Jiro Yoshino, Jonathan Yeoh Guan Aik, Khongorzul Bat-Ireedui, Krishna Prasad Kantheti, Kristen Sproat Colley, Léonie Selom Marie Allard, Matthew Clarence Bruce, Mauricio Cardenas Gonzalez, Rachel Tamar Lipson, Shravya Mallavarapu, Steven Coda Colley, Thomas Seymour Zimmerman, Weili Germaine Chua, Umar Shavurov, Sarah Golkar, Katarina Sabova, and Justin Hartley.

I also would like to thank to each and every one of the authors who contributed their time, effort, and dedication to this book: Rachel Lipson, Annie Yu Kleiman, Benjamin Goh, Lisa Lee, Umar Shavurov, Sarah Golkar, Katarina Sabova, and Justin Hartley. My sincere gratitude to the Treks' individual supporters, co-organizers, and partners who were instrumental in helping us to successfully organize our programs in various cities across Asia. The Treks wouldn't have happened without your encouragement and contribution:

Asia Leadership Trek 2016

Shanghai: Professor Li Lifan, Associate Research Professor at Shanghai Academy of Social Sciences (SASS); Dr. Wang Chengzhi, Research Fellow with the Institute of Asia and Pacific Studies at SASS; Mr. Fu Hao and Mr. Hu Wen, Directors at the Shanghai Stock Exchange (SSE); Shanghai World Financial Center Observatory (SWFC); Dr. James Geng Jing, Board Chair and President of Greenland Financial Holdings Group; Anomaly Shanghai; Guan Sheng Yuan (GSY) Group; Mr. Li Jun Wan, General Manager of GSY Group; Shanghai University of Finance and Economics (SUFE); Stone Fresh; Ms. Christine Wang, representative of the Entrepreneur Center; Ms. Joan Zhang, Chairman of the Board of Director of Library Project; Mr. Mingju Fao, Vice President of Xinxindai Internet Finance; Mr. Raefer K Wallis, Director of A00 Architecture; Director of the Xuhui Administrative District Service Center; Mr. Alan Stafford, Frog Design's Principal Strategist, Hammans Stallings, and Senior Solutions Architect; the Headmaster, teachers, and students of Shanghai Lixin University of Commerce; Shanghai Wenlai High School; Shanghai Wenlai International School; Mr. Shen Yizhen, and Founder and Headmaster of Shanghai Wenlai High School and Shanghai Wenlai International School.

Singapore: Mr. Darrel Kon, Business Development Director, *SCAPE; Ms. Elim Chew, 77th Street Founder; Professor Tan Eng Chye, Deputy President of Academic Affairs, National University of Singapore (NUS); Professor Kishore Mahbubani, Dean and Professor in the Practice of Public Policy, Lee Kuan Yew School of Public Policy, NUS; Mr. James Thong, Manager, Office of Corporate Relations, NUS; Mr. Joel Tng and Ms. Lavanya Kumaresh, Student Ambassadors of NUS; senior researchers at Singapore-MIT Alliance for Research and Technology (SMART); Mr. Reuben Wong, Manager, National Information Infrastructure, Infocomm Development Authority of Singapore (IDA); Mr. Alex Tan, Director, National Information Infrastructure, IDA; and Mr. Abel Ang, CEO, Economic Development Innovations Singapore.

Johor Bahru: Sunway Integrated Properties team; Sunway Constructions and Properties; Mr. Gerard Soosay, CEO, Sunway Iskandar; Ms. Hor Poh Choo, Principal, Sunway College Johor Bahru; Office of the Menteri Besar of Johor; Mr. Mohamed Khaled Nordin, Menteri Besar of Johor; Dr. Gerard Kho, Chief Marketing Officer, Medini Iskandar Malaysia Sdn Bhd; Ms. Zulaifah Abdul Ghani, Chief Financial Officer, Medini Iskandar Malaysia Sdn Bhd; Mr. Azlan Akil; Vice President – Stakeholder & Media Management, Medini Iskandar Malaysia Sdn Bhd;

Kuala Lumpur: Mr. Muhammad bin Ibrahim, Governor of Bank Negara Malaysia; senior management of Bank Negara Malaysia; Sasana Kijang Museum and Art Gallery, Bank Negara Malaysia; Mr. Razman M. Hashim, Deputy Chairman, Sunway Group; Dr. Ramon

Navaratnam, Corporate Advisor, Sunway Group; Professor Lin See-Yan, President of the Harvard Club and Jeffrey Cheah Foundation Trustee; Ms. Sarena Cheah, Managing Director of Property Development Division for Malaysia and Singapore, Sunway Group; Mr. HC Chan, CEO, Sunway Shopping Malls and Theme Parks; Mr. Lau Beng Long, Managing Director, Sunway Group Healthcare Services; Ms. Nadiah Wan, Chief Operating Officer, Clinical Services, Sunway Medical Centre; Mr. Idris Jusoh, Minister of Higher Education; the Ministry of Education Malaysia; Mr. Le Luong Minh, ASEAN Secretary-General; Ms. Rafidah Aziz, Chairman, Supermax Corporation Berhad; Mr. Ding Lee Leong, Executive Editor-in-Chief at Oriental Daily; Khazanah Nasional Berhad; Khazanah Research Institute (KRI); Mr. Charon Mokhzani, Managing Director of KRI; Dr. Muhammed Abdul Khalid, former Director of Research, KRI; CIMB Group; Mr. Tengku Zafrul Aziz, Group Chief Executive, CIMB Group; Ms. Ruby Khong, Past President of Kechara Soup Kitchen; Ms. Nina Teng, Vice President of Public Affairs, Grab; Ms. Shirley Maya Tan, blogger for Huffington Post; Ms. Ng Yeen Seen, Chief Operations Officer, Asia Strategy and Leadership Institute; and Mr. Tunku Ali Redhauddin Tunku Muhriz, Special Speaker at the Asia Leadership Conference 2016 in Kuala Lumpur.

Phnom Penh: Mr. Tuon Thavrak, Secretary of State, Ministry of Planning (MOP); Dr. In Channy, President and Group Managing Director, ACLEDA Bank Plc.; Mr. Ek Sonn Chan, Secretary of State, Ministry of Industry and Handicraft; Mr. Men Nimmith, Acting Executive Director, Arbitration Council Foundation (ACF); Cambodia-Korea Cooperation Center; Mr. Vongsey Vissoth, Secretary of State, Ministry of Economy and Finance (MEF) and Vice Chairman of the

Supreme National Economic Council (SNEC); Dr. Hang Chuon Naron, Minister of Education, Youth and Sport; Mr. Sun Chanthol, Senior Minister and Minister of Commerce; Mr. Samdech Techo Hun Sen, Prime Minister of the Kingdom of Cambodia; Mr. Prak Sokhon, Minister of Posts and Telecommunications; Ms. Kristina Diotima Von Knobelsdorff, United Nations Resident Coordinator of Cambodia; Mr. Om Yin Tieng, Senior Minister, Head of the Anti-Corruption Unit (ACU) and Human Rights Committee; Ms. Chea Serey, General Director, National Bank of Cambodia; Mr. Hun Many, Member of the National Assembly of Cambodia and Honorary Chairman of the Union Youth Federations of Cambodia; Mr. Hem Vanndy, Under Secretary of State, Ministry of Economy and Finance, and Country Director of Cambodia for the Asia Leadership Trek; and the leadership team of Phnom Penh Business School.

Dhaka: Senior officials of the Ministry of Foreign Affairs of the Republic of Bangladesh; Mr. Md. Shahiar Alam, MP and State Minister of the Ministry of Foreign Affairs of the Republic of Bangladesh; Mr. Md. Shahidul Haque, Secretary of the Ministry of Foreign Affairs of the Republic of Bangladesh; Professor Dr. Gowher Rizvi, Advisor to the Prime Minister and Chief of Governance Innovation Unit (GIU); Mr. Md. Abdul Halim, Director General of GIU; Mr. Devabrata Chakraborty, Director of Research and Capacity Development of the Prime Minister's Office; senior leaders, student council, and clubs of North South University; Mr. M. A. Kashem, Chairman and Board of Trustees of North South University; Dr. Hasanuzzaman, External Affairs Officer of North South University; Professor M. Emdadul Haq, Student Affairs Director of North South University; Professor M. Mahboob Rahman, Dean of School of Business and Economics,

North South University; and Professor G.U. Ahsan, Dean of School of Health and Life Sciences of North South University, and Chairman of the Department of Public Health; senior leaders and students of the Aga Khan Education Service; Mr. Amyn Saleh, Chairman of the Aga Khan Development Network; Ms. Munir Merali, Resident Representative of the Aga Khan Development Network; senior leaders of Generation Next Garment Company; Mr. Mohd Ahkter, Direction of Generation Next Garment Company; and senior leaders of BRAC.

Asia Entrepreneurship Trek

Tokyo: Representatives of #HIVE Shibuya and ABBALab; and senior management of 21 Century Club J-Seed Ventures/Venture Generation, EGG JAPAN Incubation Center of Mitsubishi Estate, 500 Startups Japan, MUJI Japan, University of Tokyo I-LAB, Justa, The Bridge, and CyberAgent Ventures.

Taipei: The Entrepreneurship and Business Administration Department of the National Taiwan University; Epoch Foundation; Garage+; Alpha Camp; Taiwan Research-based Biopharmaceutical Manufacturers Association (TRPMA); Sentri Taiwan; and senior leaders of PegaCasa.

Seoul: The Center for Creative Korea; SM Entertainment Business Center; Viva Republica; D.CAMP, LINE; and senior leaders of Fintech Asia.

Editor's Acknowledgments 299

Asia Leadership Trek VII

Dushanbe: Spitamen Bank; European Bank for Reconstruction and Development (EBRD) Tajikistan; Kazkombank; RSM Tajikistan; International Department of the Ministry of Energy; State Committee on Investment and State Property Management of the Republic of Tajikistan; and Vice Minister of the Ministry of Energy on Implementation of Energy Investment Projects in Tajikistan.

Bishkek: Osh State University; Youth of Osh; members of the Opposition Party; Ms. Roza Otunbayeva, former President of Kyrgyzstan; International Business Council Board Members; American Chamber of Commerce; Mr. Azmat Ibraimov, Associate Banker of EBRD; Transparency International Kyrgyzstan; Red Crescent of Kyrgyzstan; Mr. Omurbek Babnov, Member of Parliament; ProKG; Club of Professionals; Alumni of Ivy League Institutions; Mr. Shamil Ibragimov, Executive Director of Soros Foundation-Kyrgyzstan; Ms. Aida Kozhalieva, representative of Helvetas Swiss Intercooperation; Mr. Temirbek Azhykulov, Board Member of Business Association JIA; Mr. Sharshekeev Chingiz, CEO of QuantX; Mr. Andrew Wachtel, President of American University of Central Asia; Mr. Emil Umetaliev, CEO of Kyrgyz Concept; Mr. Azamat Dikambaev, CEO of NISR; Mr. Tolkunbek Abdygulov, CEO of NBKR; Mr. Azis Abakirov, CEO of Association of Software Developers; senior leaders of Shoro Corporation; and Bishkek International School.

Almaty: The organizing team of Almaty Universiade 2017; Mr. Margulan Seisembaev, a Business Oligarchy in Kazakhstan; Mr. Kairat Mazhibaev, Chairman of the Board at JSC Investment Financial House RESMI; Globalink; senior consultants at EBRD Almaty;

Kazkommertsbank; Mr. Timur Issatayev, CEO of Verny Investment Holdings; Mr. Kanat Nurov, President of Aspandau Foundation; and Professor Dina Sharipova, Assistant Professor of the Department of International Relations and Regional Studies, KIMEP University.

Astana: Senior management and students of Nazarbayev University; Ms. Kadisha Dairova, Vice President of Students Affairs, International Cooperation, Government Relations of Nazarbayev University; Mr. Arman Zhumazhanov, Director of the Department of International Cooperation, Nazarbayev University; Mr. Shigeo Katsu, President of Nazarbayev University; Mr. Yerzhan Ashikbayev, Deputy Minister of the Ministry of Foreign Affairs of the Republic of Kazakhstan; Mr. Meizhan Yussupov, CFO of Kazatomprom; Mr. Maxat Kabashev, CFO of Kazakhstan Temir Zholy Railway; Mr. Nurlan Kussainov, CEO of Astana International Financial Center Authority; Samruk-Kazyna Fund; AIFC Academy; Mr. Asset Yerali, CEO of Continental Logistics; and Mr. Talgat Zhumagulov, Deputy Head of the Senate Administration of the Parliament of Kazakhstan.

Tashkent: Dr. Sherzod Shermatov, Rector of Inha University in Tashkent; Mr. Fushimi Katsutoshi, Chief Representative of the Japan International Cooperation Agency in Uzbekistan; United National Development Program; Mr. Eskender Trushin, Senior Economist of Global Practice for Macroeconomics & Fiscal Management of Europe and Central Asia Region; and Mr. Olivier Durand, Senior Agriculture Economist from the World Bank.

I would like to thank several individuals who played an important role in making the Malaysian leg of the Trek a success, particularly the Asia Leadership Conference at Sunway University: Dr. Jeffrey Cheah, Founder and Chairman of Sunway Group, and Founding Trustee of the Jeffrey Cheah Foundation; Dr. Weng Keng Lee, CEO of Education and Healthcare Division, Sunway Group; Dr. Elizabeth Lee, Senior Executive Director of the Sunway Education Group; Ms. Ng Beng Lean, Director of the Office of the Senior Executive Director of the Sunway Education Group; and Professor Graeme Wilkinson, Vice-Chancellor, Sunway University.

I wish to express my sincere appreciation to Ms. Ida Fazila Ismail, Head of Acumen Case Center at CALI Malaysia for overseeing the content and applying editorial best practices in this book.

I am truly overwhelmed by the support of my brilliant team at CALI Boston, Ms. Ursula DeYoung, Advisor of Publication Affairs, and CALI Malaysia: Dr. Gin Chee Tong, Head of Strategy and Management; Ms. Jocelyn Lew En Mei, Strategy and Management Executive; Ms. Farzeera Emir, Executive Assistant to President; and the Center's interns, Michelle S Lee and Serena Kaan Tsu Li, who worked hard toward the successful publication of this book.

I would also like to thank Ms. Ruma Lopes, Assistant Director, Pre-University Studies and Director of Programme of Sunway Foundation Programme at Sunway College for providing a fresh pair of eyes in reviewing the final copy of the manuscript before it went to press.

Thank you everyone for your assistance, generosity, and commitment.

| Appendix I |
Trek and Fellowship Itinerary

∙ ∙ ●

Asia Leadership Fellowship 2016

Date	Events
July 4 – 6	**Mongolia Executive Leadership Program** New Perspectives on Leadership Ulaanbaatar, Mongolia
July 11 – 15	**Asia Leadership Youth Program** Developing a Powerful Personal Brand Kuala Lumpur, Malaysia
July 18 – 22	**Asia Leadership Scholar Program** Developing a Successful Career Path Kuala Lumpur, Malaysia
July 24 – 28	**Trilateral Leadership Summit III** Incheon, Korea
July 31 – August 4	**Central Asia Youth Leadership Camp** Pohang, Korea
August 8 – 12	**Acumen Case Center Program** Harvard's Way of Teaching and Learning Kuala Lumpur, Malaysia
	Asia Leadership Executive Program Personal Leadership: Ethics, Power and Decision Making Kuala Lumpur, Malaysia

August 15 – 30	**Global Leadership Trek** Preparing for the Next Generation Leadership New York, Washington D.C., and Boston, USA
November 24 – 26	**Asia Leadership Executive Program** Community Leadership: Leading Change for Organizational Renewal Kuala Lumpur, Malaysia

●●●

Asia Leadership Trek 2016

Sunday, December 27

	Arrival in Shanghai from Boston

Monday, December 28

8:45am	Meeting with Professor Li Lifan, Associate Research Professor & Dr. Wang Chengzhi, Research Fellow with the Institute of Asia and Pacific Studies, Shanghai Academy of Social Sciences
11:00am	Meeting with Senior Directors at Shanghai Stock Exchange
2:30pm	Guided Tour at Shanghai World Financial Center Observatory

Tuesday, December 29

9:00am	Meeting with Anomaly Shanghai
10:30am	Guided Tour and Lunch with the Chief Director Xuhui Administrative District Service Center
2:00pm	Dialogue with Frog Design's Principal Strategist, Hammans Stallings, and Senior Solutions Architect, Alan Stafford
4:30pm	Meeting & Dinner with the Headmaster and Teachers & Networking Sessions with Students of the Shanghai Lixin University Of Commerce

Appendix I | Trek and Fellowship Itinerary 305

6:00pm	Introduction of Lixin University
6:15pm	Opening Remarks by Hungsoo S. Kim, President of Center for Asia Leadership Initiatives (CALI)
6:30pm	Special Talk on Perspective on Leadership by Matthew Bruce (HKS MPP and Wharton MBA)
6:45pm	Leadership Workshops on Leadership and Management by Steven Colley (HKS MPP), and 'Transitioning from School to Work' by Carolyn Fallert (HBS MBA)

Wednesday, December 30

9:00am	Meeting with Board Chair & President of Greenland Financial Holdings Group, Dr. James Geng Jing
10:30am	Tour of Entrepreneruship & Innovation Lab at Guan Sheng Yuan
11:00am	Meeting & Lunch at Stone Fresh, F&B Startup
12:30pm	Speech with Li Jun Wan, General Manager of GSY Group & Chinese Music Performance followed by Q&A Session
3:00pm	Guided Tour of Shanghai University Of Finance And Economics and its Startup Incubation Lab
4:00pm	Pitch Presentation by Representative of the Entrepreneur Center, Christine Wang, the Chairman of the Board of Director of Library Project, Joan Zhang, and Vice President of Xinxindai Internet Finance, Mingju Fao
6:00pm	A00 Architecture

Thursday, December 31

9-3pm	**Asia Leadership Conference 2016 in Shanghai, China**
9:00am	Opening Remarks by the Founder & Headmaster, Shen Yizhen
9:10am	Welcoming Speech by Hungsoo S. Kim, President of Asia Leadership Trek (ALT)
9:15am	Forum Discussion on 'Decision Making, Social Impact, Managing Between Cultures' by Krishna Kantheti (HBS MBA), Thomas Zimmerman (Fletcher MALD), Benjamin Goh (HKS MPP)
10:00am	Group Photo

10:15pm	Career Mentoring and Networking Sessions on Finance, Writing and Publishing, Education and Social Enterprise, International Development, International Organizations, Academic Research and Think Tanks, Consulting, Non-Profits, Health Policy, Politics, and Diplomacy
11:30am	Closing Remarks by Principal, Feng Zhigang
11:40am	Guided Tour of SWIS
12:30pm	Lunch
1:30pm	Leadership Workshop Sessions on Arts of Communication, Influencing Techniques: How to be More Effective, Leadership and Management, and Applying to US Universities
3:00pm	New Year Party SWIS
5:00pm	Presentation and Guided Tour of the K11 Art Mall

Friday, January 1

9:00am	Sightseeing of Shanghai: The Bund, People's Square, and Financial Center
4:00pm	Travel to Singapore

Saturday, January 2

	City Tour of Singapore

Sunday, January 3

10:00am	Presentation on SCAPE by Darrel Kon, Business Development Director and on Social Enterprise Scene in Singapore by Elim Chew followed by Q&A
11:00am	Guided Tour of SCAPE
12:00pm	Lunch at Kokomama
2:00pm	Free Time

Monday, January 4

10:00am	National University of Singapore Campus Tour & Tour of Yale Campus

Appendix I | Trek and Fellowship Itinerary 307

11:30am	Welcome and Introduction by Prof Tan Eng Chye, Deputy President of Academic Affairs. Discussion on the topic of "NUS – Leading the Way in Asia." With Professor Kishore Mahbubani, Dean and Professor in the Practice of Public Policy, Lee Kuan Yew School of Public Policy followed by Q&A
12:30pm	Meeting with Seniors Researchers at Singapore-MIT Alliance for Research and Technology (SMART)
3:00pm	Presentation by Abel Ang, CEO of Economic Development Innovations Singapore on "Exporting Singapore's Successful Economic Development Model to Asia."
5:30pm	Tour of One-North Gallery at EDIS

Tuesday, January 5

9:00am	Guided Tour of Infocomm Development Authority of Singapore
9:30pm	Presentation on Smart Nation Initiatives by Reuben Wong, Manager, National Information Infrastructure
10:00am	Q&A Session with Alex Tan, Director of National Information Infrastructure at IDA
11:00am	Travel to Johor Bahru, Malaysia
12:30pm	Lunch Meeting with Sunway Integrated Properties team at Grand Straits Garden Seafood Restaurant
3:00pm	Guided Tour of Sunway Iskandar Gallery and Presentation on 'Property Development and Sustainability' by Sunway Constructions and Properties
4:00pm	Visit to Sunway Southern Region Office and Vantage Point; Presentation by Gerard Soosay, CEO, Sunway Iskandar on Urban Planning Landscape in Malaysia and Singapore
5:00pm	Guided Tour of Medini, a governmental agency that engages in property development, township management services, and infrastructure development of Iskandar Development Project

Wednesday, January 6

9-1pm	**Asia Leadership Conference 2016 in Johor Bahru, Malaysia**

9:00am	Welcoming Speech by Hungsoo S. Kim, President of ALT
9:10am	Opening Remarks by Dr. Elizabeth Lee, Senior Executive Director, Sunway Education Group
9:20am	Special Talk on 'Leadership in Development and Practice' by Dominique Russo (HKS MCMPA)
9:40am	Refreshments and Networking Session
10:00am	Leadership Workshops on Design Thinking & Innovation, Overcoming Immunity to Change, Political Organizing, Art of Communication, Effective Language Acquisition, Leadership and Management, Influence with Authority, Understanding Narratives, Security and Conflict in the Cyber Age, Influencing Techniques: How to be More Effective, and Cross-Cultural Communication
11:30am	Special Talk on 'Adaptive Change in Motion' by Catherine Fallert (HBS MBA)
12:00pm	Closing Remarks by Hor Poh Choo, Principal of Sunway College Johor
3:00pm	Guided Tour of Menteri Besar of Johor Bahru's Administrative Office
3:30pm	A roundtable discussion with YBhg Dato' Mohamed Khaled Nordin, Menteri Besar of Johor on "Johor – Malaysia's Economic Powerhouse"
5:00pm	Free Time

Thursday, January 7

9:00am	Travel to Malacca, Malaysia
11:00am	Tour of Malacca: A Famosa, St. Paul's Church, Queen Victoria's Foundation, Christ Church Melaka, Cheng Hoon Teng Temple, and Baba and Nyonya Heritrage Museum
4:00pm	Depart for Kuala Lumpur, Malaysia

Friday, January 8

10:00am	Dialogue with Mr. Muhammad bin Ibrahim, Deputy Governor of Bank Negara Malaysia on the topic: "Financial Market in Asia: Best Practices from Malaysia"
11:00am	Tour of of Sasana Kijang and Museum & Art Gallery of the Central Bank

Appendix I | Trek and Fellowship Itinerary 309

12:00pm	Lunch and Interaction with Senior Management of the Central Bank
2:00pm	Guided Tour of Kuala Lumpur
4:00pm	Meeting & Dinner with Sunway Group - Welcome remarks by Mr. Razman M. Hashim, Deputy Chairman of Sunway Group, followed by Keynote & Q&A by Dr. Ramon Navaratnam, Corporate Advisor - Panel Discussion on Sustainability and Women Participation in Workforce - Special Talk by Professor Lin See-Yan, President of the Harvard Club and Jeffrey Cheah Foundation Trustee

Saturday, January 9

9-5pm	**Asia Leadership Conference 2016 in Kuala Lumpur, Malaysia**
8:30am	Registration
9:00am	Opening Remarks by Hungsoo S. Kim President of ALT
9:10am	Welcoming Speech by Dr. Elizabeth Lee, Senior Executive Director of Sunway Education Group
9:20am	Keynote Address on 'Asia in the 21st Century World' by Ms. Rafidah Aziz, Chairman of Supermax Corporation
10:00am	Tea Break & Networking
10:15am	Special Talk on 'The Importance of Knowing Yourself and Your Story' by Dominique Russo (HKS MCMPA)
10:30am	Forum Discussion on 'Women in Leadership – An Asian Perspective' by Ms. Ruby Khong, Past President of Kechara Soup Kitchen; Ms. Nina Teng, Vice President of Public Affairs of Grab Taxi; Ms. Shirley Maya Tan, Blogger of Huffington Post; and Ms. Ng Yeen Seen, Chief Operations Officer of Asia Strategy and Leadership Institute
11:20am	Workshop Breakout Session 1
12:40pm	Lunch
1:30pm	Forum Discussion on 'Leadership in Asia – Insights & Inspirations' with Special Speaker, Tunku Ali Redhauddin ibni Tuanku Muhriz
2:00pm	Workshop Breakout Session 2
3:20pm	Tea Break & Networking
3:40pm	Career Mentoring Session
4:20pm	Professional Development Session

5:00pm	Closing Remarks by Professor Graeme Wilkinson, Vice-Chancellor of Sunway University

Sunday, January 10

9:00am	Tour of Kuala Lumpur: Petronas Twin Towers, Kuala Lumpur Tower, Merdeka Square, Batu Caves, and Sultan Abdul Samad Building

Monday, January 11

11:00am	"Soaring Upwards" briefing by Honorable Idris Jusoh, Minister of Higher Education followed by Q&A
12:00pm	Lunch at the Ministry of Education
3:00pm	Presentation on 'Media Landscape in Malaysia,' by Oriental Daily followed by Tea & Networking
7:00pm	Dialogue with His Excellency Le Luong Minh, ASEAN Secretary-General

Tuesday, January 12

10:00am	Guided Tour of Khazanah Research Institute
10:30am	Presentation on "The State of Households in Malaysia" by Mr. Charon Mokhzani, Managing Director of KRI, and Dr. Muhammed Abdul Khalid, Director of Research, Inequality of Wealth, Income & Opportunities followed by Q&A
12:00pm	Lunch & Networking
1:30pm	Tour of Kuala Lumpur
4:00pm	Guided Tour of CIMB Group
4:30pm	Presentation on 'Finance and Banking Industry in Malaysia and ASEAN' by Tengku Zafrul Aziz, Group Chief Executive and Management
5:30pm	Tea & Networking

Appendix I | Trek and Fellowship Itinerary   311

Wednesday, January 13

7:00am	Travel to Phnom Penh, Cambodia
9:00am	Meeting with H.E. Tuon Thavrak, Secretary of State, Ministry of Planning (MOP)
10:30am	Visit Tuol Sleng Genocide Museum or S21 Prison
12:00pm	Luncheon Hosted by Dr. In Channy, President and Group Managing Director of ACLEDA Bank Plc.
2:30pm	Meeting with H.E. Ek Sonn Chan, Secretary of State, Ministry of Industry and Handicraft
4:00pm	Meeting with Mr. Men Nimmith, Acting Executive Director of Arbitration Council Foundation (ACF)
5:30pm	Dinner on boat cruise along the Four Rivers in front of the Royal Palace, Phnom Penh

Thursday, January 14

9:00am	Meeting with H.E. Vongsey Vissoth, Secretary of State, Ministry of Economy and Finance (MEF) and Vice Chairman of Supreme National Economic Council (SNEC)
10:30am	Meeting with H.E. Dr. Hang Chuon Naron, Minister of Education, Youth and Sport
2:00pm	Meeting with H.E. Sun Chanthol, Senior Minister and Minister of Commerce (HKS, Mason Fellow)
5:00pm	Courtesy Call on Samdech Techo Hun Sen, Prime Minister of the Kingdom of Cambodia
7:30pm	Welcome Dinner hosted by H.E. Prak Sokhon, Minister of Posts and Telecommunications

Friday, January 15

9:00am	Meeting with Kristina Diotima Von Knobelsdorff, United Nations Resident Coordinator of Cambodia
11:00am	Meeting with H.E. Om Yin Tieng, Senior Minister, Head of Anti-Corruption Unit (ACU) and Human Rights Committee

12:30pm	Courtesy Call hosted by H.E. Chea Serey, General Director of National Bank of Cambodia
1:30pm	Networking Event with Major Educational Institutions in Cambodia
3:00pm	Dialogue with H.E. Hun Many, a Member of the National Assembly of Cambodia and Honorary Chairman of Union Youth Federations of Cambodia
5:00pm	Meeting with Leadership Team of Phnom Penh Business School

Saturday, January 16

8:30am – 5:00pm	**Asia Leadership Conference 2016 in Phnom Penh, Cambodia**
8:30am	Registration
9:00am	Opening Remarks: H.E. Hem Vanndy, Under Secretary of State, Ministry of Economy and Finance and Country Director of Cambodia for the Asia Leadership Trek
9:05am	Welcoming Remarks: Mr. Hungsoo S. Kim, President of ALT
9:10am	Keynote Address by H.E. Sun Chanthol, Senior Minister and Minister of Commerce
9:20am	Special Talk on 'Becoming a Leader' by Steven Colley (HKS MPP)
9:35am	Forum Talk Show on 'Perspectives on Leadership' by Shravya Mallavarapu, Kristen Colley, Aaron Kleiman moderated by Carolyn Fallert
10:30am	Tea and Networking Session
10:50am	Workshop Breakout Session 1 on 'Design Thinking and Innovation', 'Art of Communication', 'Persuasion and Change', 'Influencing Techniques: How to be More Effective', 'Introduction to Negotiation', 'Better Together: Empowering Effective Collaboration between Men and Women', 'Navigating Differ-ences in Political Cultures', 'Becoming a Better Decision Maker', and 'Adaptive Leadership'
12:10pm	Lunch
1:00pm	Workshop Breakout Session 2: Same Topics
2:20pm	Break

Appendix I | Trek and Fellowship Itinerary 313

2:30pm	Career Mentoring Sessions on Diplomacy, Education and Social Enterprise, International Organizations, Consulting, Finance (Investment Banking/Private Equity), Academic Research and Think-Tanks, Writing and Publishing, Interviewing Skills, and Applying to U.S. Universities
3:20pm	Tea and Networking Session
3:40pm	Professional Development Seminars on Interviewing Skill: Job, Interviewing Skill: Media, Essential Presentation Skills, Dressing for Success, Resume Writing, Networking and Building Contracts, Job Search Effort in the Times of Transition, Applying to U.S. Universities: finding and Choosing the Right Program, and The Secret of Getting into Harvard or Any Other Great Schools
4:30pm	Closing Remarks and Debriefing Session by Hungsoo S. Kim, President of ALT

Sunday, January 17

11:00am	Travel to Siem Reap, Cambodia

Monday, January 18

8:00am	Tour of Angkor Wat, UNESCO World Heritage Site
12:00pm	Travel to Phnom Penh, Cambodia

Tuesday, January 19

8:00am	Travel to Dhaka, Bangladesh
6:00pm	Welcoming Dinner

Wednesday, January 20

9:00am	Meeting with Senior Officials of the Ministry of Foreign Affairs of Republic of Bangladesh
11:00am	Meeting with Md. Shahiar Alam, MP and State Minister of Foreign Ministry
1:00pm	Tour of Prime Minister's Office Complex

2:00pm	Meeting with Professor Dr. Gowher Rizvi, Adivsor to the Prime Minister and Chief of Governance Innovation Unit (GIU), Mr. Md. Abdul Halim, Director General of GIU, and Mr. Devabrata Chakraborty, Director of Research and Capacity Development of Prime Minister's Office
5:00pm	Meeting with Senior Leaders of North South University

Thursday, January 21

9:00am	Meeting with Senior Leaders and Students of Aga Khan Education Service - Meeting with Mr. Amyn Saleh, Chairman and Ms. Munir Merali, Resident Representative of Aga Khan Development Network - Discussion Forum with Students and Teachers - Organized Tour of the Campus
12:00pm	Meeting with Senior Leaders of Generation Next Garment Company & Guided Tour of the Facilities
4:00pm	Meeting with Senior Leaders of BRAC - Brac School Visit - Presentation by Mr. Md. Shahidur Rabbani, Senior Manager of Production, and Guided Tour of Aarong Dairy, BRAC Dairy & Food Project
7:00pm	Hosted Dinner by Mr. Mohd Ahkter, Director of Generation Next

Friday, January 22

9-6pm	**Asia Leadership Conference 2016 in Dhaka, Bangladesh**
9:10am	Roundtable Discussion with Senior Management, Student Council and Clubs of North South University (NSU)
11:00am	Tour of Campus
12:00pm	Hosted Lunch by NSU
1:00pm	Welcoming Remarks: Mr. M.A. Kashem, Chairman and Board of Trustees of North South University, Dr. Hasanuzzaman, External Affairs Officer, Professor M. Emdadul Haq, Student Affairs Director, and Professor M. Mahboob Rahman, Dean of School of Business and Economics
1:40pm	Opening Remarks by Mr. Hungsoo S. Kim, President of ALT

Appendix I | Trek and Fellowship Itinerary 315

1:50pm	Opening Remarks by Mr. Hungsoo S. Kim, President of ALT Keynote Address by Honorable Md. Shahidul Haque, Secretary of Foreign Ministry
2:20pm	Special Talk by Mr. Benjamin Goh, HKS MPP
2:40pm	Tea and Networking Session
3:00pm	Leadership Workshops on 'Design Thinking and Innovation,' 'Art of Communication,' 'Persuasion and Change,' 'Influencing Techniques: How to be More Effective,' 'Introduction to Negotiation,' and 'Adaptive Leadership'
4:00pm	Leadership Workshops on the same topics above
5:30pm	Closing Remarks by Professor G.U. Ahsan, Dean of School of Health and Life Sciences and Chairman of Department of Public Health

Saturday, January 23

Travel to Boston

•••

Asia Entrepreneurship Trek

Friday, March 11

Arrival in Tokyo from Boston

Saturday, March 12

9:00am	Tour of Meiji Jingu, Harajuku and Omotesando
1:30pm	Meeting with #HIVE Shibuya
3:30pm	Meeting with ABBALab

Sunday, March 13

9:00am	Guided Tour and a Dialogue with Senior Executives of the EGG JAPAN Incubation Center of Mitsubishi Estate
12:00pm	Uniqlo Japan Headquarters
2:00pm	Meeting with 21 Century Club
4:00pm	Meeting with J-Seed Ventures/Venture Generation

Monday, March 14

9:00am	Meeting with 500 Startups Japan
12:00pm	Meeting with Directors at MUJI Japan
2:00pm	Meeting with University of Tokyo I-LAB
4:00pm	Meeting with the Justa
5:30pm	Meeting with the Bridge
7:30pm	Reunion Gathering with the Harvard Kennedy School Alumni of Japan

Tuesday, March 15

9:00am	Meeting with Cyber Agent Ventures Japan
12:00pm	Travel to Taipei, Taiwan
6:00pm	Welcoming Dinner and Tour of the Night Market

Wednesday, March 16

8:30am	Meeting with the Entrepreneurship and Business Administration Department at the National Taiwan University
10:30am	Meetings with Epoch Foundation on Young Entrepreneurs of the Future and Garage+ on Startup Global Program
2:00pm	Meeting with Senior Leaders of the PegaCasa affiliated with ASUS
4:30pm	Meeting with Alpha Camp

Appendix I | Trek and Fellowship Itinerary 317

Thursday, March 17

9:00am	Meeting with Taiwan Research-based Biopharmaceutical Manufacturers Association (TRPMA)
11:30am	Meeting with Sentri Taiwan
2:00pm	Guided Tour of Hsinchu Science Park
4:00pm	Sightseeing of Chiang Kai-shek Memorial hall, Taipei 101, and Lungshan Temple of Manka
11:50pm	Travel to Seoul, Korea

Friday, March 18

9:00am	Meeting with Center for Creative Korea
11:00am	Meeting with SM Entertainment Business Center
2:00pm	Meeting with Viva Republica
5:00pm	Meeting with D.Camp

Saturday, March 19

9:00am	Guided Tour of the Samsung Innovation Museum
11:30am	Meeting with Senior Leaders of Fintech Asia
2:00pm	Meeting with LINE
4:00pm	Sightseeing of Insadong, Gwanghwamun, and Myungdong
7:00pm	Farewell Dinner

Sunday, March 20

Travel back to Boston

Asia Leadership Trek VII

Tuesday, May 31

	Arrival in Dushanbe from Boston

Wednesday, June 1

9:00am	Meeting with Spitamen Bank
11:00am	Meeting with State Committee On Investment and State Property Management of the Republic of Tajikistan
2:00pm	Meeting with European Bank for Reconstruction and Development (EBRD) Tajikistan
4:00pm	Meeting with Kazkombank

Thursday, June 2

9:00am	Meeting with RSM Tajikistan
11:30am	Meeting with the International Department of the Ministry of Energy
2:00pm	Meeting with Vice Minister of the Ministry of Energy on Implementation of Energy Investment Projects in Tajikistan
4:00pm	Tour of the Tajikistan National Museum
6:00pm	Farewell Dinner
7:00pm	Football Match between the Tajikistan National and Bangladesh National Teams

Friday, June 3

9:00am	Departure for Bishkek, Kyrgyzstan

Saturday, June 4

8:00am	Travel to Osh, Kyrgyzstan

Appendix I | Trek and Fellowship Itinerary 319

10:00am	Visited Osh State University
11:00am	Tour of Sulayman Sacred Mountain
2:00pm	Town Hall Meeting with Youth of Osh on 'Ways to Promote a Public Participation in Social Change'
5:00pm	Dinner with Members of the Opposition Party

Sunday, June 5

	Tour of City of Bishkek: Ala-Too Square, Oak Park, Kyrgyz National Philharmonic Hall, and Town Market Hiking of Ala Archa National Park

Monday, June 6

9:00am	Meeting with H.E. Roza Otunbayeva, Former President of Kyrgyzstan
11:00am	Meeting with International Business Council Board Members and American Chamber of Commerce
1:00pm	Meeting with Mr. Azmat Ibraimov, Associate Banker of EBRD
2:00pm	Meeting with Transparency International Kyrgyzstan & Red Crescent of Kyrgyzstan
4:00pm	Meeting with Honorable Omurbek Babnov, Member of Parliament
6:00pm	Meeting with ProKG, Club of Professionals and Alumni of Ivy League Institutions – Mr. Shamil Ibragimov, Executive Director of Soros Foundation-Kyrgyzstan, Ms. Aida Kozhalieva, Representative of Helvetas-Swiss Intercooperation, Mr. Temirbek Azhykulov, Board Member of Business Association JIA, Mr. Sharshekeev Chingiz, CEO of QuantX

Tuesday, June 7

9-5pm	**Asia Leadership Conference 2016 in Bishkek**
9:00am	Welcoming Remarks by Mr. Andrew Wachtel, President of American University of Central Asia

9:05am	Opening Remarks by Mr. Hungsoo S. Kim, President of ALT
9:10am	Panel Discussion: Central Asia 25 Years Since Gaining Independence: New Perspectives on Leadership and Practice with Mr. Emil Umetaliev, CEO of Kyrgyz Concept, Mr. Azamat Dikambaev CEO of NISR, and Mr. Tolkunbek Abdygulov, CEO of NBKR, moderated by Mr. Umar Shavurov, HKS, MCMPA
10:30am	Tea Break and Networking Session
10:50am	Special Talk by Ms. Katarina Sabova, Columbia MBA, and Mr. Aaron Kleiman, HKS MCMPA
11:20am	First Round of Leadership Workshops on 'Power and Influence,' 'Strength-Based Leadership,' 'Authentic Leadership,' 'Public Narrative,' 'Managing Innovation in Cyber Age Controlled Chaos,' 'Building an Organizational Culture,' 'Adaptive Leadership,' 'Language Acquisition Skills,' 'Leadership Role in the Public Sector,' and 'The Practice of Negotiations'
12:30pm	Lunch
1:00pm	Second Round of Leadership Workshops on the Same Topics
2:30pm	Professional Development Seminars on 'Dressing for Success,' 'Social Media – How to Make or Break Your Life,' 'Applying for Schools in the U.S.,' 'Be Remembered: Building Your Personal Brand,' 'Storytelling,' 'Interviewing Skills,' 'Building a Resume,' and 'Becoming an Effective Orator'
4:00pm	Career Mentoring Sessions: Management Consultant, International Development Expert, Social Entrepreneur, Lawyer, Finance Investor, Marketing Strategist, Academician, Foreign Service Officer, and IT Engineer
5:00pm	Closing Remarks by Mr. Umar Shavurov, HKS MCMPA
6:00pm	Farewell Dinner at Khan Tenir

Wednesday, June 8

9:00am	Meeting with Mr. Azis Abakirov, CEO of Association of Software Developers
11:00am	Meetings with Senior Leaders of Shoro Corporation
1:00pm	Lunch Meeting with and Tour of the Bishkek International School
2:00pm	Travel to Almaty, Kazakhstan
7:00pm	Welcome Dinner

Thursday, June 9

9:00am	Meeting with Almaty Universiade 2017 Organizing Team
11:00am	Meeting with Mr. Margulan Seisembaev, a Business Oligarchy in Kazakhstan
2:00pm	Meeting with Mr. Kairat Mazhibaev, Chairmn of the Board at JSC Investment Financial House RESMI
5:00pm	Sightseeing of Almaty: Almaty Tower, Zenkov Cathedral, and Central State Museum

Friday, June 10

9:00am	Meeting with Globalink
10:30am	Meeting with Senior Consultants at EBRD Almaty
1:30pm	Meeting with Kazkommertsbank
3:00pm	Meeting with Mr. Timur Issatayev, CEO of Verny Investment Holdings
5:30pm	Meeting with Mr. Kanat Nurov, President of Aspandau Foundation

Saturday, June 11

9-1pm	**Asia Leadership Conference 2016 in Almaty, Kazakhstan**
9:00am	Welcoming Remarks by Professor Dina Sharipova, Assistant Professor of Department of International Relations and Regional Studies, Kimep University
9:05am	Opening Remarks by Mr. Hungsoo S. Kim, President of ALT
9:10am	Special Talk by Ms. Emilie Valentova, HBS MBA
9:30am	First Round of Leadership Workshops on 'Power and Influence,' 'Strength-Based Leadership,' 'Public Narrative,' 'Language Acquisition Skills,' 'Leadership Role in the Public Sector,' and 'The Practice of Negotiations'
10:50am	Tea Break and Networking
11:10am	Second Round of Leadership Workshops on the Same Topics
12:30pm	Closing Remarks by Mr. Hungsoo S. Kim, President of ALT

Sunday, June 12

9:00am	Travel to Astana, Kazakhstan
3:00pm	Sightseeing of Astana:, Palace of Peace and Reconciliation, Khan Shatyr Center, and Nur-Astana Mosque

Monday, June 13

9:00am	Meeting with Nazarbayev University Senior Management and Students - Meeting with Ms. Kadisha Dairova, Vice President of Students Affairs, International Cooperation, Government Relations & Mr. Arman Zhumazhanov, Director of Department of International Cooperation - Organized Tour of the Campus - Meeting with Mr. Shigeo Katsu, President of Nazarbayez University
1:30pm	Guided Tour of Expo 2017 Sites
3:30pm	Meeting with Honorable Yerzhan Ashikbayev, Deputy Minister of Ministry of Foreign Affairs of the Republic of Kazakhstan
5:00pm	Sightseeing of Astana: Bayterek Tower and National Museum

Tuesday, June 14

9:00am	Meeting with Mr. Meizhan Yussupov, CFO of Kazatomprom
10:30am	Meeting with Mr. Maxat Kabashev, CFO of Kazakhstan Temir Zholy Railway
1:00pm	Meeting with Mr. Nurlan Kussainov, CEO of Astana International Financial Center Authority
2:00pm	Meeting with Samruk-Kazyna Fund and AIFC Academy
4:00pm	Meeting with Mr. Asset Yerali, CEO of Continental Logistics & Guided Tour of the Complex
7:00pm	Dinner Meeting with Mr. Talgat Zhumagulov, Deputy Head of the Senate Administration of the Parliament of Kazakhstan

Appendix I | Trek and Fellowship Itinerary   323

Wednesday, June 15

9:00am	Travel to Tashkent, Uzbekistan
3:00pm	Tour of Tashkent: Friday Mosque, Khazrati Imam Complex, The St. Alexander Nevsky Cathedral, Amir Temur Square, Independence Square, and Monument to Courage

Thursday, June 16

9-5pm	**Asia Leadership Conference 2016 in Tashkent, Uzbekistan**
9:00am	Welcoming Remarks by Dr. Sherzod Shermatov, Rector of Inha University in Tashkent
9:05am	Opening Remarks by Mr. Hungsoo S. Kim, President of ALT
9:10am	Special Talk by Mr. Justin Hartley, HKS MCMPA
9:30am	First Round of Leadership Workshops on 'Power and Influence,' 'Strength-Based Leadership,' 'Public Narrative,' 'Language Acquisition Skills,' 'Leadership Role in the Public Sector,' and 'The Practice of Negotiations'
10:50am	Tea Break and Networking
11:10am	Second Round of Leadership Workshops on the Same Topics
12:30pm	Closing Remarks by Mr. Hungsoo S. Kim, President of ALT
1:30pm	Meeting with Mr. Fushimi Katsutoshi, Chief Representative of the Japan International Cooperation Agency in Uzbekistan
2:30pm	Meeting with United National Development Program
3:00pm	Meeting with Mr. Eskender Trushin, Senior Economist of Global Practice for Macroeconomics & Fiscal Management of Europe and Central Asia Region, and Mr. Olivier Durand, Senior Agriculture Economist from The World Bank
4:00pm	Travel to Samarkand, Uzbekistan

Friday, June 17

8:00am	Sightseeing: Imam al-Bukhari Mausoleum, St. Daniel's Tomb, Ulughbek Observatory, Gur Emir Mausoleum, Bibi Khanoum Mosque, Shahi Zinda Ensemble, and Registan Square
5:00pm	Travel to Tashkent, Uzbekistan

Saturday, June 18

Depart for Boston

| Appendix II |
List of Trekkers and Fellows

● ● ●

Asia Leadership Trek 2016

Aaron Jay Kleiman, *American*
MPA, Harvard Kennedy School of Government

Adam Malaty-Uhr, *American*
Ed.M., Harvard Graduate School of Education

Afsha Akhter, *Bangladeshi*
BA (Hons.), Sunway-Lancaster University

Annie Yu Kleiman, *American*
MALD, Tufts Fletcher School of Law and Diplomacy

Benjamin Goh, *Singaporean*
MPP, Harvard Kennedy School of Government

Carolyn Elizabeth Fallert, *American*
MPA, Harvard Kennedy School of Government
MBA, Harvard Business School

Chow Shenn Kuan, *Malaysian*
BSc (Hons.), Sunway-Lancaster University

Clare Claro, *American*
MALD, Tufts Fletcher School of Law and Diplomacy

Daniel Junghyun Kim, *Korean*
BA, Handong University

Dominique Liana Russo, *American*
MPA, Harvard Kennedy School of Government
MBA, MIT Sloan School of Management

Elsa Babette Kania, *American*
BA, Harvard College

Esther Cho, *Korean/Guatemalan*
BA, Handong University

Eunhae Grace Oh, *Korean*
MPP, Harvard Kennedy School of Government

Hazel Yek Kai Jeng, *Malaysian*
MBA, Sunway-Victoria University

Hungsoo S. Kim, *Korean*
President, Center for Asia Leadership Initiatives
MPA, Harvard Kennedy School of Government

Jiro Yoshino, *Japanese*
MPA, Harvard Kennedy School of Government

John Lim, *Canadian/Filipino*
Yonsei/Fletcher, Harvard Extension School

Jonathan Yeoh Guan Aik, *Malaysian*
BSc (Hons.), Sunway-Lancaster University

Katie Yao, *Chinese*
BA, Xi'an International Studies University

Khongorzul Bat-Ireedui, *Mongolian*
MALD, Tufts Fletcher School of Law and Diplomacy

Krishna Prasad Kantheti, *Indian*
MBA, Harvard Business School

Kristen Sproat Colley, *American*
MSc, University of Oxford

Léonie Selom Marie Allard, *Korean/French*
MA, School of International Relations & Public Affairs, Science Po

Matthew Clarence Bruce, *American*
MPA, Harvard Kennedy School of Government
MBA, The Wharton School, University of Pennsylvania

Mauricio Cardenas Gonzalez, *Colombian*
MALD, Tufts Fletcher School of Law and Diplomacy

Rachel Lipson, *American*
MBA, Harvard Business School
MPP, Harvard Kennedy School of Government

Shravya Mallavarapu, *Indian*
Ed.M., Harvard Graduate School of Education

Sok Lor, *Cambodian*
LL.M., Harvard Law School

Somnieng Hoeurn, *Cambodian*
MPA, Harvard Kennedy School of Government

Steven Coda Colley, *American*
MPP, Harvard Kennedy School of Government

Taeyoung Kim, *Korean*
BA, Handong University

Thomas Seymour Zimmerman, *American*
MALD, Tufts Fletcher School of Law and Diplomacy
Vannoy Hem, *Cambodian*
MPA, Harvard Kennedy School of Government

Weili Germaine Chua, *Singaporean*
MA, Harvard Graduate School of Arts and Sciences

●●●

Asia Entrepreneurship Trek 2016

Adnane Meziane, *American/French/Algerian*
MPA, Harvard Kennedy School of Government

Afsha Akhter, *Bangladeshi*
BA (Hons.), Sunway-Lancaster University

Christine Thuy-Anh Vu, *American*
MPA, Harvard Kennedy School of Government

Daniel Junghyun Kim, *Korean*
BA, Handong University

Galia Levi, *Israeli*
MPA, Harvard Kennedy School of Government

Haydeeliz Carrasco Nunez, *Dominican*
MPP, Harvard Kennedy School of Government

Hungsoo S. Kim, *Korean*
President, Center for Asia Leadership Initiatives
MPA, Harvard Kennedy School of Government

Jane Park, *Korean*
Professional Diploma, Berklee College of Music

Jiro Yoshino, *Japanese*
MPA, Harvard Kennedy School of Government

Kethanjali Sanjkar, *Malaysian*
BSc, Sunway University

Russell Saito, *American*
BA, University of California, Berkeley

Sheikh Mohammed Irfan, *Bangladeshi*
Director of Admin-Research and Development at Cyber Giant

Songi Ryu, *Korean*
MBA, Harvard Business School

● ● ●

Asia Leadership Trek VII

Adamas Belva Syah Devara, *Indonesian*
MPA, Harvard Kennedy School of Government
MBA, Stanford Graduate School of Business

Asset Nakupov, *Kazakh*
LL.B., Kimep University

Asset Yerali, *Kazakh*
MPA, Harvard Kennedy School of Government

Azim Usmanov, *Kazakh*
Partner, Centil Law Firm

Dauren Leskhan, *Kazakh*
BA, Nazarbayev University

Elsa Babette Kania, *American*
BA, Harvard College

Emilie Valentova, *Czech*
MBA, Harvard Business School

Farrukh Bulbulov, *Tajik*
BA, American University of Central Asia

Hungsoo S. Kim, *Korean*
President, Center for Asia Leadership Initiatives
MPA, Harvard Kennedy School of Government

Hyun Sung, *Korean*
BA, Brigham Young University

Justin Hartley, *Australian*
MPA, Harvard Kennedy School
Research Fellow, Center for Public Leadership, HKS

Katarina Sabova, *Slovakian*
MBA, Columbia Business School

Michael Koichopolos, *Canadian*
MBA, Harvard Business School

Sarah Golkar, *American*
MALD, Tufts Fletcher School of Law and Diplomacy

Shirinbek Milikbekov, *Tajik*
MLB, Bucerius Law School

Soojin Park, *Korean*
BS, Duke University

Tatsuo Sakai, *Japanese*
MALD, Tufts Fletcher School of Law and Diplomacy

Umar Shavurov, *Kyrgyz*
MPA, Harvard Kennedy School of Government

Yerzhan Ashikbayev, *Kazakh*
MPA, Harvard Kennedy School of Government

Yunjae Kim, *Korean*
BA, Saint-Petersburg State University of Russia

● ● ●

Asia Leadership Fellowship 2016

Hungsoo S. Kim, *Korean*
President, Center for Asia Leadership Initiatives
MPA, Harvard Kennedy School of Government

John Lim, *Canadian/Filipino*
Yonsei/Fletcher, Harvard Extension School

Lisa Lee, *American*
Ed.M, Harvard Graduate School of Education

Panche Kralev, *Macedonian*
MPA, Harvard Kennedy School of Government

Randy Tarnowski, *American*
Ed.M, Harvard Graduate School of Education

| Appendix III |
List of Conference Topics

• • •

Asia Leadership Conference

Workshop Topics

1. Addressing Cognitive Biases in Decision Making
2. Adaptive Leadership
3. Art of Communication
4. Authentic Leadership
5. Becoming a Better Decision Maker
6. Better Together: Empowering Effective Collaboration between Men and Women
7. Building a Public Narrative
8. Building Bridges through Inter-Cultural and Ethnic Dialogue
9. Campaigns 101: How to Run and Manage a Campaign
10. Creating and Claiming Value in Negotiations
11. Creating Inclusive Workplaces–Targeting and Minimizing Conflict
12. Creating Shared Value
13. Cross-Cultural Communication: Embracing Others and

Debunking Stereotypes
14. Decision Making
15. Design Thinking and Innovation
16. Designing a 21st Century Learning Environment
17. Disciplined Entrepreneurship
18. Effective Language Acquisition
19. Entrepreneurial Venture Evaluation
20. Entrepreneurship in Developing Countries
21. Financing Entrepreneurial Ventures
22. How to Give an Impromptu Speech
23. How to Lead High-Impact Meetings
24. How to Use Behavioural Insights to Become a Better Leader
25. Improving Performance and Outcomes in Negotiation
26. Influencing Techniques: How to be More Effective
27. Leadership and Identity
28. Leadership and Management
29. Leadership in Sustainable Urban Planning
30. Making of a Politician
31. Managing Innovation in the Cyber Age: Controlled Chaos
32. Measuring Performance of Non-Profits
33. Navigating Differences in Political Cultures
34. Negotiation Strategies for Managers
35. Overcoming Hidden Barriers to Change (Immunity to Change)
36. Persuasion: An Everyday Exercise to Rally Opinions
37. Political Organizing
38. Public Speaking and Media Training
39. Social Change Starts with Good Intentions

40. Social Entrepreneurship: From Idea to Realization
41. The Art of Effective Advocacy
42. The Reflective Leader
43. Transformational Leadership
44. Using Stories to Mobilize Change
45. Women and Leadership

Career Mentoring Topics

1. Applying to US Universities: General
2. Applying to US Universities: Finding and Choosing the Right Program
3. Applying to US Universities: MBA, MPA or JD Programs
4. Career in Academics, Research and Think Tanks
5. Career in Advocacy and Campaigning
6. Career in Education
7. Career in Engineering-General
8. Career in Finance & Banking
9. Career in Foreign Service
10. Career in International Development & Aid
11. Career in Legal
12. Career in Marketing
13. Career in Management Consulting
14. Career in Medicine & Health
15. Career in Nonprofit
16. Career in Politics
17. Career in Social Entrepreneurship
18. Career in Sports

19. Leadership Coaching
20. Tech Start-ups

Professional Development Topics

1. All About Publishing Your Own Book
2. Building a Personal Branding
3. Building Resume
4. Creative Writing
5. Developing a Powerful and Persuasive Voice
6. Dressing for Success
7. Essential Presentation Skills
8. Giving an Elevator Pitch
9. Giving an Impromptu Speech
10. Interviewing Skills: Jobs
11. Interviewing Skills: Media
12. Job Search Efforts in the Times of Transition
13. Managing Your Online Presence: LinkedIn
14. Managing Effective Small Talks
15. Networking and Building Contacts
16. Social Media–How to Make or Break Your Life
17. Transitioning from School to Work or Vice-Versa
18. Writing a Business Plan
19. Writing a Great Op-ed
20. Writing a News Article
21. Writing a Powerful Speech
22. Writing a Statement of Purpose
23. Writing Good Recommendation Letters

| Appendix IV |
List of Contributors

∙∙∙

Introduction, Key Leadership Insights from ALT & Afterword

Hungsoo S. Kim, *Korean*
President, Center for Asia Leadership Initiatives
MPA, Harvard University Kennedy School of Government

∙∙∙

Asia Leadership Trek 2016

Rachel Lipson, *American*
MBA, Harvard Business School
MPP, Harvard Kennedy School of Government

Annie Yu Kleiman, *American*
MALD, Tufts Fletcher School of Law and Diplomacy

Benjamin Goh, *Singaporean*
MPP, Harvard Kennedy School of Government

Asia Leadership Fellowship 2016

Lisa Lee, *American*
Ed.M., Harvard Graduate School of Education

Asia Leadership Trek VII

Umar Shavurov, *Kyrgyz*
MPA, Harvard Kennedy School of Government

Sarah Golkar, *American*
MALD, Tufts Fletcher School of Law and Diplomacy

Katarina Sabova, *Slovakian*
MBA, Columbia Business School

Justin Hartley, *Australian*
MPA, Harvard Kennedy School
Research Fellow, Center for Public Leadership HKS

www.ingramcontent.com/pod-product-compliance
Lightning Source LLC
Chambersburg PA
CBHW052140220526
45471CB00004B/1457